THE POLITICS OF
CULTURAL
SUB-NATIONALISM
IN AFRICA

ABOUT THE CONTRIBUTORS

VICTOR A. OLORUNSOLA was born in Mopa, Nigeria, in 1939. He received his Ph.D. in Political Science from Indiana University in 1967, and has lectured at various American universities, including the University of California at Los Angeles, Howard University, and Indiana University. He is presently an Associate Professor of Political Science at Iowa State University. Last spring, he was Visiting Associate Professor at Ohio University.

NELSON KASFIR was Lecturer in Political Science at Makerere College, Uganda. Currently, he is an Instructor in Government at Dartmouth College, Hanover, New Hampshire.

DONALD ROTHCHILD was Professor of Political Science at the University of California, Davis. He is currently Ford Professor of Political Science at the University of Zambia.

DICK SIMPSON was a Foreign Area Fellow in Sierra Leone. He is now an Assistant Professor of Political Science at the University of Illinois at Chicago.

THOMAS TURNER is a Professor of Politics at the Université Libre du Congo, République Démocratique du Congo.

THE POLITICS OF CULTURAL SUB-NATIONALISM IN AFRICA

Edited by Victor A. Olorunsola

ASSOCIATE PROFESSOR OF POLITICAL SCIENCE
IOWA STATE UNIVERSITY, AMES

WITHDRAWN

ANCHOR BOOKS
DOUBLEDAY & COMPANY, INC.
GARDEN CITY, NEW YORK
1972

The Anchor Books edition is the first publication of THE POLITICS
OF CULTURAL SUB-NATIONALISM IN AFRICA

Anchor Books edition: 1972

Library of Congress Catalog Card Number 75–150932
Copyright © 1972 by Victor A. Olorunsola
All Rights Reserved
Printed in the United States of America
First Edition

This book is dedicated to the

memory of

Chief Thomas Bello Olorunsola

ACKNOWLEDGMENTS

In this volume, acknowledgment is not a meaningless exercise. In a very real sense, I am indebted to my wife, Carol, for acting as my research assistant and undertaking the less glamorous but very vital tasks. Professors Hadwiger, Liebenow, Crawford Young, Fikry, Rothchild, Talbot, and Mr. Holmquist offered me encouragement and support. I am grateful to Cambridge University Press for permission to use the article on Kenya and to Miss Hickey for her administrative help.

CONTENTS

in Uganda up to 1966; Six Cases of Cultural Sub-Nationalism; The Impact of the Confrontation of 1966; Ethnic Composition of Politicians, Bureaucrats, and University Students; Political Development in Uganda; Notes.

Colonial Impact; Political Subcultures; Development of Political Parties; Distribution of Rewards; Election and Military Coup of 1967; Ethnicity and Future Development; Notes.

The Facts of Inequality; African Attitudes Toward Tribal Inequality; African Attitudes Toward Racial Inequality; Government Responses
to Claims for Equity; The Balance Between
Equity and Development; Notes.

TABLES

LIST OF MAPS

INTRODUCTION

The essential element of society is the interaction of human beings in such a manner as to mutually benefit and support one another. But if man is to live in society, he must have some way of steering it so that the society can collectively make decisions about its public posture and policies. The decision-making process must take place in and be part of a general cultural pattern of a society. Political culture is not radically divergent from general culture, rather it is an aspect of it. The political culture of a community includes such diverse elements as its history, religious beliefs, familial organizations, role expectation, values, and structures of government. Furthermore, political culture has an added dimension —deep emotional aspects involving individual security, identity and sentimental attachments, geographic location, and even rituals. Since these factors "give meaning to the polity, discipline to the institutions, and social relevance to the individual acts,"[1] they are very important considerations if we are going to concern ourselves with the problem of national integration.

There are multivarious definitions of nationalism; Fichte, Hayes, Deutsch, Kohn, Hertz,[2] to mention a few, are familiar names in this connection. However, no matter how differently writers define nation, all are agreed that the nation is a cohesive human community. Therefore, instead of belaboring the definition, I will simply say in the words of Rupert Emerson that "the nation is today the largest community which, when the chips are down, effectively commands men's loyalty overriding the claims of the lesser communities within it . . ."[3] That a state is not necessarily coterminous with a nation should be axiomatic in the light of political history. The Republic of Congo (Kinshasa) and Nigeria, to mention a few current examples, have demonstrated the fact that the achievement of formal political independence by a country does not necessarily lead simultaneously to the emergence of a nation. It is conceded, however, that, except in the case of Israel and perhaps Pakistan, states are historical antecedents of nations.

Building a nation-state is not only a slow but also a complicated process. In countries where the emergent state is co-extensive with old political units, where the peoples have a history and experience of living together for generations within the same political framework and have done so peacefully, or where there is coincidence between the political unit and roughly distinct cultural area, there has traditionally existed a greater propensity for national integration. On the other hand, it is suggested that the states which have been born under less fortunate conditions will find the achievement of nationalism and national integration a very herculean task. Strayer contended that because of the absence of these factors, most of the political entities created in the past fifty years are never going to complete this process of building a nation.[4]

An examination of African politics vis-à-vis the problem of integrating sub-national groups into the nation is most important because many African countries are creations of colonial masters. Thus, we have the names Nigeria, Ivory Coast, Upper Volta, Sierra Leone, Rhodesia. In the scramble for Africa the colonial powers cut out enclaves for themselves with an absolute disregard for tribal loyalties and ethnic compatibilities. The phrase "one state—many nationalisms" may be an appropriate designation of political systems of many developing countries, but it is particularly appropriate in describing the new states of Africa. To this extent, African states are most vulnerable to tension, malintegration, and even fragmentation. Under these conditions, a country's nationalism can be jeopardized by its cultural sub-nationalisms, for the right of every cultural group to autonomy and self-determination, or self-assertion, laudable as it seems, may lead either to the existence of the multinational states or to the perpetual fragmentation of sovereign states. It must be quickly added, however, that on occasions a forceful patch-up of recalcitrant groups into a single state may be ill-advised in the long run. This is particularly true if the political actors are shortsighted or if they should allow their objectivity to be obfuscated in the heat of emotions.

Realizing that this is not a zero-sum game, we shall raise questions and attempt a critical analysis of the ways in which the selected African countries have attempted to deal with cultural sub-nationalism. In the final analysis, both of them are not mutually exclusive; in fact they are both necessary for the general welfare of the citizens in the political community. After all, some countries have been able to achieve a level of integration which seems surprisingly quite out of proportion to the degree of their cultural homogeneity.

This then is not a book about secession. Neither is it the ambitious general's devil's advocate. It underscores the complexity of national integration and sympathizes with all the peoples of developing countries who are under fire in this regard. The problems posed by cultural sub-nationalism are not those which will disappear with time if left unattended. Failure to attend to them may be disastrous and an attempt to gloss over them may be fatal in the end. Without envying the politicians who must somehow find a political formula, we wish them all the best in this all-important endeavor.

In discussing this topic, anthropology, history, political science, and sociology have equal relevance. The contributors have relied heavily and quite appropriately on the interdisciplinary approach. This book appeals to a broad audience, all who seek to understand the current political phenomenon in Africa and those interested in political development. One note of caution is in order: the fact that we stress cultural conflict does not imply that this is the only source of conflict in Africa. There are military-civilian and political interest group conflicts, for example. It appears to us that ethnic conflict is a cantankerous cancer with an amazing ability to grab and use these other sources as reinforcements.

On the whole, our goals are modest and we shall be gratified if this volume succeeds in contributing to our knowledge of comparative political development.

In the treatment of each country the contributors:

(1) discussed the various traditional political cultures found in the state;

(2) emphasized the degree of homogeneity, heterogeneity, and compatibility among these cultures;

(3) elaborated upon the colonial administrations' treatment of the various cultures within the state's framework;

(4) pointed out the absence or presence of ethnic arithmetic in the public institutions;

(5) sought to discover efforts made by different traditional cultural groups to insure their survival within the framework of the independent state;

(6) outlined the historical experiences, in the post-independent era, which point to the incompatibilities or intensification of the politics of sub-nationalism;

(7) delineated the ramification of these experiences;

(8) showed the methods used successfully or unsuccessfully to keep cultural sub-nationalism from destroying the state;

(9) suggested solutions to the problems posed by cultural sub-nationalisms; and considered how sub-nationalism can be made compatible with a country's nationalism.

The contributors seem to agree that ethnic conflicts can block development and that effort should be made to overcome the destructive dimensions. The ideal that one can hope for is the modification, transformation, and incorporation of ethnic goals, steadily, into a national framework. Different countries are applying differing techniques. These case studies analyze these attempts in the hope that the lessons from the failure of the past will contribute to the success of the future.

All of the contributors have had research experience in Africa: Kasfir has researched and taught in Uganda; Rothchild has had several years of research experience in Kenya; Simpson was a Foreign Area Fellow in Sierra Leone; Turner is currently teaching and researching in Congo; and I have done research in Nigeria under the auspices of the Ford Foundation.

It is not my purpose to force a monistic view. To do so would have been pretentious. Each contributor is an authority in his area. The plurality of opinion is not only natural but it should be rewarding.

One final note, the choice of the five countries was suggested by the topic under investigation. Nigeria, Congo-Kinshasa, Uganda, Sierra Leone, and Kenya are examples *par excellence* of countries striving to achieve nationalism in the face of strong sub-national consciousness. I felt fortunate to have the voluntary cooperation of these contributors.

NOTES

1. Lucian Pye and Sidney Verba, eds., *Political Culture and Political Development* (Princeton: Princeton University Press, 1965), p. 7.

2. Hans Kohn, *Nationalism: Its Meaning and History* (Princeton: D. Van Nostrand Company, Inc., 1955).

Karl W. Deutsch, "Some Problems in Nation-Building" in Deutsch and William J. Foltz, eds., *Nation-Building* (New York: Atherton Press, 1966), pp. 11–12. Here he extrapolated five variables from Carl Friedrich's definition of a nation. The variables are: independence, cohesiveness, political organization, autonomy, and internal legitimacy.

Also see: Deutsch's *Nationalism and Social Communication: An Inquiry into the Foundations of Nationality* (New York: John Wiley & Sons, Inc., 1954).

Fichte and Herder in Elie Kedourie, *Nationalism* (London: Hutchinson & Co., 1961), pp. 62–67.

Friedrich Hertz, *Nationality in History and Politics* (London: Routledge & Kegan Paul, 1944).

Carlton Hayes, *Essays on Nationalism* (New York: The Macmillan Co., 1926).

James Coleman and Carl Rosberg, eds., *Political Parties and National Integration in Tropical Africa* (Los Angeles: University of California Press, 1964).

Emerich Francis, *Ethose & Demos: Soziologische Beiträge zur Volkstheorie* (Berlin: Duncker & Humblot, 1965), pp. 69–87.

3. Rupert Emerson, *From Empire to Nation: The Rise to Self-Assertion of Asian and African Peoples* (Cambridge: Harvard University Press, 1960), pp. 95–96.

4. This is a paraphrased position of Joseph Strayer in Karl Deutsch, *Nation-Building, op. cit.,* p. 25.

I
NIGERIA

❖ ❖ ❖

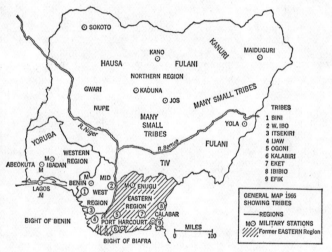

NIGERIA—General Map Showing Tribes, 1966

EDITOR'S INTRODUCTORY NOTE

Nigeria contains three major traditional political cultures: the Hausa-Fulani, which is essentially theocratic, the Yoruba, which tends to be gerontocratic, and the Ibo, which is often referred to as democratic or "parademocratic."

Unfortunately, the colonial administration did little to reconcile these varied political cultures in order to create an integrated Nigerian nation. The Richards Constitution attempted to promote Nigerian unity, but it did not provide adequate political representation for the majority. The question of unequal representation as well as the issue of the allocation of financial resources never was resolved to the satisfaction of all concerned. Furthermore, the impact of Westernization was not felt equally by all tribal groups. As each ethnic group acquired modern skills through Western education, the competition for limited jobs increased. Nigerian leaders inherited this state of affairs from the British upon independence. Their inability to cope effectively with these seemingly overwhelming problems permitted the continued expression of regional and ethnic hostilities. Political parties, even those with national pretensions, appeared concerned with the maximization of regional security. This could only be achieved by obtaining the political power necessary to control the nation's resource allocation. The 1964 federal elections and the events following the elections intensified political struggles between regions to such a point that military coups resulted, and ultimately civil war broke out.

Nigerian leaders presently are saddled with the task of creating a Nigerian nation. Structural rearrangements done within democratic norms are useful. Where regional hostilities have been intense, however, citizens must be politically resocialized to accept and vigorously work for the development of a strong nation-state. Modern political behavior must be reconciled with traditional political behavior and norms so that all people may participate fully in political life. Finally, the leaders of the state must continue to promote the expansion of financial resources so that the needs of all the sections can be met. This would eliminate a paramount source of regional conflict: competition for extremely scarce resources.

NIGERIA

By Victor A. Olorunsola
IOWA STATE UNIVERSITY, AMES

To avoid duplication, I should not undertake any formal introduction of this chapter. Rather, I should like to go directly into an examination of the major traditional groupings in Nigeria. Part 2 of this chapter is a juxtaposition of the traditional political cultures. In Part 3 an attempt is made to examine the colonial government's treatment of the major cultural groupings within the framework of a dependent state and the response of these peoples to such treatments. The desperate efforts of various groups to achieve or maintain political security during the period immediately preceding the attainment of independence and in post-independent era, constitute the subject matter of Part 4. Part 5 appraises the attempts made to insure that cultural sub-nationalism did not prevent the attainment of Nigerian nationalism. A most significant component of Part 5 is the analysis of the reasons for the failure of these sometimes gallant attempts.

1. DISCUSSION OF MAJOR TRADITIONAL NIGERIAN GROUPINGS

The Hausa-Fulani[1]

The Fulanis had established themselves in Kano as early as the fifteenth century. The early relationship between them and the Hausa rulers, who were indigenous to the area, was a mixture of dependence and detachment. They moved through the territories acknowledging the sovereignty of these

Hausa leaders and paying tribute to them. Gradually but persistently, increasing numbers of Fulanis became urbanized, for no sooner did they turn toward a more settled life than they absorbed the Hausa culture. They eventually succeeded in converting some Hausa chiefs to the Islamic religion.

By the turn of the nineteenth century increasing numbers of Fulani clans had settled in Hausa cities and occupied positions of importance. Not only did they begin to gain important council positions, but they also embarked on a wide campaign to convert the urban Hausas to Islam. A crisis point was reached in 1804 when the Hausa chief of Gobir, fearing the increasing political strength of the Fulani, forbade any further Moslem observances. He threatened not only to expel the Fulani clerics from his domain but also to send word to other Hausa chiefs to do the same.

Under the pretext of reviving religious fervor among the Hausas, Othoman dan Fodio, the head of the local Fulani clan and a fervent Moslem scholar, declared a jihad. With the help of urbanized Fulanis and some Moslem Hausas, the Hausa chiefs were overthrown one after the other, and the Fulani leaders were installed as local emirs in their place. The new leaders and emirs were appointed by and owed their allegiance to dan Fodio and later to his son, Bello, who became Sultan of Sokoto. From then on, the Sultan of Sokoto became the political and religious leader of all Mohammedan Fulani-Hausa emirates.

This jihad had profound effect on the authority system of Northern Nigeria. First, it reversed the relationship among the Hausas and Fulanis. Second, it changed the pattern of authority which existed prior to the holy war. The movement resulted in the creation of the largest empire in Nigeria, an empire in which obedience was demanded outside of kith and kin. It established the political supremacy of the Fulanis.

The Fulani Empire, in the Northern Region of Nigeria, had as its distinguishing quality the large-scale state form of political organization. It was composed of about thirty emirates. Although each emirate differed in certain forms, all shared certain principles. But in all of these there was a lack of clear distinction between religious and political authority; the emir personified both. The ruling emirs were chosen from royal families, and the titled officials as well as traditional offices of the states were heirarchically organized. The principle of clientage—an exclusive relation of mutual benefit that stresses the solidarity between two persons defined as socially and politically unequal—was the orientational focus in the territorial organization.[2]

Looking at emirate rule from the standpoint of the commoner, Richard Sklar and C. S. Whitaker indicated that "emirate rule was despotic in form," because "the personal security of the commoner depended wholly on the uncertain benevolence of his overlords."[3] Concerning the nature and structure of emirate rule, they continued, "Fief-holders residing at the capital of an emirate were clients of the emir; they were in turn patrons of subordinate agents through whom they administered and exploited the subject communities within their jurisdiction. The concentration of 'de jure' power and authority in the hands of the emir tended to inhibit any opposition to him, even from those within the ranks of the ruling stratum."[4] The emirs, unlike the Yoruba oba, therefore, tended to be despotic. In short, the Hausa-Fulani Empire was a theocratic dynasty, for the emir claimed unquestioned religious sanctions derived through divine delegation. Here then is a fusion of the sacred and the secular without constitutionality. Whereas the Hausa-Fulani cannot claim to be involved in a representative system nor claim to engage in a participatory democracy, the Yoruba is not a total alien to representative government.

The Ibo[5]

Prior to European advent the Ibos consisted of over two hundred independent territorial groups divided into villages. The internal organization of these groups rested upon patrilineal clans and lineages.[6] The groups were autonomous with regards to governmental processes, but social and commercial bonds were strong among them.

The degree of political independence of the Ibo communities is underscored by Meek:

> It may be said generally that the most characteristic feature of Ibo society is the almost complete absence of any higher political or social unit than the commune or small group of continuous villages, whose customs and cults are identical, who in former times took common action against an external enemy (though they frequently also fought amongst themselves), and whose sense of solidarity is so strong that they regard themselves as descendants of a common ancestor.[7]

Notwithstanding the political independence of these Ibo communities one from another, there were certain things common to the political system of all. Traditional leadership was vested in the Okpara, who was the equivalent of lineage head. The Okpara was the onunne—head of the lineage—as well as the umunne—ritual leader in the lineage cult of ancestors. The position of the Okpara was structurally relative because many extended families had their own Okpara. Among a group of lineage Okparas, the oldest resident lineage's Okpara was given seniority. His seniority is one of *primus inter pares*. Meek wrote, "It may be said generally that among the Ibo government is based on the family organization, and that the controlling authority is the general body of family heads, the senior Okpara acting as ceremonial president."[8]

However, it would be erroneous to think that traditional political recruitment among the Ibos is primarily ascriptive. Stevenson wrote, "Leadership and political office among the Ibo seem even in the pre-colonial period to have been much more largely based on achievement and wealth as opposed to lineage ascription . . ."[9]

Meek was more specific:

> In all society the possession of wealth confers power, and so we find that, if in any group there was a personage of outstanding wealth, that personage obtained a measure of authority within the group which overshadowed that of the Okpara. Such a personage could, if he were able and

generous, obtain a position of chieftainship of his local group (*nchi*) and be styled the *"Onyisi"* or head of the group. He might even be regarded as the *"Onyisi"* of the whole village-group.[10]

To avoid misunderstanding, the role of the Ibo village chief must be clearly spelled out. "Typically, the Ibo village chief is the head of a specified lineage; the chief of a senior village in a group may preside at meetings of the village group. In some cases, village-group heads enjoy great prestige, but their authority never reaches beyond the village group. Indeed, there are parts of Iboland where chieftaincy is virtually unknown, and 'tribal government is thought of as the collective rule of the senior age grades.' "[11]

On the whole, then, when one considers the traditional political culture of the Ibos, the largest ethnic group in Nigeria's Eastern Region, one discovers neither a constitutional monarchy nor a theocracy. Instead, one is confronted with a strong republicanism which features a wide dispersal of tribal authority based on patrilineal kinship groups.

Unlike the Hausas and the Yorubas, the Ibos never developed permanent large-scale state systems. Equalitarianism, individualism, and achievement were highly placed in their value system, and there was a high degree of popular participation in the process of policy-making. It is for these reasons that the political culture of the Ibos is often referred to as "parademocratic" at least, if not "democratic."

The Yorubas[12]

Oduduwa was the progenitor of the Yorubas, and the Yoruba rulers were regarded as the direct lineal descendants of the Oduduwa of Ile-Ife. Legitimacy of the Yoruba oba rested, to a large extent, upon the solidity of his claim and that of his lineage to the Oduduwa. If Oduduwa was regarded as the founder of the Yorubas, the oba was looked upon as the founder of the town. The Yorubas regarded the chiefs as the representatives of the people. To this extent, then, the chiefs as representatives of the people must be involved, at least precariously, in the selection of an oba. Although each royal house in the community reserved the right to present a candidate, the final selection of the oba rested with the chiefs. Once selected, however, an oba assumed a sacred status. But at the same time he remained a public property, lived in a palace, and all the goods acquired by him during his reign remained public property after his death. Seemingly, there was a fusion of the secular with the sacred. The oba was a sacred king, but the pervasiveness of beliefs and rituals in the governmental institutions of the society should not obfuscate the secular aspect of the actual governmental processes.

Patrilineage was the basic element in the Yoruba political system. The lineages headed by the oldest member of the descent groups clustered together to form politically unified towns. There was a functional distribution of power between the lineage head and the lineage chief. The former concerned himself primarily with matters affecting the group, whereas the latter was concerned with the government of the town. Generally, the oba or king, who as noted earlier was selected by the senior chiefs, was regarded as the father of all the towns' people but not as the head of a particular descent group.

There existed among the Yorubas what one might call a check-and-balance machinery through which political excesses by the oba were controlled. The senior chiefs, who represented the major lineages, furnished one such legal check. Peter Lloyd wrote, "There has always been a delicate balance of power between the chiefs who made the policy and the oba whose sacred status commanded such authority as will ensure obedience. If the oba misused his power he might be deposed by his chiefs who would 'ask him to die.' "[13]

Moreover, in the Yoruba towns, policy was made by the senior chiefs. "In the past they used to meet on the palace veranda sending their decisions to the oba, secluded inside, who would in turn (through the slaves) announce the decision as his own, giving the necessary accompanying orders."[14] Of course, they may issue orders contrary to the advice of their chiefs. However, this very seldom happens because the council will refuse to cooperate and ultimately it may impose the political sanction on the oba.

In short, then, one may correctly regard the Yoruba state as a constitutional monarchy. The obas were limited, hence, they could not afford to be despotic without recriminations. Great obas lived in the midst of their people and chiefs as well as lineage heads who controlled the political process were close to their people. "Government was a communal interest and at some point every adult had a say . . . fear of authority does not appear to have been a normally important factor in tribal government."[15]

2. JUXTAPOSITION OF THE CULTURES

Political recruitment in Yoruba land was not totally ascriptive. There were shaded spots of achievement recruitment criteria. In contrast, however, the political recruitment in Ibo land was heavily dependent upon the possession of achievement criteria with a very light sprinkling of ascriptive prerequisites. The Ibo value system heavily rewarded aggressiveness. Whereas the Ibos might be concerned about the prospect of being the village big man, the Yorubas would be preoccupied with the prospect of being the wise old man. For the former, wisdom did not reside necessarily in old age. The Yoruba oba's limitations notwithstanding, he was by far a more powerful political figure than the Ibo village chief. Finally, the Ibo demanded and received greater grass roots participation in the political process, and he was more individualistic. It is therefore not surprising that the Ibo village was traditionally more autonomous than its Yoruba counterpart.

The Yoruba political culture tended to be a mix of certain aspects of the Ibo and the Hausa-Fulani political culture. The Yoruba oba like the Fulani emir was both secular and sacred. In spite of the fusion of both the sacred and the secular, the Yoruba oba was not absolute. Traditionally, he was a constitutional monarch who, more often than not, accepted the policy advice of the senior chiefs. Effective check-and-balance machinery operated upon him. Unlike the Yoruba oba the emir operated in a theocratic social system, one in which he was recognized as the representative of God on earth. Consequently, one dared not question the authority or the wisdom of God's appointed. Thus, dissimilar political cultures— parademocratic versus monarchial versus theocratic-autocratic —were juxtaposed within the state of Nigeria.

3. COLONIAL GOVERNMENT'S TREATMENT OF MAJOR CULTURAL GROUPINGS

In his lecture at Saint Pancras Town Hall in London, Awolowo noted:

(1) that Nigeria is a British creation,

(2) that Nigeria consists of a multiplicity of races who are as different from one another as races of Europe,

(3) that for about forty-three years past, British have striven to unite all these diverse peoples . . . and to infuse in them a sense of common nationality . . .[16]

Perhaps many will contest the validity of the first two points, but most have wondered to what extent the last contention is tenable. This brings up a crucial dimension in this discussion: the colonial administration's treatment of these cultures within the state framework. Following the acknowledgment of British claims by the Berlin Conference, the British sphere of influence entered into a period of expansion. The Northern Protectorate and the Southern Protectorate were proclaimed in 1900. Thus, the British superstructure was imposed on three separate territories of Nigeria: Southern Protectorate, Northern Protectorate, and Lagos Colony.

In April 1912 Sir Frederick Lugard took control of two separate administrations, and in May 1913 he presented his program for the amalgamation of North and South. His proposal, which was accepted, took effect on January 1, 1914. It would appear that Lugard's decision was affected by the cutthroat competition between the two rail lines and a consideration of fiscal efficiency.[17] However, it is crucial to note that this amalgamation was only formalistic because "different policies and conceptions of colonial administration . . . continued to dominate official thought and action."[18] Administrative individuality of the separate territories continued in practice.

The speech of Governor Sir Hugh Clifford before the so-called Nigeria Council on December 29, 1920, is more enlightening:

> . . . the suggestion that there is, or can be in the visible future, such a thing as a "West African Nation" is as manifest an absurdity as that there is, or can be, an "European nation," at all events until the arrival of the Millennium . . . The peoples of West Africa do not belong to the same stock and are not of common descent; . . . (they have) no common language . . . and no community of religious beliefs . . . As a matter of fact, the Hausas of Zaria, the Bantu tribesmen of the Valley of the Benue, and say the Fantis of Cape Coast are less nearly allied to one another than are, for example, the Scandinavians of the Baltic, the Slavs of Bulgaria and the Semitic peoples of Egypt and Morocco . . . Any advancement or recognition of . . . these ridiculous claims and pretensions . . . is mischievous, because they are incompatible with that natural development of real national self-government which all true patriots in Nigeria . . . should continue to secure and maintain . . . It is the consistent policy of the government of Nigeria to maintain and support the local tribal institutions and the indigenous forms of Government . . . which are to be regarded as the natural expression of (African) political genius . . . I am entirely convinced of the right, for example, of the people of Egbaland, . . . of any of the great Emirates of the North, . . . to maintain that each one of them is, in a very real sense, a nation . . . It is the task of the Government of Nigeria to build up and fortify these national institutions.[19]

But Sir Hugh did not stop there:

> Assuming . . . that the impossible were feasible—that this collection of self-contained and mutually independent Native States, separated from one another, as many of them are, by great distance, by differences of history and traditions, and by ethno-logical, racial, tribal, political, social and religious barriers, were indeed capable of being welded into a single homogenous nation—a deadly blow would thereby be struck at the very root of national self-government in Nigeria, which secures to each separate people the right to maintain its identity, its individuality and its nationality, its own chosen form of government; and the peculiar political and social institutions which have been evolved for it by the wisdom and by the accumulated experience of generations of its forebears.[20]

In view of these statements by the Governor, who was the highest territorial representative of the colonial government in the territory, it is fair to say that until this time at least it was not the conscious policy of Britain to form a united, free Nigerian nation.

The principle of indirect rule did not contribute much to a forging of a Nigerian nation. Coleman underscores the point succinctly:

> In the balance, the overwhelming emphasis has been upon greater tribal integration. Whatever else might be said of the application of indirect rule in Nigeria—and a very strong case can be made for it—there can be little doubt that it has complicated the task of welding diverse elements into a Nigerian nation.[21]

Sir Hugh finally established a Legislative Council as a result of the 1922 Constitution, but essentially the Northern Region was excluded from the area of legislative competence of the Council. Therefore, we cannot assert that there was any central representative institution between 1922 and 1947. The liability of this fact seems obvious; it means that there was no history of Nigerian unity during this crucial period. Moreover, the Nigerian educational system was sectionalized, and the goals and philosophies underlying the educational system were conflicting in many instances. Coleman writes:

> In short, before 1947 there was little opportunity for a Nigerian to feel that he was under a common government which commanded his obedience, allegiance, and loyalty. The situation was further aggravated by the educational system . . .[22]

Quite apart from the absence of common central institutions, the expected political behavior varies from one section to another. The function of political recruitment is a case in point. Election into the Eastern House under the 1951 Constitution went through two stages; in the West, through three stages; and in the North, through several stages. In addition, the native authorities were given an additional privilege of adding to the final college 10 per cent of the total membership. Under this Constitution, the election of members to the House of Representatives was done on the basis of regional representation.

When Sir Arthur Richards became Governor, he introduced a new Constitution. The stated objectives of the new Constitution were:

(1) to promote Nigerian unity,

(2) to secure greater participation by Africans in the decisions of their own government,

(3) to provide adequately for the diverse elements in the country.

Thus, on the face of it, Sir Arthur recognized the fact that in practice a Nigerian nation did not exist. While Nigeria had been administratively unified at the top and economically more unified as a result of trade, up to the war years it remained an amalgam of distinct political and constitutional entities. Furthermore, the Governor was cognizant of the diverse political cultures within this British colony. However, he did not carry out prior consultation with the peoples who must live under this new Constitution.

Nigerian nationalists had mixed attitudes toward the Richards Constitution. All of them denounced its arbitrary introduction without prior consultations. They also felt that it would create a false impression of providing for unofficial majoritarian rule. The opportunity to discuss cannot be equated with genuine political participation. However, they all hailed the Constitution because they felt that it provided, for the first time, for the integration of the North and the South for legislative purposes.

In 1948 John McPherson became Governor of Nigeria. He proceeded to announce his intention to revise the Richards Constitution. The new Governor was careful to avoid the mistake of Governor Richards. Unlike his immediate predecessor, McPherson made sure that there were long deliberations, from the local level up, to give Nigerians an opportunity to articulate their views on the new Constitution. Of course, general guidelines were set down by the Governor and the Colonial Office concerning the limits of freedom accorded to the deliberative bodies and the area of their constitutional competence.

By 1950 it had become very evident that the proposed Constitution would not eradicate regions as structural entities but would increase their power. Yoruba leadership was busy laying the groundwork for a modern political organization which would play a new role in the struggle for the survival of Yoruba cultural nationalism. In 1945 the Egbe Omo Oduduwa was formed abroad, and it functioned in London until 1948 when it was introduced into Nigeria as a cultural organization. Three of the five major goals of this new organization were:

(1) the emergence of a virile, modernized, and efficient Yoruba state with its own independence within Nigeria,

(2) the protection of Yoruba chiefs,

(3) the protection of the interest of the Yorubas so that future generations of Yorubas would have a secure place in Nigeria.

In 1951 the Egbe Omo Oduduwa formally converted itself into a political organization called the Action Group (AG).

It is an irrefutable fact that the membership of the organization even at its inception included non-Yorubas such as the Edo, Ishan, and Jekiri leadership. However, it could be argued with considerable merit that this was enlightened self-interest. It was necessary for the AG to have the support of these people in order to ensure the control of political power in the region. But of greater relevance to our discussion are the two most valuable weapons used by the Action Group. The first was the assertion of the dissimilarity of traditional political culture between the West and the East. The AG leadership asserted that the leadership of the NCNC—the National Council of Nigeria and Cameroons—was dominated by the Ibos, and in the Ibo traditional political culture, as we have pointed out, there was no place for chiefs. The AG leadership pointed out that the NCNC, because of this factor, would not be expected to show respect for elders or protect the chieftaincy institution of Yorubas. Secondly, they pointed to the aggressiveness of the Ibos and their drive, and then they interpreted these as indications that in terms of political and administrative recruitment as well as economic security, the future of Yorubas and the Western Region minority groups, rested not with the NCNC but with the AG.

The NCNC was formed earlier as a result of the Constitutional Convention of 1945. At its inception, the organization had nationalistic pretensions. It wanted to extend democratic principles, to advance the interests of the people, to adopt suitable means for the purpose of imparting political education to the people of Nigeria with the view to achieving self-government, to afford their members the medium of expression in order to secure political freedom, economic security, social equality, and religious tolerance in Nigeria and in the Cameroons under the British mandate as a member of the British Commonwealth. Although its early membership included Middle-belters and many Yoruba Lagosians, an overwhelming proportion of the membership was Ibo. (This in spite of the fact that membership was extended only to tribal unions, professional associations, and trade unions, but not to individuals. In Nigeria, tribal origin has always been a significant determinant of organizational identification.) We must say that the national image portrayed by these lofty goals of the NCNC can be very misleading. The national pretensions of the NCNC appear to be enlightened self-interest.

Many contend that since the majority of NCNC members were Ibos, and since they were the people most scattered throughout Nigeria, it should not be surprising that at that time the NCNC claimed a nationalistic orientation. An organization with nationalistic pretensions and significant political claims might offer to the dispersed Ibo significant security and official protection in alien cultural areas. In fact, some prominent leaders of the NCNC and the Ibo State Union gave credence to this interpretation of events in speeches such as the one made by NCNC leader Azikiwe who was the President of both the Ibo State Union organization and the NCNC.

> It would appear that the God of Africa has created the Ibo nation to lead the children of Africa from the bondage of the anguish . . . the Ibo nation cannot shirk its responsibility from its manifest destiny.[23]

One might quietly ask the question: How many nations does the leadership want out of a Nigerian country? Can this be a realization of the gravity of cultural sub-nationalism?

The McPherson Constitution is a watershed within our general framework because it succinctly pinpoints the efforts of different cultural groups to insure their survival within the framework of the independent state prior to October 1960.

First let us mention some features to underscore the elaborateness of the process of making this McPherson Constitution. (1) There was a Constitutional Draft Committee which consisted of official and nonofficial members. (2) The Committee was guided by the Chief Secretary's list of questions to be answered. (3) The General Conference which met in January 1951 consisted of twenty-five unofficial members of the Legislative Council; unofficial members were drawn proportionately from the regions.

The Draft Committee recommended:

(1) regional autonomy within a united Nigeria,

(2) giving Nigeria ministerial responsibility which would give them full share in shaping the central course of governmental action,

(3) creation of a larger, more representative legislature.

The Committee was unable, however, to make recommendations with regard to a number of crucial issues. These issues are very important because they affect the distribution of power. They are the issue of geographical boundaries between regions, the issue of financial allocation of funds, and the issue of regional representation at the center.

At the Ibadan Conference of 1950 the leader of the Northern delegation demanded that financial allocation of funds as well as regional representation at the center be done on the basis of population estimates. This would have given the veto to the Northern Region since it would then be able to control economic and political power. Mallam Balewa threatened that if the demands of Northern Nigeria were turned down, "I am afraid, gentlemen, to think of what will be the result." Again Balewa said:

> People speak of the fear of the North being dominated by the South, but at the same time they should speak of the fear of the South being dominated by the North. We have been told many times that it is impossible to put Northern provinces in a dominating position in the Legislative Council. Well, I will say, vice versa. We do not ask anything which is not reasonable. If we work on the population basis, the North will get more than 50%, but we have come down and we say, well, we are asking for 50%.[24]

Stephen Awokoya said that the West could not accept the Northern proposition that fifty per cent of the Central Legislature be given to the Northern Region. If the Northern proposition was accepted then the West would have to pursue the policy of complete regional autonomy. Furthermore, the West insisted that the regions should be granted rights to secede once self-government was attained.

What the McPherson Constitution unwittingly did was to

give the cultural groupings not only the opportunity to demonstrate their incompatibilities and mutual distrust but also the
opportunity to view the mirror of things to come in terms
of ethnic competition for power. Political parties and regions
were dominated by cultural groups which tended to give them
their character. To this extent, regions and political parties
are operationally vertical pressure groupings on the national
scene. In any culturally pluralistic national system where vertical pressure groups are the only vehicle for grasping and
maintaining political power, considerable havoc is done to nationalism and national cohesion.

The politics of cultural sub-nationalism would henceforth
be cast as a struggle among the three regions, each primarily
concerned with maximization of its own security. The implied
goal of each region became the control of the largest share
of the country's resource allocation. As a result, each region
became concerned with who gets what, how, and by how
much.

The failure of the Northern Elements Progressive Union
(NEPU) as a Northern political party is due partially to its
association with the NCNC, an alien political party. In addition, the party was made more unacceptable to the Northern
establishment because it appealed to the commoner and advocated democratic principles which ran into direct conflict with
the Northern political culture. To the extent that its ally, the
Ibo-dominated NCNC, earned the reputation of being anti-
aristocratic and anti-theocratic, it is easy to understand the
Northern establishment's strong anti-NEPU and anti-Ibo
sentiment.

On the whole, the demand for independence was lethargic
in the North until the 1950s. Hence, the Northerners were
understandably the favorites of the colonial administrators.
Very little was done to eradicate the somewhat rigid class
structure which was supported by the theocratic nature of the
society. The British saw in the Northern rulers a class of black
squires. Conscious efforts were made to insulate the North
from Western influence. They created an "Eton" in Northern
Nigeria, a place where children of the rulers could be edu-

cated in order to bolster and perpetuate the traditional hold on the society. Since most of the few educated people did not experience discrimination and were absorbed into the native administration system, Northern nationalism did not arise out of discontent with the British rule. (To be sure, there were demands for reforms in the native administrative system. However, vigorous Northern cultural sub-nationalism received its impetus from the activities of Ibo and Yoruba cultural sub-nationalisms.) When national political consciousness began to develop in the North, it was due primarily to a reaction against the threat of southern domination. This reaction was triggered by the presence of southern pariah groups, civil servants, and southern politicians in the North. Thus, the idea of separatism and a feeling of Northern identity, which to a certain extent was unwittingly encouraged by the colonial administration, received a powerful momentum from the activities stemming from Ibo and Yoruba cultural nationalisms.

Cultural sub-nationalisms would not have been so damaging to national cohesion but for the fact that the implied goal for each of the active cultural groups increasingly became the control of the largest share of the country's resource allocation. Thus, each component, each constituent became interested in the personnel of government as well as the direction of governmental activities and policies.

Because a "largest tribe" dominated political and cultural life, each region acquired a tribal political culture, thus accentuating regional competition and conflict among the North, West, and East. Often, at the federal level, "regionalism" was used coterminously with "ethnicity." The Yorubas denounced the "aggressiveness and clannishness" of the Ibos.

The Ibos detest the Hausa-Fulani easy acquiescence to authority. They cannot understand why the individual should not be allowed to participate in the political affairs of his community. Each group collects a dictionary of stereotypes of the other. Nevertheless, the fact that these are stereotypes does not make them insignificant. One must remember that verbal interactions, like actual interactions, are modes of behavior.

A man's behavior is conditioned by what he thinks of the man with whom he interacts.

When these different peoples with different political cultures and with a history of animosities have to interact, these political cultures, if not reconciled, these animosities, if not checked, may lead to violent confrontations. But conflicting political cultures quite apart, the accident of history made a more harmonious interaction among the three major ethnic groups difficult to achieve.

The Yorubas were the first to come into contact with Western influences, and they seized the advantage to advance themselves in the area of Western education and the acquisition of modern skills. The Ibos were rather late in coming into contact with Western influence. But once they had come in contact with the West, they redoubled their efforts in order to catch up with the Yorubas who had acquired Western education and Western skills. Increasing numbers of them were going overseas, some to the United States, many to the United Kingdom. Even at home the ratio of the Ibo students in the higher institutions of learning had been favorably tilted toward the Ibos. The acquisition of these skills meant that the Ibos must migrate to other regions of Nigeria to look for jobs and to further their education. Ibo migrations this time, unlike in the early twentieth century, were not in pursuit of land, but in search of new skills which they defined as prerequisites for meaningful participation and leadership in the new society. It should be noted that most of the Ibos migrated to other regions of Nigeria and notably to the urban centers where the Hausas and Yorubas, who have largely been an urban people, had to compete for the limited number of job opportunities available in the cities. Later, many of the recruits in government service in the North, West, and Lagos were no longer Yoruba but Ibo.

This, then, was the beginning of the race for ethnic security. The Yorubas, suddenly realizing the "ubiquity, ambition, and drive" of the Ibos and remembering only too well that the Yoruba upper hand had been so quickly reversed, reacted. From then on, the tribes paid greater attention not only to "who gets what and how" but also to "who gets the most, why, and by how much." This is the story of the intensification of ethnic hostilities.

With the approach of independence and the consequent intensification of ethnic hostilities, the politics of cultural subnationalism took on a new dimension. The Yoruba and Ibo political actors realized that neither of them could control national political power without securing a significant political foothold in the Northern Region, which alone had about half of the national electoral seats. Thus, a scramble began for the control of those electoral seats.

4. THE ATTEMPTS OF EACH GROUP TO ACHIEVE AND MAINTAIN ITS POLITICAL SECURITY

Following Chief Enahoro's self-government motion in the Central House,[25] the NCNC and the AG parliamentarians walked out. The leaders of both parties undertook to send delegations to the Northern cities to campaign for self-government for Nigeria in 1956. When Chief Samuel L. Akintola, the deputy leader of AG, reached Kano, it was at the height of North-south tension. His speech led to a chain of events which culminated in four days of riots in the Kano (Sabon Gari area) and which resulted in 277 casualties including at least thirty-six deaths.[26]

The reports on the Kano disturbance placed the cause of the riots on the contact between dissimilar cultural groups and the burgeoning of latent hostilities. The point most germane here is the naïve assumption that all that was needed was a public education of the Northern mass by their Southern brothers, and the former would give the Southerners the required mandate. The violent atrocities and mutilations which followed as the aftermath of this 1953 constitutional crisis underscores the invalidity of this presumption. It took the

combined efforts of the administration, police, and army to
restore peace to Kano.

The truth of the matter is that in their efforts to gain political power, Ibo political leaders as well as the Yoruba Action Group operated in the Northern Region as if an
autocratic-theocratic political culture would willingly permit
the open-market concept of political power to operate. The
NCNC and AG activities in the North during the 1954 federal
election campaign is a case in point.[27]

Given the Northern social system, which I have mentioned,
and the great deference which the British colonial officials
had for the Northern political actors as well as for the traditional establishment, these efforts were bound to fail.

On the basis of cultural or ethnic compatibility one would
have expected, if there was going to be an alliance during
that period, an alliance between the Western and Eastern regions against the Northern Region. Let us remember that one
way in which conflict is waged is through cooperation.[28] The
two southern peoples could have cooperated in waging the
conflict against the Northern group. But the Ibos chose to
form an alliance with the Hausas following the abortive efforts
of the former to gain power. The politics of ethnic security
momentarily forced the Ibos and the Hausas to ignore their
deep cultural differences. The Ibos anticipated a larger "pay
off" from the partnership with the Hausa-Fulani federal power
elite. The latter probably always expected the marriage to be
tentative.

Some believe that the AG had approached the NPC—the
Northern People's Congress, which was the political party of
the Northern establishment—with a plea for the formation of
a coalition between both the NPC and the AG—a coalition
which would be designed to eliminate the NCNC as a viable
political party. If the above contention is correct the similarity between the politics of 1953 and that of 1964–65 should
be obvious. This point will be pursued presently. In doing so,
however, I shall address myself rather broadly to the events
during the post-independent era which contributed to the intensification of the politics of cultural sub-nationalism.

Following the 1959 federal election, which was to be the last election before Nigeria became independent, the NCNC and the NPC formed a coalition, and the Action Group constituted the opposition. To the extent that the North, which was the senior partner in this coalition, did not have the educated manpower to fill the administrative and quasi-governmental positions, the junior partner benefited immensely. There was a marked overrepresentation of Ibos and Easterners in influential positions. Whereas the NCNC and the NPC were able to forge a cordial working relationship at the center, considerable conflict continued between the Hausa-Fulani and the Ibo residents in the North. Most of these conflicts can be traced to conflicting traits and values held by both groups. Ibo pariah groups in the North felt there was no reason why they should not be allowed to participate fully in Northern political life since they were residents of the region. Moreover, they found the Northern system of justice, as witnessed by the Alkali courts, at odds with their own. These conflicts came to a head during the Nigerian Census Crisis. The NPC had ordered a recount of the census undertaken in 1962 because the result was adverse to the North.[29] The recount was carried out, but the result was rejected by the Eastern Region because it was adverse to it. There were reports that Ibos in the North did not cooperate with Northern authorities, and the Hausa-Fulanis believed that they did so on orders from their home region.

The weight of the cultural dissimilarities was being felt increasingly by both the North and the East. The regional political elites were communicating their displeasure to their federal representative. The Ibo pariah groups in the North were especially vulnerable to the mounting antagonism. The difference in political-cultural orientations was a constant additive to the abrasive relationship. Consequently, the coalition government of NPC (predominantly Hausa-Fulani) and NCNC (predominantly Ibo) was subjected to greater strain. The senior partner began to inject more of its men into governmental positions, but it was doing so at the expense of the Ibos.

The NPC recognized that although it could muster enough

seats from the Northern Region to govern the whole of Nigeria, it needed a southern ally in order to guard against an alliance of the two southern regions; although the North was more numerous, the south still controlled the talent, a greater rate of economic development, and, possibly, the preponderance of valuable natural resources. The Easterners were becoming dissatisfied with their ever-decreasing political influence, and the North was finding its Eastern ally burdensome. Consequently, the North was looking with interest at the possibility of political alliance with some faction of the Yoruba.

The Yoruba Action Group rift of 1963, which led to the imprisonment of Chief Obafemi Awolowo and the polarization of Yoruba leadership, precipitated a Western Region crisis that afforded both the Hausa-Fulani and the Ibos the opportunity to seek new allies. One of the reasons for the rift between Awolowo and Chief Akintola concerned the question of AG strategy in the political struggle. Akintola was perturbed by the elimination of Yorubas from political and administrative sinecures and the diminuation of Yoruba political influence. He advocated cooperation with the North (a reversion to the 1952–53 strategy which failed) as the method for Yoruba security, but Awolowo rather adamantly adhered to a policy of oppositionalism and eventual cooperation among Southern peoples against the North. Ultimately, the rift became irreconcilable, and Awolowo was jailed.

The NCNC was rather ambivalent on the whole issue affecting the Western crisis. On the one hand, in its enthusiasm to get back at the Yoruba AG, it unwittingly voted along with the NPC at the House of Representatives to declare that a state of emergency existed in the Western Region. On the other hand, it realized that in terms of cultural compatibility, most of the rank and file members of the party did not feel comfortable with the Northern establishment. Hence, the NCNC as a party was also interested in passing as the friend of the West.

The Northern People's Congress teamed up with the faction of the Yoruba Action Group under the leadership of Chief Akintola which called itself the Nigerian National Democratic Party. The NCNC allied itself with the other faction of the AG which (in the absence of Chief Awolowo) was led by D. S. Adegbenro and retained the name AG. The alliance between NCNC and AG was called the United Progressive Grand Alliance (UPGA) and that of the NPC and the NNDP was called the Nigerian National Alliance (NNA). The latter won the 1964 federal elections.

This election, more than any before it, witnessed more intense disregard for the rules governing elections in democratic societies. The elections were neither free nor peaceful. Candidates of opposing parties received technical knockouts simply by the NNDP's use of obstructionist practices. Each competing group hired gangs to beat up and victimize its opponents and their supporters. Campaign permits were not issued to the opposing parties. Arbitrary arrests, wrongful imprisonment, assaults and killings were not uncommon.

Faced with this situation, UPGA appealed for a postponement of the election. Neither the Electoral Commission nor the President was competent to do this. The UPGA leadership threatened secession just as the Northern leadership had done in 1953. By the eve of the election, the party's representative on the Electoral Commission had resigned, and the UPGA had ordered a boycott of the election. The boycott was totally effective in the Eastern Region but only partially effective in the West. In any case, the boycott made it quite easy for the NNDP to win the federal elections in the North and in the West.

The President, himself an Ibo, tendered his resignation rather than call upon the deputy leader of the successful party, Sir Tafawa Balewa, to form the government. He believed that although he might not have the constitutional authority to declare the election null and void, he had the obligation to resign because of the circumstances under which the elections were held. But two prominent Nigerians, a Yoruba and an Ibo, intervened. After persistent negotiation, they succeeded in breaking the deadlock between the Prime Minister and the President.

Two points in the agreement are of interest. It was agreed

that a broad-based national government should be formed on the basis of the results of the controversial election so as to avoid chaos. Second, it was decided that new elections must be ordered in areas where the elections had been successfully boycotted so as not to make a mockery of the democratic process.

The Ibos and their allies seemed frustrated at the apparent denial of the opportunity to operate in the North under the open-market concept of power. Hence, they felt doomed. Perhaps, in desperation they appealed to the President, who himself was an Ibo. The power of the President could not give them adequate redress. Nevertheless, it could be argued that the UPGA's partial boycott of the federal election robbed Nigeria of the opportunity to mitigate the bad effects of cultural sub-nationalism. They argued that had the party participated despite the odds against it, it would have emerged as a very strong opposition in the Federal House and that the ruling party would not have been deluded into interpreting its success as a vindication. However, it must be recalled that in 1959 the NCNC got the majority in both Western and Eastern regions in the federal elections, but this did not even adumbrate cultural sub-nationalism. Perhaps the fact that the UPGA seemed to be an alliance of concerned Yorubas and Ibos, coupled with the probability that an UPGA victory in the Western federal election would have ensured the ousting of the NNDP, would have forced a realignment of Nigerian political parties less along tribal lines. But this is by no means certain. In any case, considerable care must be taken not to overestimate the potentiality which such a structural realignment may have had for Nigerian unity. After all, there have always been Yorubas in the membership of the NCNC, but that has not had any overwhelming positive contribution to Nigerian unity.

The census crisis is an interesting case in point. This crisis split the NCNC along ethnic lines. Most Yorubas in the NCNC bolted the party and opted for Yoruba solidarity. Whereas the Yorubas seemed satisfied with the results of the second census, Eastern Nigerians, especially the Ibos, were dissatisfied with it. Thus, many prominent NCNC legislators joined the NNDP as the party which would best represent Yoruba interests. The Nigerian census crisis reflects the politics of cultural sub-nationalism. Extreme attachment to one's cultural group at the expense of national identity requires that one pays most meticulous attention to who gets what, how much, and by what means. In a society that has democratic pretensions, census is important not only for the purpose of political recruitment but also as a basis for the allocation of resources. Naturally, therefore, each group would have to pay great attention not only to its own population but also to the accuracy of those of the other groups.

The Western regional crisis has been alluded to several times in this discussion. One of the six points of agreement reached in order to avert the constitutional crisis, which was a consequence of the 1964 federal elections, was the dissolution of the Legislature of Western Nigeria to enable the people of that region to express their wish regarding who should govern them. On October 11, 1965, the Western elections were held. This election proved to be the most controversial in Nigerian history. There were many electoral irregularities. Electoral officers were kidnapped. Many electoral officers deserted their posts to avoid receiving nomination papers from UPGA candidates. The appointments of electoral officers who had been impartial were revoked, and the certificates of validity they had issued to opponents declared null and void. Thus, many seats were declared unopposed, and in accordance with the Western Nigeria Electoral Regulation sections 19b and 14 (3), the validity of the proceeding cannot be questioned in any legal proceedings.[30] Furthermore, unauthorized persons, including local government police officers, contrary to the law, were caught in possession of several ballot papers which they allegedly intended to dump into the ballot boxes. "The most notorious example of this travesty was the case of a man who won the election in one of the Owo constituencies. His opponent was declared the victor. He thereupon announced that he decided to join the NNDP. A few days after this announcement the Electoral Commission declared him

the successful candidate and quietly dropped his opponent."[31]
The first indication that the system was reaching the elasticity
limits of grace can best be glimpsed from the fact that the
defeated candidates did not seek redress in the courts as was
customary, but took the law into their own hands. Inciden-
tally, this may also be an index of the level to which esteem
for the judiciary had fallen.

The Northern Region had the most at stake in the Western
election. If the UPGA had won the election, it would have
had ominous implications for the North. A UPGA victory
would mean that the southern cultural groups had arrived at
an apparent solidarity. The AG controlled Lagos; the NCNC
controlled the East and Midwest. An UPGA victory in the
West would have wrapped things up. In the event of such a
victory, minority groups in the North might become bolder
in their demands. Through their allies in the minority areas of
the North, the NCNC and the AG might effect a defection.
Consequently, Northern group solidarity would be severely
threatened. The control of the North by the aristocracy and
the Northern establishment would be severely put to the test.
Ultimately, the Hausa-Fulani cultural group might find its
security and commanding position rocked and even reversed.

It must be recalled that the East had slowly but consistently
fallen from the grace of the North which controlled political
power in Nigeria. It was imperative for them, the Ibos, to seek
a more compatible ally if they were going to ascertain not
only a more lasting political influence but also their very survival. Their boycott of the federal election robbed them of the
opportunity to test the strength of the new coalition and possibly denied them the opportunity to protect their own security
solidly.

The Yorubas themselves could not reach a unanimous
agreement on a course of action. However, it seemed clear
that the majority of Yorubas were more inclined, although
reluctantly, to support the Ibo-Yoruba coalition. They were
willing to seek their security without sacrificing cultural
compatibility.

The Nigerian National Alliance won the Western Region

election. The conduct of these elections is still widely criticized. The victory of the North accentuated the fears of the East. It was the last straw which set in motion a train of tragic events.

In manners almost characteristic of the revolt of the masses, frustrated Western Nigerians took the law into their own hands. Disillusioned candidates and their supporters seemed to have lost interest in the judiciary as an unbiased adjudicative institution. Travelers on the major roads were at the mercy of roaming gangs. The police could no longer cope with the situation in many areas. As if to confirm the partiality that had been long suspected, the Prime Minister was not going to intervene in this case despite the killings. He would intervene only if there were two persons who declared themselves premier of the region. Most people saw in the Prime Minister's reluctance a double standard. After all, the Prime Minister did intervene in 1962. Could his reluctance in the present circumstance be traced to the fact that the NNDP was an ally of his party? Many Nigerians have answered this question in the affirmative. But friends of the Prime Minister have pointed out that he endeavored to be an informal mediator. Reportedly he had suggested a broadly based government in which both camps would be represented. However, the NNDP leadership was intransigent and unwilling to compromise. The Prime Minister had hoped that such a compromise would cool tempers, assure representation, and pave the way to a fair Western Region election in the near future.

The NNDP and the leader of the NPC had reportedly reached an agreement on what measures would be taken to stamp out the disturbances. It was felt that the Western government with the strong backing of the Northern government was prepared to use extreme measures. If this had been allowed to happen, it would have, as usual, rendered the federal government impotent; the senior partner in the federal government consisted of the less powerful members of the NPC whereas the more powerful members of the party were to be found in the Northern Region. Thus, in a sense Western Nigeria was being used as the political pawn around which the survival of Northern cultural sub-nationalism revolved.

It is unfortunate for Nigerian unity that most of the time and energy of the Prime Minister was spent reconciling conflicts which had been set in motion by cultural sub-nationalism. Few will doubt his sincere commitment to Nigerian unity. But like some other supporters of Nigerian unity, the Prime Minister was hardly ever on the offensive. Some have argued in the Prime Minister's defense that whereas he was theoretically the most powerful individual, in practice the most powerful individual was the Sardauna of Sokoto, the pivot of Northern cultural sub-nationalism. In any case, once again cultural sub-nationalism was allowed to take precedence over national unity. The Prime Minister let the "sleeping dog lie."

On January 15, 1966, a group of young army officers executed a coup d'état. Most of the officers involved in the coup d'état were Ibos. However, it should be mentioned that a majority of the Nigerian officers at the time were Eastern Nigerians. In the execution of this takeover, the Sardauna of Sokoto, the leader of the Northern Region, Tafawa Balewa, the Prime Minister, and Chief Akintola, the controversial Premier of Western Nigeria, were killed. On the other hand, Chief Osadebey and Dr. Okpara, the premiers of the Midwest and Eastern regions respectively, were spared somehow. Moreover, the overwhelming majority of the senior military officers killed were Northerners.

In retrospect, there are three schools of thought regarding the motivating forces behind the coup d'état. The first takes the words of the leader of the coup d'état at face value. At the conclusion of the coup, the leader, Major Chukwama Nzeogwu, announced that the participants were concerned with stamping out tribalism, nepotism, and regionalism.[32] But when it became clear that not all the regional premiers and that very few Ibo officers had been killed, many Nigerians became skeptical. Thus, within the rubric of the politics of cultural sub-nationalism such Nigerians felt that the Ibos, having found themselves at the lowest ebb of political influence and having been frustrated in their attempts to seek redress through legitimate channels, must have resorted to violence as an interest-aggregating instrument. There are still others who are not quite prepared to lump all the participants in one group. They admitted that there were some officers who might have been motivated by love of country but that there were still many others who were definitely influenced by cultural sub-nationalism. The majority of the people who held this opinion subscribed to the notion that most of the participants in the coup d'état were motivated not by love of country but by cultural sub-nationalism. At the risk of oversimplification, it would seem today that the Ibos held the first view, the Hausas the second, and the Yorubas the third. It was not always this way, however. Surprisingly, the reaction of the overwhelming majority immediately after the coup d'état was one of relief and appreciation because this military takeover meant a restoration of law and order, security, and perhaps justice. In the North the majority of the people were illiterates, and they were concerned more with Northern Nigerian politics. Most of the illiterates felt it was a mistake for the North to be tangled up in the affairs of the West. The Northerners who were apprehensive from the beginning were the educated Northerners who had found themselves rather rapidly in very high administrative and political positions because of the political power that the North held in Nigeria. The latter group of Northerners has been credited with inciting the riot of May 24, 1966, and precipitating the counter coup of July 29, 1966. Admittedly, the counter coup d'état was undertaken to restore Northern political influence, or, at least, to ensure that the region's freedom of action as a political entity would be restored. The last event which led to the May riot was the declaration of Decree Number 39 of 1966.[33] This decree abolished the regions of Nigeria and the federal form of government; it unified the top grades of the public services and introduced a provincial system of administration. The riots which broke out in the major cities of Northern Nigeria led to the loss of property and the death of many southerners, mostly Ibos.

Major General J. T. U. Aguiyi-Ironsi, the head of the Federal Military Government, while on a reconciliation tour of Ibadan was abducted on July 29, 1966, and was eventually killed by Northern Nigerian soldiers. Many Ibo officers and recruits were killed along with him. In his first broadcast, the successor, Lieutenant Colonel Yakubu Gowon, who was a Northerner, proceeded to revoke Decree Number 39 and stated that "the basis for trust and confidence in our unitary system of government has not been able to stand the test of time." But this did not seem to satisfy all Northerners. So again, in September, civilians as well as some Northern soldiers went on a rampage, killing, looting, and destroying property of the Ibos or those they believed to be Ibos.

Is it a coincidence that the person and the property of the Ibos have always been a target of Northern anger? Is it a coincidence that many northern Ibos after the first coup d'état continued to brag about the active part played by their Ibo officers, as if by the act the Ibos had achieved collective pride?

There are common features of both coups which seem relevant to our interest in cultural sub-nationalism. A common feature of the first and the second coups was the fact that in each case the political change was accompanied with changes in the assignments of the higher civil servants. Since the Nigerian bureaucracy is a career bureaucracy, neither appointed nor elected, administrators cannot be dismissed, as long as they conduct themselves well. They can, however, be relegated to unimportant offices.

Following the January event, the North began to lose its political influence. Some Northern higher civil servants were transferred to less powerful positions and ministries. Efforts were made to centralize the political decision-making machinery as well as the entire civil services.

In some quarters it was felt that one of the reasons why the First Republic was doomed was because of the divergence between the constitutional power-holder and the actual power-holder. In theory, the Prime Minister was powerful, but in reality the Sardauna had greater power. Furthermore, it was believed that tribalism was anchored in regionalism, and that if you could somehow get rid of that structure called the region, then tribalism would cease to be a problem child. Of course, this is a gross simplification.

Many Northern civil servants, following the coup d'état, expressed grave fears about their future. Personal secretaries to the ministers lost their positions. Those of them who had good qualifications were given positions commensurate with their academic and professional qualifications. Since Northern Nigeria ranked lowest in the possession of high educational qualifications, many Northern personal secretaries were demoted to junior service positions. To the extent that they were not able to readjust to this low status and style of life, many of them went back to their villages and towns in the North. This fact added to the waning influence of the North made the Northern higher civil servants and educated elite unkindly disposed toward the Ironsi regime.

We do not have the complete data which would enable us to make a correct assessment of the role which the Northern educated elite played in the second coup d'état. However, it must be reported that they took an active part in the negotiations which ended up in the emergence of a Northerner as the successor of Major General Aguiyi-Ironsi.[34] Many of them were rather outspoken about their dislike for the Aguiyi-Ironsi regime. Perhaps many of them aided and abetted the protests which took place in major Northern cities during the month of May. In fact, most Northerners sympathized with the most common slogan of the protestors which demanded separation or secession.

After the second coup d'état, Ibo higher administrators suffered similar reverses. They were relegated to the background or "kicked upstairs." As a result of the bloodshed which followed the second coup d'état, Ibos in Eastern Nigeria began to agitate for redress or separation. The refugee problem put a significant pressure on the regional government. It has been argued by Father James O'Connell that the Ibo civil servants who were forced to flee to the East contributed greatly to the somewhat uncompromising attitude of the East.[35] It seemed that the East, particularly the Ibos, somehow decided that they could no longer protect and pursue their communal and individual goals within the framework of a Federal Nigeria.

5. APPRAISAL OF THE ATTEMPTS MADE TO INSURE THAT CULTURAL SUB-NATIONALISM DID NOT PREVENT THE ATTAINMENT OF NIGERIAN NATIONALISM

Let us now pinpoint some of the efforts made in order to keep cultural sub-nationalism from destroying national integration. After the self-government motion of 1953, the subsequent political deadlock, and the Kano riots which followed, the colonial administration made a major adjustment in the structure of government. It felt that unity could be achieved without getting rid of diversity. By implication, it was felt that there might be virtue in keeping unlike things apart. Thus, the Constitution which replaced the McPherson was not a central Constitution but a federal one which gave more power to the regions. However, in retrospect, we find that this new arrangement did not succeed where its predecessor failed. Although it allowed the communities greater latitude, it ignored the question of unequal representation. No section of a federal country should have been allowed to hold political power which would permit it to control federal power without regard to the other components. The new Constitution harbored inconsistencies. Granted that one must respect the cultural values of a society in determining the method of representation, but representation in such a competitive heterogeneous society should be based on a computation of the registered eligible voters. For example, if women and children are not allowed to vote because of the tradition of a society, is it fair to count them as relevant when it comes to representation?

Perhaps, for a society with great conflict potential, it is absolutely important that the society agree on basic goals and the procedure and rules governing the pursuit of such goals.

The advantage in this is that many areas of intrinsic conflict would be foreseen and efforts would be made to reconcile them. Instead of doing this, efforts were made to cover up areas of deep conflict because of deliberate speed to achieve Nigerian self-government. Unequal representation of major cultural areas may not be damaging in countries where a political party or political organization genuinely national in scope, concern, and performance exist. However, in a system where cultural sub-nationalism engulfs newer institutions and tribal loyalty takes precedence over national attachment, it is fatal.

A popular instrument of the late Prime Minister is the formation of a broadly based government as a method of reconciliation of sectional conflict. To be truly effective in stamping out cultural sub-nationalisms, there must be a conviction that the head of such a government is truly his own man. It is not enough for him to show concern for national unity; he must act to vindicate his authority and power to act positively in the interest of national unity. The Prime Minister was not successful in his method because he was generally accepted as a lieutenant of Sir Ahmadu Bello, who was regarded as the pivot of Northern cultural nationalism. Furthermore, Balewa's broadly based governments have been dominated by one group. Those persons included in such all-party governments should be people who will continue to have enough credit with their people as to be able to influence them positively toward deeper national commitment.

Two political parties have tried to become national in terms of influence. However, the means they have used have been a liability to national unity. Appealing to tribal sentiment, tribal exclusivism, and complete disregard for cultural sensitivities are harmful to national unity. In short, the type of alliance which the AG and NPC sought in 1953, the type of politics which the NPC and NCNC played with Western Nigeria in 1962–65, and AG activities in minority areas from 1954 to 1959 could not make positive contributions to national unity.

It is naïve to look at structural rearrangement as the only solution to Nigerian problems. There must be a structural rearrangement arrived at as much as possible within acceptable democratic norms. Otherwise, the methods used in effecting such a restructuring become an added bone of contention and an aggravated source of future conflict. Attitudes have to be changed. In addition to political resocialization which must take place to effect the change of attitude, there must be a reconciliation of the modern political behavior with the traditional political behavior. For example, if the future Nigeria is going to be a democratic society, ways must be found for all Nigerians irrespective of their place of origin to participate fully in the political life of the community of their residence after satisfying certain residency requirements. For example, it will be absurd to say that a Western Yoruba who has lived in Northern Nigeria for twenty years cannot stand for an election in Northern Nigeria.

This chapter would be deficient if it does not attempt an analysis of General Gowon's efforts to preserve the Nigerian state. Here an analogy between Uganda and Nigeria is in order. Despite the many similarities between both countries, early indications are that Uganda is succeeding where Nigeria is not making spectacular progress. Generally, the essence of the difference seems to lie in the ability of President Apolo Milton Obote to take successful initiative. The factors responsible for this capability were:

(1) the thrust of ethnic coalition which cemented most Uganda sub-national groups solidly behind him,

(2) the quick, short, and decisive military victory of Uganda's army over the ex-servicemen of the Buganda kingdom.

The violent encounter caused a disequilibrium in power relationships. President Obote seized upon this disequilibrium to press for a new authority in the form of a new Constitution designed to reduce the political importance of sub-national movements.

In the case of Nigeria, one can view General Gowon's declaration of twelve states as an attempt to engineer a temporary disequilibrium. This attempt did not succeed immediately due to circumstantial and temporal factors. It was ill-timed because it came after the Aburi Conference which was anticipated as the basis for the resolution of conflict for both sides but which significantly did not intimate the further division of states. Moreover, it should be noted that Ibo sub-nationalism was sufficiently well nourished by a feeling of self-righteousness on the part of its members. Ibos in the Eastern Region were not extremely enthusiastic about secession until after the August riots which sent to the Eastern Region many more refugees than the May riots and which saw many more Ibos massacred. In one sense, then, and in the perception of most Ibos, Biafra was a forced last defensive stand. Apparently, Nigerians did not fully imagine the bolstering effect in the conviction of such perceived righteous posture. In addition, perhaps an urge for vendetta secretly lurked in the minds of many whose friends or relatives had been victims.

Unlike Obote, General Gowon's thrust to public life was circumstantial, and he needed to build a basis of power. He had come to power as a result of a military coup d'état against a military government. At the time, at least, one could argue that the military institution like most Nigerian institutions had only national pretensions, at best. Some unsympathetic observers whispered, "Physician heal thyself." But even a kind observer would have to admit that the existence of such a state in the military complicated matters and made the job of General Gowon difficult. For a while, the Nigerian military had a credibility gap.

Furthermore, unlike the Baganda, the Ibos had a well-trained officer corps, a comparatively sophisticated array of military hardware, and dedicated and bitter recruits. Despite the fact that some new Ibo leaders had a Messianic complex, there is no evidence to suggest a very serious gap between the elite and the masses. A bond of common experience had forced itself upon all Ibo refugees; the former higher civil servant and the former steward from Lagos now shared essentially the same fears. The phrase "Ojukwu and his clique" is a gross underestimation of Ibo unity. Such underestimation handicapped those intent upon dealing with this Nigerian problem.

The Uganda political game is not over yet. It is therefore difficult to separate temporary success from a lasting one. In any case, one must note that forceful integration is a most dangerous approach because the permanence of success is not assured. Besides, it can exacerbate matters. For the country which feels compelled to resort to it, such a country must take stock of (a) the institutional viability of the military; (b) the will of the sub-national group(s) to secede; (c) the skill of the political leaders of the sub-national group. In addition, it is well to remember that a long-drawn-out civil war, an underestimation of the military capability of the sub-national group, and a brutal domestic military confrontation can be self-defeating to those eager to create a nation.

An aggravating source of ethnic conflict revolves around the determination of who gets what, how, and by how much. In many cases, friction would be minimized if the leaders of the independent state can continue to provide the expanding resources needed. In short, if the less-developed sub-national groups can be lifted from the doldrums without taking away from the more fortunate groups, sub-national movements should lose some of their luster. Finally, political actors must lead the way in showing tolerance and in manifesting the desire for a more harmonious national community.

The surrender of Biafran forces on January 12, 1970, meant that the civil war had come to an end with a military victory for the Nigerian Federal Military Government. Undoubtedly, the Gowon government can claim credit for this achievement. But, does this demonstration of military competence amount to an assertion of political credibility with reference to the role of the military in the creation of Nigerian nationalism?

The *Nigerian Tribune* of March 23, 1969, demanded from the military government an immediate transfer of power to civilians. Influential opinions in the Western State were sympathetic to this position. It is therefore irrefutable that even during the period of the civil war serious attempts were made to pressure the military to relinquish political power. Perhaps, in order to assuage the fears of many, generate sufficient internal solidarity in Nigeria—for the purpose of the war—and dampen the impatience of ambitious politicians, the military leaders were constrained to give the impression of an eagerness to return to the barracks once the civil war was over and a feeling of uneasiness about wearing the political hats. The impression that the most important goal was the successful prosecution of the war and that thereafter normalcy would return, was created.

Ironically, then, the military victory must have rejuvenated high expectations in many quarters. Many old politicians, nascent politicians, and political entrepreneurs must be impatient. The Nigerian case is further complicated by the fact that the tradition of military intervention in sub-Saharan Africa has been followed in a relatively short time by a return to civilian rule. Consequently, it will represent a departure from the trend.

This is not to argue that there are not some who would rather have the military continue to rule as long as "it is necessary." The *Nigerian Daily Times* has expressed a similar sentiment. In any case, the military has clearly indicated its intention to continue in power until 1976. It is not the purpose here to say whether or not the military will fulfill this goal. However, it is proper to mention some of the problems and difficulties the military may face in its political role. In doing so, it must be conceded that it has not been possible to have General Gowon's complete political blueprint. The outline we have—published in *West Africa*—is as follows:[36]

(1) the desire to implement the National Development Plan of 1970–76,

(2) the ambition to "retrain" and reorganize the army and to readmit "former rebels,"

(3) the desire to freeze the number of states until 1974,

(4) the goal to establish a panel to draft a new Constitution and a constitutional assembly which will consider the

draft (the composition and the time of these bodies are not known),

(5) the promise to establish a **Revenue Allocation Committee** linked to the constitutional proposal,

(6) the desire to have national political parties and eradicate corruption,

(7) the preference for a Federal Constitution which will provide for elected ministerial government in the states.

Finally, the author of the article in *West Africa* wrote: ". . . it is clear that General Gowon is wedded to the idea of states of the present kind, with at least some of the attributes of the old regional government."[37]

The deadline of 1976 means that Nigeria will remain under a military rule for over ten of its sixteen years of independence. Even if one were to grant the very controversial contention that military regimes can bring about high political capability such as is necessary to promote nationalism, there are particular notes of caution which the experiences of other countries suggest. In a state with very ambitious and experienced politicians and a populace unused to military discipline, a period of ten years may do havoc to the "good name" of the military. Since the second general task to which the military seems committed is essentially political, and it requires political strategies and solutions, might not the military men be perceived as "politicians"? On the other hand, if the populace becomes "accustomed" to the military in politics, it is entirely possible that they will develop skeptical attitudes about politics. Pervasive political skepticism about the state cannot contribute to meaningful political development.

Those who want the military to remain in politics for as long as it is necessary are expressing their faith in the political capability of the military because of the military's performance during the civil war. However, the performance required of a military regime to end the civil war is markedly different from the one needed to engender nationalism. Unless the military can demonstrate the latter competence, then the vagaries of public opinion will become sadly evident. Even a reputable newspaper like the *Nigerian Daily Times* has demonstrated an ability to change horses in midstream and sail with the wind. During this period of continued military governance, the resilience and viability of the Nigerian military as a truly national institution may be tested.

On the positive side, one must note that delicate political decisions were made during the civil war. It can be argued, therefore, that what the military needs is the wisdom and support of the bureaucracy. Indeed, some believe that the higher civil servants, more than the military leaders, are reluctant to return the government to the civilian politicians. But such a line of reasoning must be balanced with a realization that such cooperation was easy to achieve in a war situation and that over a longer period it might become strained. Bureaucrats are not incapable of shifting alliances. More importantly, however, the military leaders can no longer be looked upon as novices. An apparently sophisticated "military bureaucracy" is developing. It is therefore conceivable that there will be conflict between the military and the civilian bureaucracy. There is also the possibility that that which one seeks to tame might become one's master; parochial loyalty may forcefully and overtly reassert itself.

At the present, the popularity of General Gowon and his good intentions are not seriously questioned by Nigerians. It may well be that he might become a political leader following the tradition and style of Gamal Abdel Nasser and Joseph Desire Mobutu. In any case, the political future of Nigeria and Nigerian nationalism may be entering a most crucial stage.

NOTES

1. This subsection has drawn upon several sources including:

Margery Freda Perham, *Native Administration in Nigeria* (London: Oxford University Press, 1937).

Ahmadu Bello, *My Life* (London: Cambridge University Press, 1962).

James Coleman, *Nigeria: Background to Nationalism* (Berkeley and Los Angeles: University of California Press, 1958).

Michael G. Smith, *Government in Zazzau 1800–1950* (London: Oxford University Press, 1960).

Economy of Hausa States, Report to the colonial Social Science Research Council (London: Her Majesty's Stationery Office for the Colonial Office, 1955). Colonial Research Studies No. 16.

Richard L. Sklar and C. S. Whitaker, "The Federal Republic of Nigeria" in Gwendolen Carter, ed., *National Unity and Regionalism in Eight African States* (Ithaca: Cornell University Press, 1966).

E. R. Yeld, "Islam and Social Structure in Northern Nigeria," *British Journal of Sociology*, XI, 2, 1960.

2. Michael G. Smith, *Government in Zazzau 1800–1950*, p. 8.

3. Sklar and Whitaker, *op. cit.*, p. 12.

4. *Ibid.*, p. 12.

5. The following authors should be helpful in this subsection:
Robert F. Stevenson, *Population and Political Systems in Tropical Africa* (New York: Columbia University Press, 1968).

Kenneth O. Dike, *Trade and Politics on the Niger Delta, 1830–1885* (London: Oxford University Press, 1956).

Coleman, *op. cit.*

Charles K. Meek, *Law and Authority in a Nigerian Tribe* (London: Oxford University Press, 1937).

Margaret M. Green, *Ibo Village Affairs* (New York: Frederick A. Praeger, Inc., 1964).

Simon Ottenberg, "Ibo Receptivity to Change" in William R. Bascom and Melville J. Herskovits, eds., *Continuity and Change in African Cultures* (Chicago: University of Chicago Press, 1959).

G. I. Jones, "Report of the Position, Status, and Influence of

Chiefs and Natural Rulers in Eastern Region of Nigeria" (Enugu Government Printer).

6. Ottenberg, *op. cit.*, p. 130.

7. C. K. Meek, *op. cit.*, p. 3.

8. *Ibid.*, pp. 110–11.

9. R. F. Stevenson, *op. cit.*, p. 200.

10. C. K. Meek, *op. cit.*, p. 111.

11. G. I. Jones quoted in G. Carter, *op. cit.*, p. 15.

12. The following sources should be helpful:

Peter C. Lloyd, *Yoruba Land Law* (London: Oxford University Press, 1962).
Daryll Forde, *The Yoruba-Speaking Peoples of South-western Nigeria*, Ethnographic Survey of Africa (London: International African Institute, 1951).
Coleman, *op. cit.*

13. Lloyd, *op. cit.*, p. 46.

14. *Ibid.*, p. 46.

15. *Ibid.*, p. 46.

16. Awolowo quoted in Donald S. Rothchild, *Toward Unity in Africa: A Study of Federalism in British Africa* (Washington: Public Affairs Press, 1960), p. 142.

17. *Ibid.*, p. 144.

18. Coleman, *op. cit.*, p. 46.

19. *Ibid.*, pp. 193–94.

20. *Ibid.*, p. 194.

21. *Ibid.*, pp. 52–53.

22. *Ibid.*, p. 50.

23. *West African Pilot*, July 8, 1948.

24. See Proceedings of the General Conference on Review of the Constitution held at Ibadan, January 1950 (Lagos), Report of the Drafting Committee on the Constitution (Lagos, 1950), Review of Constitutional Proposals by Colonial Secretary (Lagos, 1950).

For a continuous narration of Nigerian political history, the reader may want to read:

Coleman, *op. cit.*

Richard L. Sklar, *Nigerian Political Parties: Power in an Emergent African Nation* (Princeton: Princeton University Press, 1963).

John P. MacKintosh, *Nigerian Government and Politics* (London: George Allen & Unwin, Ltd., 1966).

Kalu Ezera, *Constitutional Developments in Nigeria* (London: Cambridge University Press, 1964).

Okoi Arikpo, *Modern Nigeria* (Baltimore: Penguin, 1966).

25. The self-government motion of 1953.

26. Coleman, *op. cit.*, pp. 399–400.

27. Sklar, *op. cit.;* Coleman, *op. cit.*

28. Georg Simmel, *Conflict* (Kurt H. Wolff, tr.) and *The Web of Group Affiliation* (Reinhard Bendix, tr.) (Chicago: The Free Press, 1955).

29. James O'Connell in Arthur Hazlewood, ed., *African Integration and Disintegration* (London: Oxford University Press, 1967).

30. Arikpo, *op. cit.*, p. 140.

31. *Ibid.*, p. 141.

32. Radio broadcast on January 16, 1966, following the coup d'état.

33. Decree no. 39, May 24, 1966, *Nigerian Official Gazette*, Supplement A153.

34. *West Africa*, August 13, 1966.

35. James O'Connell, *Africa Report*, February 1968.

36. *West Africa*, October 10, 1970.

37. *Ibid.*

II
UGANDA

❖ ❖ ❖

EDITOR'S INTRODUCTORY NOTE

In Uganda, ethnic political behavior suggests a typology (a modification of Clifford Geertz's typology) based on several differentiating factors. On the basis of this typology, six subnational movements come into focus: Kabaka Yekka, Sebei, Rwenzururu, the "Lost Counties" controversy, the Mbale controversy, and the anti-Baganda coalition. The roots of these movements date back to the struggles for territory and military superiority in pre-colonial time. The policies of the British Colonial Administration tended to give increased strength to cultural sub-nationalism. Indirect rule not only tampered with ethnic boundaries but also actually organized people into tribal units. Under the Colonial Administration, educated Africans were encouraged to participate in local government as a preparation for self-government. As a result, power was shifted from traditional rulers to democratically elected representatives without eliminating the ethnic basis of their power. Moreover, when nationalist parties were developed, the district rather than the nation was the organizational focus. Politics, therefore, became preoccupied with local issues and politicians were susceptible to the appeals of sub-national movements. In their preferential treatment of the Baganda, the British further intensified the ethnic basis of Ugandan politics. Baganda was not only granted more autonomy than other districts but also enjoyed more educational opportunities and a faster rate of economic growth.

With the approach of independence cultural sub-nationalism was given additional impetus by the departure of the colonial authorities, by minority groups who feared that the government would not respect their rights, and by a willingness on the part of people to regard civil servants and ministers from their districts as "their representatives" in the central government. Independence, therefore, was accompanied by the heightened saliency of ethnic identity.

As a result, the forces of fragmentation were quite operative in Uganda even though President Apolo Milton Obote had indicated his strong opposition to cultural sub-nationalism. The occasion of factional disputes within Uganda's majority political party gave Obote an opportunity to consolidate the support of military and political leaders and to challenge the privileged position of Buganda. Obote used this confrontation to develop a greater sense of national consciousness among the Ugandans. A new Constitution was adopted which greatly centralized the political system and gave increased power to the President. It also removed many legal provisions encouraging the expression of sub-nationalist tendencies, such as the autonomous powers of districts.

The official policy of the Ugandan government is that ethnicity no longer exists. However, if national unity is to remain a reality in Uganda, the government must eliminate resentment bred by ethnically differentiated educational and economic development inherited from the past. Such resentment can be appeased most successfully by greatly expanding the resources available for distribution. Only then can the government ignore ethnic considerations while redressing the inequities of the past. Under the central government, the Ugandans appear to be developing a political structure which permits Uganda to achieve its intended goals and to attack ethnicity, a central problem of most new states of Africa, with encouraging success.

CULTURAL SUB-NATIONALISM IN UGANDA

By Nelson Kasfir*

DARTMOUTH COLLEGE, NEW HAMPSHIRE

Competition among ethnic groups has marked politics in almost all the new states of Africa and Asia. Becoming the focus of intense loyalties these groups often challenge the legitimacy of state authority. The clash between cultural sub-nationalism and civil order, each making an absolute moral claim on its adherents, reduces the possibilities of national integration.[1] This problem of dual loyalty has plagued political leaders searching for institutions to contain sub-nationalisms. By and large the political structures bequeathed by colonial rulers have proved inadequate. Yet the effort to replace imitations of European representational patterns of government with more realistic substitutes immediately raises the suspicion that one ethnic group may be favored at the expense of another. In addition the virtually universal moral argument that all groups have some sort of right to self-determination[2]—an essential weapon of the independence struggle—limits the choices open to governments hoping to curb assertions of cultural identity.

* I have greatly profited from the comments and reactions of those who read an earlier draft of this chapter, and would particularly like to thank Michael Davies, Bryan Langlands, Yash Tandon, Crawford Young, and Richard Hook for the close and painstaking scrutiny they generously provided. Since I rejected their criticisms as often as I accepted them, I alone remain responsible for all opinions expressed.

I am further indebted to the Department of Political Science and Public Administration at Makerere University for financial assistance.

The arrival of independence has tended to further stimulate ethnic rivalry and consciousness of cultural differences at the expense of national unity. The problem, however, is not limited to the new states. One writer has argued recently that "no multination structure has been immune to this surge of nationalism. . . . No government of a multination state has found the solution to the dilemma . . ."[3]

Uganda has been no exception to these centrifugal tendencies through most of her first years of independence. The prospects for national unity were considered discouraging at the time the British departed.[4] Later commentators noted that ". . . local nationalism remains an essential element of the Uganda scene."[5] A Ugandan Member of the Legislative

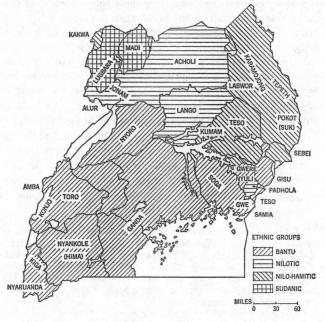

ETHNIC AND LANGUAGE GROUPS IN UGANDA
Source: Department of Geography, Makerere University.

Council declared: "All Uganda is advocating parochial institutions."[6]

Like many other African states Uganda was the product of borders drawn in Europe (and later adjusted by Protectorate officials) without much regard for the ethnic identification of the peoples in question. This resulted in two anomalies. First, many border peoples were divided between two or more states. Second, a variety of ethnic groups with unlike cultural practices were included in the same state. However, Uganda differs from many of her African neighbors in later governmental development, since British colonial authorities emphasized certain legal institutions that separated and encour-

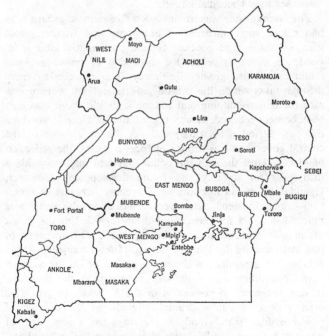

UGANDA—Districts and District Capitals after 1967
Source: Department of Geography, Makerere University.

aged ethnic identity. The result was a semi-federal form of government at the time of independence.

Under British rule "District Councils . . . [became] the repositories of local power in defense against central power."[7] The 1900 Agreement with Buganda that made Uganda a Protectorate instead of a Crown Colony was largely responsible for the development of this state of affairs, as we shall see later.[8] The Baganda came to regard themselves as equals with the British in governing Buganda. As time passed, they demanded more autonomy in various spheres of government. Other ethnic groups saw themselves in competition with the Baganda and began to demand similar privileges for themselves. Thus, demands for federalism were also indigenous responses to a historical situation.

The consequence was to embolden those ethnic groups who had gained some measure of autonomy and frighten those who had none. The political system, particularly after independence, came to reflect the dispersion of power as local sentiments gained greater legitimacy. The capacity to carry through tasks which the central government felt were necessary for nation-building and economic development was correspondingly reduced. It was argued that if Uganda survived this first period with widespread popular acceptance of the central government as arbiter of local disputes, the reflection of local interest through the political system might provide a firm basis for stability and future development. However, Uganda almost did not survive. Plagued by threats of secession—which in some cases were acted upon—the nadir was reached in a bid for power, popularly regarded as the thrust of an ethnic coalition, in February 1966. The recovery of political initiative by Prime Minister (later President) Apolo Milton Obote resulted in the arrest of five of his ministers, a new Constitution and a military victory over the Baganda, leaving the army in possession of the Kabaka's palace. This brief violent encounter dramatically altered the balance of power within Uganda and set the stage for a new form of government consciously designed to reduce the political importance of sub-national movements.

Ugandan political developments between 1962 and February 1966 provide an excellent case for S. Eisenstadt's proposition that in the new states "the high level of political demands, the possible cleavages among the elites in their pursuit of popular support, may easily create conditions under which they themselves are unable to assure the initial institutionalization of political frameworks capable of absorption of change."[9] There is little that is unexpected in Uganda's political behavior during this period.

What is surprising, and calls for close study, is the way in which the Ugandan polity subsequently was restructured. Instead of further escalating ethnic fears and reactions, instead of deepening primordial ties, Uganda has entered into a period of relative calm with a noticeable reduction in the emphasis on ethnic considerations in political life. This is *not* to suggest that feelings of cultural sub-nationalism are not harbored by many Ugandans, nor that the government can ignore these feelings in the allocation of development projects or in the employment of civil servants. But a breathing space has emerged and it may give the state the opportunity to realize more fully its national identity. In this change lies Uganda's potential contribution to overcoming an important obstacle facing most new states.

The general argument of this chapter is that a series of changes in political structure, initiated by the confrontation of 1966, reversed the emphasis on the political role of cultural sub-nationalism that had marked earlier Ugandan development. I shall look at the problems of defining ethnic groups, suggest typical patterns of ethnic political behavior, and explain why ethnic factors came to be politically salient in Uganda. I will then investigate some of the reasons contributing to a reduction of their importance in national and local politics, and discuss the extent to which Uganda has relied on "ethnic arithmetic." Finally, I will suggest some aspects of political development on which the experience of Uganda casts some light.

To single out the role of ethnic assertion in national politics can be subject to serious misinterpretation. First, it tends to magnify one basis of political conflict at the expense of several others. Politics in Uganda has been extraordinarily complex. Sharp discord has arisen over land ownership, religious competition, wealth, economic ideology, and race.[10] The appearance of ethnic competition often masks (or echoes) rivalries involving other social and economic issues. Second, use of the word "tribe" conjures images of primitive behavior and lack of capacity to manage the political apparatus of the modern state. Nothing of the sort is intended here. It would be wrong to ignore the political dynamics of ethnicity for either of these reasons. They have played an important role and the government has responded creatively in its efforts to curb them.

1. Identifying the Groups Involved in Ethnic Politics

Given the salience of ethnicity in African politics, one might assume that the nature and boundaries of cultural units asserting their rights to privileges or autonomy would be relatively well-defined. Yet, not least of the uncertainties that mark politics in new states is the shifting nature of what is taken to be the ethnic group, and the extent to which participation of members is forthcoming.

Several criteria have been put forward to define ethnic groups in Africa. Language, territory, social structure, cultural patterns (particularly authority relationships), external administrative classification, and an active sense of identification have been suggested. May Edel, an anthropologist, points out that it would be difficult to find a single definition that would fit all Ugandan peoples.[11] More complex is the problem of determining what the groups are that have united effectively to take political action.

A brief examination of the suggested criteria will demonstrate the problems involved in relating organized political assertions to ethnic groups. As will shortly become apparent, each basis of classification may help in certain cases, but the last—an active sense of identification with a particular group —is the most conclusive indicator of political behavior.

The language spoken can provide a definition of the ethnic group. However, the degree of emotional attachment to the language is an equally important criterion for identifying groups. When little importance is placed on the language spoken, "foreign" words and expressions may become so prevalent as to greatly obscure group boundaries determined on this basis alone. The use of official (but "foreign") vernacular languages in primary school instruction, the requirement that central government business be conducted in English, and widespread use of Luganda and Swahili have introduced changes into traditional languages. Thus, language becomes a less certain guide to ethnic determination.

However, when a sub-national movement is begun, language policy is generally one of the first political issues. Widespread use of Luganda due to missionary policies and the introduction of Baganda administrative agents outside Buganda created resentment among those whose mother tongue was subordinated. The use of Lutoro in Toro District and Acholi in schools in Lango District also became grievances as soon as ethnic consciousness developed.

The four major language families spoken in Uganda— Bantu, Nilo-Hamitic, Nilotic, and Sudanic—are often regarded as major factors in the formation of ethnic coalitions in national politics. However, at best they have been potential groupings with little popular support due to an enormous variety of conflicts within the ranks of each group.[12]

The fact that Batoro and Banyoro regard themselves as separate "tribes" due to possession of separate administrative structures in spite of speaking the same language and sharing the same customs is a good indication of the limits of language as a basis of solidarity. On the other hand, some groups, such as the Baamba, speak two languages of their own, and speakers of one may not be able to understand speakers of the other.

Territoriality has also been a powerful basis for organization for certain ethnic groups. This is particularly relevant when sacred shrines are in an area subject to dispute between two ethnic groups. Much of the political salience of Banyoro and Baganda cultural sub-nationalisms stemmed from a territorial controversy. On the other hand, some groups like the Bakiga (at least when they were studied in the 1930s) and the pygmies are identifiable, but have little sense of possession of territory.[13] Others traditionally had migrated from one area to another (particularly in eastern Uganda) and accidentally settled in a particular place because colonial administrators introduced order and established boundaries at that moment.

Traditional customs and social structure are a third, and perhaps the most popular, basis of "tribal" classification. However, even if we accept this approach, we still have to determine which customs or obligations should form the basis of classification. For example, Immanuel Wallerstein warns us to keep separate three levels of loyalty: (1) to the extended family; (2) to the tribal community; and (3) to the tribal government.[14]

Since we are investigating ethnic politics, differences in traditional political culture seem a sensible method to classify groups. It is attractive, because it permits us to hypothesize that differences in traditional cultures will produce different political values which, in turn, will create conflict when integrated in a new state. A further reason for adopting this criterion is that virtually every ethnic group operating in the modern arena justifies its demands in traditional terms.

Apter's interesting formulation of different types of cultural patterns varying according to authority systems (segmentary, pyramidal, and hierarchic) and to value systems (consummatory and instrumental) offers possibilities to guide empirical research.[15] Robert LeVine's analysis of achievement motivation in three Nigerian ethnic groups demonstrates that differences in traditional patterns of authority remain important today and produce significant variations in attitudes toward status mobility.[16]

But, beyond suspecting that there may be a relationship between traditional political culture and modern political behavior, there is little we know for certain.[17] What is known suggests that other factors, particularly the degree of the threat to security and the spread of modern influences which undermine traditional values, are probably more important determinants of present-day political activity. The factors shaping political positions taken by leaders of ethnic groups depend heavily on the immediate protection of the group. Thus *Kabaka Yekka* (KY)—"Kabaka Only," a Baganda neotraditional sub-national movement—was willing to unite in a coalition with the more progressive Uganda People's Congress (UPC) in order to join the government in 1962. In addition ethnic groups in Uganda have tended to emulate whichever one is most successful, without paying much attention to the traditional implications. Finally, it could be argued that parallels in behavior in national politics of Hausa-Fulani in Nigeria, Ashanti in Ghana, and Baganda in Uganda owe less to their different traditional values than to the position in which each group found itself—the largest group, but not a majority, in a fragmented country.

Changing social and administrative structures in both town and countryside have greatly modified belief in traditional customs in general and traditional authority relationships in particular. Indeed, "tribes" today are as much a product of the economic, social, and political influences of the colonial and independence period as of their traditional past. In Uganda, for example, the use of Baganda agents to administer areas outside Buganda resulted in new definitions of tribal units both because of and in reaction to the agents.[18] Baganda agents introduced a more precise notion of the concept of tribe into the vocabularies of peoples in the former Eastern Region through new history textbooks as well as administrative control. They also became a reference group emulated by some of the people they ruled, thus increasing the importance of ethnicity. In addition there was active resentment against the often rapacious conduct of these agents and fear of their potential acquisition in freehold of land traditionally belonging to those they administered. The reaction of the Bagisu and others living in this area was to revive and deepen their attachment to their own traditional rituals.

Those who move from the countryside to towns confront a radically different social structure and must adapt their values accordingly.[19] This does not mean, however, that their concern with ethnic identity has diminished, though the group to which they will give allegiance may change. In trade unions, voluntary associations, and urban councils, they find that "tribal" identification is politically potent.[20] Alur immigrants to Buganda have experienced an increase in tribal feeling from that felt by Alur who remain in their home area. Forced to cluster together for security in a "foreign" area, they have a ". . . recognition of 'tribal' belongingness far beyond the limits of any earlier community."[21] The reverse phenomenon has often been noted of Banyaruanda immigrants. After living for some time in Buganda, they often desire (and sometimes achieve) assimilation into the Baganda group.[22]

Max Gluckman insists on a distinction between the meaning of ethnic identity in rural areas (where it is based on participation in traditional customs) and in towns (where identity may be reformulated as the work situation and available voluntary associations require).[23] For example, men from various ethnic groups in Nyasaland (now Malawi) who came to work on the Copperbelt were regarded as "Nyasalanders" in daily life and for census purposes.[24] Thus, a man can be "detribalized" when he comes to live in the city, and then "supertribalized" when he takes on obligations to a new urban group.[25] When a migrant laborer (or civil servant) returns to his home area, he may (or may not) readopt his former obligations and loyalties. With the introduction of cash crops and increased primary schooling, however, rural life may have undergone equally complex changes in the ways in which people relate to traditional customs.

Because of these ambiguities some social anthropologists have abandoned the notion that "tribe" refers to an integrated group sharing social values and instead use the term to refer to categories of people, however they have come to be classified together. For example, J. C. Mitchell argues that in the town ethnic identifications operate to permit a person to put the various people he meets into manageable categories.[26] A more extreme view holds that:

> Specifically "tribe," to take the example of a basic "unit," would appear to be a concept which was intellectually imposed on Africa by its early foreign visitors . . . Between such "tribes" it was imagined that there must be defined territorial boundaries, which it remained merely to demarcate . . . Yet certainly in Anglophone Africa, what happened was rather that the colonial regimes administratively *created* tribes as we think of them today . . .[27]

If ethnic groups are to be understood as categories, then it is important to learn how these categories come to be formed. Apthorpe suggests the importance of administrative classifications and the Ugandan experience demonstrates how important a factor this has been. The use of "tribal" classifications in gathering census information and establishing county and district boundaries has reified ethnic consciousness along official lines. In eastern Uganda, for example, Baganda agents made their own determination of which peoples belonged to which tribes. This classification was later adopted by the Protectorate government.[28] Sub-national movements have developed around these basically administrative determinations, though they adopt traditional justifications for their claims. The behavior of inhabitants of Bukedi District during the Mbale controversy (discussed in section 4) is a typical case. Crawford Young has found similar ethnic responses to administrative boundary-making in the Congo.[29]

Sometimes the impact of administrative classification has unexpected ethnic repercussions. Fred Burke reports that when East Budama became a separate county in Bukedi District in the early 1940s in recognition of the claims for administrative autonomy of Iteso living in the area, many other Iteso who had previously assimilated into the Japadhola tribe reclaimed their original identity.[30]

External classifications may have an effect on redefinition

of ethnic groups, but it seems unlikely that they created such strongly felt solidarities out of whole cloth. This is particularly true of the centralized kingdoms like Bunyoro and Buganda, which could call on widespread loyal response to an identifiable head of state for payment of taxes, military activities, and the like. The case for segmentary systems is much less clear, of course, though customs and language were not unimportant in creating some precolonial unity as well.

Thus, each of these objective criteria—language, territory, customs, and administrative (and social) categories—provides limited benefits in attempting to work out political involvement on the basis of ethnicity. They cannot explain the new situation to which leaders and aroused followers are reacting.

Ultimately, if we are to unravel the politics of subnationalism, we must rely on the subjective criterion of an active sense of identification of the ethnic group member.[31] The conception of the group so identified may be based on any of the objective criteria mentioned above—or, on a fictional equivalent to one of them. An ethnic group becomes politically potent, when it is perceived as a group by its followers and outsiders, and when it can command the effective loyalty of the individual in the rivalry for political advantages within the state or the refusal to accept the authority of the state. If it is successful, it may become "the group within which common moral fellowship is acknowledged."[32] Or, it may simply be seen as the vehicle for advancing one's self-interest.

In either case cultural sub-nationalism is being used here to refer to political assertions by self-aware groups within the state. These groups have usually coalesced on the basis of some presumed or actual traditional heritage or territorial claim. Their political assertions include demands for greater autonomy in local government, a greater share of national economic rewards, or a defense of such advantages already acquired.

We should not overlook the problems that accompany this formulation, however, as the perceived boundaries of modern ethnic groups are virtually never distinct. First, the perceptions of the ethnic group may vary from insider to outsider. The Baganda, for example, are more likely to regard the Banyaruanda living in Buganda as a separate ethnic group than are the Banyaruanda themselves. Second, the boundaries of the group (in terms of perception and loyalty) may change over time, or in response to different issues. As groups gained more political sophistication during the late colonial and early independence periods, they tended to become more aware of the advantages of coalitions to defeat political enemies. On some issues an ethnic group, which was commonly perceived as a single unit, found itself bitterly divided, only to unite when challenged from the outside. Different ethnic groups may compete for control of a district in which both are located, only to coalesce when an issue affecting the status of the district is posed. A man may be a member of one ethnic group in the town and a somewhat different one in his rural home area. In short, ethnic affiliation may vary with the situation.

Third, it is not always clear whether an ethnic group is united or whether its leaders are simply putting forward claims in the hopes of galvanizing potential members. In discussing the politics of Bukedi District, Burke wonders whether "tribal nationalism is as strongly entrenched among the peasants as it obviously is among the political activists."[33] In a survey among rural Iteso carried out in 1956 asking who was the leader of the Iteso people, over 50 per cent of the respondents stated that there was none. The political elite of Teso, however, called for union of all Iteso in Kenya and Uganda, purging the language of Luganda words, and giving traditional names to thirty-five towns.[34]

All these problems in using the individual's sense of identification as the basis for establishing the boundaries of ethnic groups hinge on the question of determining his perceptions and loyalties. Only in this way can we determine who belongs to which ethnic group. In principle there is no difficulty in developing the requisite measures. Impressionistic data may be sufficient to suggest the broad outlines of groups involved in issues of high intensity, but more precise instruments will be necessary to establish some of the variations in degree of identification and participation created by changes in tradi-

tional loyalties occurring over the past one hundred years.
Consequently, in the remainder of this chapter groups will
not be determined as precisely as would be desirable. But
since Ugandans accept certain sets of people as possessing
both ethnic identity and social solidarity, an explanation of
the rise and decline of sub-nationalism must take these
"groups" into account.

2. Typical Patterns of Sub-national Activity

Besides identifying the members of ethnic groups, it is necessary to isolate and explain the widely different organizational
and behavioral characteristics of the sub-national activities in
which they participate. Ultimately, it would be useful to develop a full typology of sub-national groups, particularly as
more comparative data from other countries become available. For the moment, however, it may be sufficient to indicate some of the factors that differentiate Ugandan sub-
national movements.

Geertz has developed a relatively simple typology that
isolates five patterns of politics based on primordial ties.
These are:[35]

(1) a majority set against a single large minority (Cyprus,
    Ceylon);
(2) one central group opposed to several medium-sized
    peripheral groups (Indonesia, possibly Ghana and
    Uganda);
(3) two evenly balanced major groups (Lebanon, possibly
    Pakistan);
(4) gradation of groups from large ones to small ones
    (India, the Philippines);
(5) multiple small groups (Tanzania).

This classification is limited to the relative sizes of groups
within the national state. For Uganda this is an important
consideration, as size has affected both goals and organization
of sub-national movements. The differences between the Sebei

and Baganda movements (discussed below) illustrate how significant this factor can be. However, Geertz's scheme must be expanded before it can be fruitfully employed in explaining the complex differences and interrelationships between Ugandan movements.

In the first place the context in which a sub-national movement has meaning may vary from local to national. In Bukedi District, for example, various ethnic groups attacked each other within district politics, but banded together to defend the rights of Bukedi in the Mbale controversy. For some, though certainly not all, Bakonjo and Baamba the Rwenzururu movement made sense in local terms as a struggle against the Batoro, and not at the national level. At the same time, of course, locally oriented movements will often affect politics in the national arena.

A second additional consideration is that many subnational movements are oriented to the international arena, as well as the national and local levels. This can happen either because an ethnic group is split by national borders and becomes self-aware as a consequence of irredentist elements, or because the group feels itself a persecuted minority, declares its independence, and appeals for recognition from other national states and international organizations. Uganda has faced both problems. The Sebei, the Iteso, and the Bakonjo have given warning at one time or another of their desire for trans-national ethnic unity. Both the Buganda and Rwenzururu governments declared their areas independent though without receiving any international recognition.

Third, and most important, it is necessary to introduce several internal dimensions to account for the nature and degree of organization, the political style, and the spread and intensity of grass-roots support. The degree of organizational control of sub-national movements has varied from spontaneity to firmly established control over a segment of a movement with virtually all Ugandan sub-national movements plagued by a variety of competing part-time "leaders." The nature of the political style employed by the leaders varies from total passivity with respect to national issues to demands that their adherents accept their absolute sovereignty in all matters.

The quality of grass-roots support can also vary in kind and in salience. One basic distinction must be drawn between loyalty that seems so overpowering as to be a moral absolute,[36] and loyalty that is offered because political benefits may follow. Ethnic claims based on relative deprivation of prestige might fall somewhere in between. In Uganda, the *Kabaka Yekka* and Rwenzururu movements are based on moral absolutes (see the discussion in section 4 below), while district nationalism—particularly in multitribe districts like Bukedi and West Nile—appears to be a shrewd strategy for gaining a larger share of available resources for the people of the district.

But there is only one national political arena, and all of these groups whatever the differences among their movements must compete against each other for wealth and prestige. Inevitably this results in each group copying successful tactics used by another group, even if the tactic makes no sense in its new context. The result is the development of a variety of spurious "traditions" to justify the existence of ethnic subnationalisms.

For example, the Acholi, who traditionally possess a segmentary system of political authority, insisted on choosing a *Laloyo Maber* ("Good Ruler") as constitutional head, after seeing the benefits the possession of a *Kabaka* brought to the Baganda. For the same reason councillors in Bukedi District also installed a constitutional head as their "traditional monarch" even though the occupant had to represent seven tribes with widely varying traditional cultures.

Under these circumstances it is not surprising to discover that while traditional customs may no longer be a good indication of the ethnic group to which a man gives his political allegiance, leaders must still demonstrate their regard for "tradition." A survey of candidates for the 1961 Legislative Council elections indicated that most either possessed important traditional qualifications or were related to chiefs.[37]

Thus a more exhaustive typology might include:

A. External dimensions
  1. Relative size
  2. Context or arena in which dispute is meaningful (local, national, international)
  3. Distinctiveness of ethnic membership boundaries
B. Internal dimensions
  1. Nature and degree of organization
  2. Political style
  3. Spread and intensity of grass-roots support.

Applying these dimensions to Ugandan sub-national movements, we can construct several typical patterns of behavior. The following three indicate some of the major differences.

The Karamojong, Jie, Dodoth, and Suk of northeastern Uganda represent a pattern of sub-nationalism which has deviated little from precolonial times. The groups demand highly intense association at the grass-roots level, based on traditional organization. Their political style is completely passive with regard to district and national politics. It is reinforced by their small size relative to other Ugandan ethnic groups. International borders with Kenya and the Sudan are ignored. Ethnic membership boundaries are highly distinct due to the emphasis on traditional values.

The Baganda have formed a different pattern of sub-nationalism. Twice as large in population as the second ranking ethnic group, and the recipients of more favorable colonial treatment, the Baganda have become the most developed ethnic group in Uganda. They have operated in both national and international arenas with a political style that has tended to become more and more defensive, as the Baganda try to hold on to privileges which their minority position can no longer justify. Intermittently an extremely intense association of all Baganda reaches the level of moral obligation. A variety of competing organizations, including the Buganda government itself (until its demise), support the sub-national movement by using modern methods while calling for a return to traditional values. Territoriality, language, and the *Kabaka* as a focus of loyalty help to make ethnic membership boundaries relatively distinct.

A third sub-national pattern, organized around the district, could be found (before 1966) all over the country outside Buganda. In the typical case its demands are presented in terms of a (usually fictional) traditional culture. Its ethnic justification is vague and consequently the boundaries of the group are indistinct. It is generally met with moderate to intense response from ordinary people depending on the nature of the issue. It evokes a low level of organizational activity based mainly on the district council and administration as fulcrum of the movement. It tends to operate intermittently, as it is limited to specific issues manipulated by local politicians. Its major concern up to 1966 was either emulation or control of Buganda. When the local groups in the district are willing to cooperate, it is oriented to the national arena. It takes no interest in promoting its demands internationally.

A final consideration in discussing sub-national movements in Uganda is that one tends to consider only those that make at least some public impact at the national level. However, often the sub-national movements themselves are little more than coalitions of an incredible variety of even smaller groups. In Ankole, for example, there are memories of formerly independent kingdoms which are now counties. They fuel a distinct sense of economic rivalry that is expressed on a county basis. In one instance such a rivalry provoked an attempted secession from the local cooperative union over the siting of a coffee factory. At the same time Ankole was deeply split by ethnic rivalry between the Bairu (agriculturalists) and the Bahima (pastoralists) living in these counties.[38]

In Teso a dispute over local appointments between the northern and southern areas of the district led to the breakdown of local government.[39] Acholi has been the scene of geographical and clan rivalries.[40] The petty kingdoms amalgamated into the district of Busoga have continued their competition, as the dispute over the *Kyabazingaship* (kingship) demonstrated.[41] In multitribal districts, such as Bukedi, Kigezi, and West Nile, relatively sophisticated ethnic arithmetic in allocating district political and administrative posts was necessary to maintain a minimal level of unity. During those periods when one ethnic group monopolized the posts, the severe resentment of other tribes tended to fuel sub-national movements. Many more examples could be given, but it should be clear that one of the factors moderating the intensity of sub-national feeling is the difficulty of coordinating these smaller entities for any length of time.

3. Causes of the Rise in Cultural Sub-nationalisms in Uganda up to 1966

Several general propositions help to explain the proliferation of sub-national movements which developed during the colonial and independence period until the confrontation between the central government and the Baganda took place in 1966.

A. STRUGGLES FOR TERRITORY AND MILITARY SUPERIORITY IN PRECOLONIAL UGANDA PRODUCED RIVALRIES THAT ARE REFLECTED IN THE POLITICS OF THE PRESENT DAY

Most ethnic groups in Uganda have brought grievances forward from the past which they attribute to the actions of members of some other "tribe."[42] Memories of traditional antagonisms, among others, have contributed to ethnic tensions in the post independence period.

When European explorers first entered the Lake Victoria area, forces led by Mutesa I, *Kabaka* of Buganda, were expanding Buganda's hegemony at the expense of the empire of Bunyoro-Kitara. Baganda were also claiming parts of Busoga. In about 1830 a kingdom was established in what is now Toro District by a Munyoro prince who broke away from the Bunyoro *Omukama* (king). He also asserted hegemony over areas occupied by Bakonjo and Baamba tribesmen.

The Nilotic migration from the north through Eastern Uganda deposited several groups in the area around Mt. Elgon among Bantu-speaking tribes with different customs. This led to intermittent warfare suppressed under British rule, but not forgotten. Intermittent disputes marked relationships between the Acholi and the Langi over the location of the border between them.

B. THE BRITISH COLONIAL POLICY OF INDIRECT RULE TENDED TO INCREASE CULTURAL SUB-NATIONALISM

With the arrival of colonial authority ethnic boundaries were either frozen in order to better maintain law and order, or changed in order to reward one ethnic group at the expense of another. Indirect rule was justified mainly on the argument that it would be cheaper to permit traditional authorities to carry out administrative tasks under British supervision than to have British officers do it themselves. Reliance on traditional authorities meant organizing administrative units in traditional or "tribal" terms (as the British perceived them).

In Buganda the British found a well-organized traditional state on a relatively large scale. Having allied with the Baganda in the military expeditions against the Banyoro, and having deported one *Kabaka* and installed an infant in his place, a treaty negotiated with important Baganda chiefs seemed the most expedient basis of securing the British presence in this traditional kingdom. This treaty, the Buganda Agreement of 1900, rewarded the chiefs with grants of freehold land (contrary to traditional custom) and rewarded the Baganda generally by giving them administrative control over large areas of land taken from the defeated Banyoro. The Agreement guaranteed the position of the *Kabaka* and accepted a modified version of the traditional Baganda hierarchy of chiefs, acting under the supervision of British officers. This treaty has been central to the development of Baganda separatism, as it gave an important administrative role to traditional chiefs, which in practice resulted in a delegation of considerable autonomy. Lord Lugard regarded Buganda as a good example of successful indirect rule.[43] The Baganda regarded the Agreement as a contract between equals which could be terminated by either party. The contradiction in these views did not become fully apparent until Uganda gained its independence.

From their base in Buganda the British set out to introduce a pattern of rule over the rest of the "tribes" of Uganda that reflected aspects of their relationship with the Baganda. Agreements were signed with the other three kingdoms (though many years later in Bunyoro)—which meant largely reconstructing them in order to recognize them as ethnic entities and administrative units. Semei Kakunguru, an important Muganda chief, was sent to Busoga to "weld scattered chiefships into a tribal organisation,"[44] and also to Teso and Bukedi. Baganda agents were sent to Lango and Kigezi as well. Each of these areas was separately administered on the assumption that indirect rule required a tribal unit governed by traditional authorities.

In practice there were several difficulties with this assumption. First, many Ugandan tribes were too small to warrant a separate district and thus were gathered together for administrative purposes. In these districts counties were often demarcated on tribal lines and named after the tribe that occupied them. Second, in some cases the kingdoms asserted sovereignty over other tribes—Buganda over Banyoro in the "Lost Counties" (the territory ceded in the 1900 Agreement), and Toro over Baamba and Bakonjo. Third, Baganda agents were sent out to establish hierarchic chiefly rule in many areas which had no tradition of hierarchy (Teso, Kigezi). Fourth, the introduction of a bureaucratic style of administration—standing orders, salaries, and transfer—further vitiated whatever traditional obligations of loyalty remained. Outside Buganda, and to some extent the other kingdoms, indirect rule meant little more than direct rule by Africans rather than Europeans.

The Ugandan version of indirect rule made several contributions to the growth of cultural sub-nationalism. Most importantly, it sanctioned the notion that the existence of an ethnic group was a valid basis for an administrative unit. Indirect rule provided an institutional expression for cultural unity. This was most obvious in Buganda where top local government officers were ever watchful for encroachment by British authorities. However, in all four kingdoms the traditional identification between chiefs and people were strengthened beyond precolonial levels by British policy (though economically the two were becoming more stratified). Greater unity within the ruling ethnic group in the kingdoms became possible, because the British refused to tolerate military rivalries for the throne. Ethnic identity was also increased by establishment of clear territorial boundaries between "tribes," thereby eliminating the fluid situation typical of the earlier period.[45] At the same time British policy increased frustration of ethnic groups who in accepting the equation between cultural unity and administrative boundaries felt that they had lost territory rightfully theirs.

Indirect rule also enhanced the position of local rulers as the focus of cultural identity. This was immediately true in the four kingdoms, and later—as we shall see—in many of the districts as well. As President Obote has commented, the doctrine of prohibiting a commoner to hold a position above the king "enriched indirect rule and the operations of separate development."[46] Finally, by using Baganda agents and by giving Buganda a degree of self-government denied all other kingdoms and districts, the British contributed to the sense of resentment other peoples felt for the Baganda and to their growing awareness that only by demonstrating a cultural unity approximating that of the Baganda could other ethnic groups wring similar concessions from the British.

C. COLONIAL ADMINISTRATIVE TECHNIQUES TO ACHIEVE LAW, ORDER, AND DEVELOPMENT OFTEN STIMULATED CULTURAL SUB-NATIONALISM

One important reason for drawing district and county boundaries along tribal lines was to reduce ethnic antagonism between tribes and make the task of maintenance of order easier for colonial officers. Application forms for government employment included a question on the "tribe" of the prospective job-seeker.[47] Census data provided similar information. Colonial administrators—particularly when the rationale of indirect rule was the basis of policy—put heavy emphasis on the role of customary law in settling disputes.[48] By institutionalizing traditional legal practices and by giving administrative sanction to the collection of information about ethnic identity, the legitimacy of local feelings was strengthened.

In encouraging development, colonial officers often emphasized tribal identity in an explicit effort to build a greater sense of collective participation.[49] Thus, the Iteso were urged to grow more cotton and collect more taxes so as not to fall behind the Langi. Policy toward Karamoja for much of the colonial period sacrificed development for a minimal level of order by leaving the various tribes of the district alone. The decision not to bring in administrators, technical officers, and schools followed the murder of a British-appointed chief in 1923. Not until the 1950s were developmental resources invested in Karamoja, and then only because the tribesmen drew attention to themselves through intertribal cattle raiding.[50] The result has been the preservation of tradition in Karamoja.

D. THE INTRODUCTION OF LOCAL GOVERNMENT BASED ON DISTRICTS AND KINGDOMS INCREASED SUB-NATIONALISM

As conceptions of indirect rule gave way to preparation for self-government after World War II, the Protectorate authorities began to emphasize the development of local government as a training ground in democracy and administration. National self-government, even in the early 1950s, was felt to be decades away. Educated Africans were encouraged to seek work in district government and leave central administration to British officers. Thus local government became a focus of loyalty and African participation, while the central government remained distant and aloof.

The 1949 Local Government Ordinance and its successors determined that the district (or kingdom) would be the basic local government unit. This meant that power would be shifted slowly from chiefs to democratically elected representatives, but without disturbing the ethnic basis of their rule. Introduction of the electoral principle in these circumstances tended to exacerbate ethnic feelings.

Once again Buganda led the way. In the 1955 Agreement (which replaced the 1900 treaty and paved the way for the *Kabaka*'s return from exile) the central government's control over the Buganda government was greatly reduced. Buganda gained the right to select its chiefs and other officers through its own Appointments Board. It was also permitted to introduce government by ministers on the pattern of English national government rather than local authority. Baganda civil servants who had been posted to other districts returned to take up newly created positions in the *Kabaka*'s government. "Tribalism and local service appointment were brought together as never before."[51]

The other kingdoms and districts were immediately anxious to acquire the same governmental structure and autonomy: ". . . both the colonial administration and non-Ganda political leaders [saw] political development in terms of building up the other kingdom and district administrations to a comparable level of competence and vigour."[52] Since competition with Buganda was by definition ethnic, the rivalry took on overtones of cultural sub-nationalism.

The struggle to achieve "federal status" and a "constitutional head" by the districts illustrates this desire to emulate Buganda.[53] Under the 1962 Constitution, districts and kingdoms had three different kinds of relationships to the central government. Only Buganda had a truly federal relationship implying separate spheres of autonomous power. The three western kingdoms of Ankole, Bunyoro, and Toro had also signed agreements with Britain, but gained far less autonomy. The three kingdoms had demanded full federal status in discussions on local government in 1953.[54] This issue increased in intensity as independence approached. But they ultimately

settled for a "semi-federal status," which involved less independent political power than Buganda, but gave them strong
protection of their traditional customs, their king, and the
trappings of local government rather than local administration (e.g., "ministers" heading departments and the like).
Busoga—unified only under British colonial rule—insisted on
a similar status. In 1961 local councillors made their preferences clear by speaking "of the division of 'states in Uganda'
into federal, semi-federal, and 'others, the despicable unitary.'"[55] Busoga also managed to achieve semi-federal status
under the independence Constitution.

The remainder—"mere" districts (except Karamoja, a "Special District" more closely administered by the central government)—were concerned over their lack of status, both for
reasons of prestige, and because the example of Buganda suggested that greater power and economic rewards would accrue
to districts that gained greater autonomy. They could not,
however, point to a traditional unity either because there were
several tribes living in the district, or because the tribe was
not united under a single traditional authority prior to the
arrival of the British.

However, they agitated for constitutional heads for their
districts. As Leys puts it, these were to be "Kabaka-substi-
tutes."[56] Finally in 1963 an act was passed giving district
councils the right to establish the position of constitutional
head and to elect its occupant for a term of five years.[57] In
what might be termed the high-water mark of legal recognition of ethnicity as a basis for politics in Uganda the first
amendment to the 1962 Constitution limited the choice of
President and Vice President of Uganda to "the Rulers of
the Federal States and the constitutional heads of the Districts."[58]

Having achieved and acquired a pseudo-traditional monarch, the next logical step for each district was to agitate for
federal status, which several did. Thus, in the first four years
of independence Uganda experienced growing *district* nationalism (among other types) clothed in traditional garb.

E. UNEQUAL EDUCATIONAL AND ECONOMIC DEVELOPMENT AROUSED FRUSTRATIONS AND CONSEQUENTLY INTENSIFIED FEELINGS OF CULTURAL SUB-NATIONALISM

The optimal combination of factors producing modernization is a subject of much debate, though the availability of modern resources and traditional receptivity to using them are both felt to be important.[59] However, in Uganda (with the possible exception of the southeastern area) geographical distance from the capital city is sufficient to provide a rough indicator of the degree of modernity. Most Ugandans are fully aware that the Baganda profited more than others from their close proximity to the administrative center of the country.

Apter's argument,[60] therefore, that the rapid Baganda acceptance of western religions, modern education, and cash crops resulted from the essentially secular character of their traditional value system integrated by a hierarchic pattern of authority cannot be proved or disproved by historical evidence. The Baganda may have been motivated by their culture, by their advantageous relationship to the colonial rulers (buttressed by the favorable treaty signed in 1900), or both. Whether or not the argument can be resolved, overcoming or at least equaling the economic advantages of the Baganda has become a potent political goal for other Ugandans.

Several external influences gave the Baganda a one to two generations' headstart on the rest of the country. Missionaries, responding to Henry Stanley's appeal, came first to Buganda. Rivalry between Catholics and Protestants ensured that mission work would be well established in Buganda before other regions were penetrated.[61] The schools and hospitals built by missionaries were thus disproportionately available to Baganda. Today the best equipped hospitals in the country are in Kampala.

In a country with an enormous income gap between peasant farmer and civil servant the importance of gaining a place in secondary school and in university can scarcely be underestimated. Up to independence the Baganda filled a disproportionate number of secondary school places. As Table 2 indicates, in 1960 the Baganda had slightly less than twice as many school places in comparison to their share of the country's population. However, visible discrimination in favor of the Baganda probably was felt to be much higher, since they occupied three out of every ten places.

However, disproportion in secondary school places is not a sufficient explanation of the resentment of Baganda felt by other Ugandans. For example, it is less well known, perhaps, that the Acholi were also overrepresented by only a slightly smaller proportion relative to their share of the population. The Samia, surprisingly, were more overrepresented than any other ethnic group. The Banyoro, Batoro, Iteso, Kumam, and Langi were also slightly overrepresented. If the secondary school population is divided into major language groups and compared to the general population, the factor of overrepresentation virtually disappears, as the index of dissimilarity indicates. (See Table 2.)

At this time more secondary schools were located in Buganda than anywhere else (though the situation has changed considerably since independence). This factor worked in favor of secondary school entry of slightly less well-qualified Baganda compared to other groups. While students are admitted primarily on the basis of a Junior Secondary Leaving Examination (JSLE), headmasters have some discretion and often tend to choose the pupil living nearer the school. Thus, in 1961, "more than half the boys who entered senior secondary school from junior secondary schools in Buganda had JSLE marks of less than 168, as compared with less than a quarter of the boys from junior secondary schools in other districts."[62]

Baganda overrepresentation at Makerere University College, the only university in East Africa during the colonial period, has been far more striking. Considering that university degrees were the gateway to the most powerful positions and greatest economic opportunities, the fact that 40 per cent of the 1698 persons who entered Makerere before 1954 from all parts of East Africa were Baganda explains much of their predominance today.[63] While Baganda overrepresentation at Makerere has fallen (and continues to fall), they still provided over 50 per cent of the Ugandan entrants as late as 1950–53.[64]

Based on data taken from the College's nominal roll, Table 2 presents the students from each ethnic group figured as a percentage of all Ugandan African students attending Makerere in 1959/60. The Baganda possessed a higher disproportion of university places in comparison to the secondary school places they held in the same year. This comparison suggests (as Table 5 proves) that their university percentage would fall during the 1960s, as the changes in ethnic composition in secondary schools were reflected in university attendance. The Baganda percentage of Ugandans at Makerere in 1959/60 was almost three times their percentage of the general population and amounted to only slightly less than half the total Ugandan contingent in the College. All other ethnic groups, with the exception of the Bagwere, Banyole, Banyoro, Jonam, Kumam, and Samia, were underrepresented. In terms of language groups the Bantu-speakers held four fifths of the places against two thirds of the general population, and the Nilotic, Nilo-Hamitic, and Sudanic tribes were significantly underrepresented in varying degrees.

In addition to higher studies in Ugandan secondary schools and Makerere an increasing percentage of students have gone overseas for training. While no breakdown by ethnic groups exists for those abroad, the Baganda probably possessed a disproportionate share of these also. Of Ugandan students abroad in the last quarter of 1960, 143 were sponsored by the then *Kabaka*'s government, as compared to only 106 sponsored by all the rest of the districts and kingdoms.[65] Of the 103 students sponsored by the Ugandan and foreign governments, and the 124 students studying on private resources, the Baganda also probably took more places than their numbers alone would warrant.

Baganda parents who have gone to school demand similar

privileges for their children. Goldthorpe, and later Pierre van den Berghe, found a strong and growing tendency for Makerere students to have educated parents, brothers, and sisters.[66] Built-in, therefore, to the early provision of education to Baganda is a demand for its continuation.

In economic development and consumption patterns the Baganda also forged ahead of their neighbors. The Baganda were given cotton seed in 1904 to encourage them to grow cash crops to generate funds for the payment of poll tax.[67] Farmers from other ethnic groups received seed later. The first Ugandan cooperative union was begun by Baganda in 1923.[68] Later, the first ginnery to be turned over to Africans was run by this union.

The existence of freehold land in Buganda (there is very little in other districts) also has created opportunities to grow wealthy for some Baganda. Large plots were given to chiefs to persuade them to sign the 1900 Agreement. The rental income was sufficient to provide school fees for their children and investment in trade. Chiefs sometimes sold their land to peasants who had become wealthy growing cotton or coffee.

When the capital city of Kampala—already offering many central government jobs—attracted industry, the Baganda were more available to take up wage employment. They continue to get the higher-paying jobs, because they are better educated and because they can commute to work and still grow their own food on plots near Kampala. Thus, they tend to be more stable employees and advance more rapidly into skilled positions.[69] The inequality in wage opportunities favoring (the former) Buganda Region is now quite pronounced (though a large number of these jobs are held by non-Baganda).

Consequently, a market catering to fairly sophisticated tastes developed in Buganda, but not elsewhere. As Walter Elkan puts it, "everybody [in Uganda] needs money to pay their poll-tax, and in most areas there is a sale for cloth, cigarettes, soap and bicycles. In Buganda there is also a sale for refrigerators, motor-cars and dinner jackets."[70]

TABLE 1

African Employees by Region, 1967[a]

Region	Private Industry	Public Services	Total
Buganda	75,000	34,800	109,800
Eastern	34,000	24,700	58,800 [sic]
Western	31,800	21,600	53,300 [sic]
Northern	9,300	10,700	20,000

[a] *Enumeration of Employees: June 1967* (Statistics Division, Ministry of Planning and Economic Development: Entebbe), August 1968, p. 1.

Members of other ethnic groups became acutely conscious that they had to become strangers in the home of the Baganda to earn high incomes. They resented the fact that the development of their schools and hospitals lagged behind those of Buganda. They watched the Baganda consolidate their population advantage by becoming the educational and economic elite as well. By demanding an equal share of the benefits of development, they necessarily intensified the ethnic basis of Ugandan politics.

One important exception to the pattern of economic opportunities favoring the Baganda was recruitment into the police and army. The British set a height requirement which tended to discriminate against the shorter Bantu groups. They also recruited more vigorously in the northern parts of the country among ethnic groups possessing a reputation for martial skills and few other economic opportunities.

The data presented in Table 2 confirms the widespread belief that the Acholi (at least in 1960) occupied a disproportionate share of positions among the nongazetted ranks in the police force. They were the largest group both in absolute numbers and one of the largest in comparison to their share of the general population.[71] The Alur, Japadhola, Iteso, Jonam, Kakwa, Kumam, and Madi were also heavily over-represented. Contrary to general belief the Langi produced only a few more policemen than their population percentage would have suggested. The Baganda were severely underrepresented.[72] As a whole the Bantu groups provided less than half the number of policemen that one would predict on the basis of their share of the population. The Nilotics, Nilo-Hamitics, and Sudanic speakers were correspondingly overrepresented.

By examining the data for secondary schools, university, and police comparatively against population in a given year, the wide ethnic variations become readily apparent. The only groups which were overrepresented in all three institutions were the Acholi and the Kumam. A comparison of the indices of dissimilarity shows that in the late colonial period secondary school places were more representatively allocated in ethnic terms than were university places. The police had the worst "fit," and were more than twice as unrepresentative as the secondary schools. The dissimilarity of the three institutions is even more marked when the major language groups are compared to their percentages of the general population. It should be kept in mind that the ethnic identifications in each column may have been based on a different criterion, and in any case are subject to all the problems discussed in section 1.

Even though Buganda's greater wealth created frustration everywhere else, the same differential developmental process also created resentment on a smaller scale within several of the districts and kingdoms. Rural social structure has been changing all over Uganda, though at varying rates of speed, as new educational and economic opportunities become available. In Toro, for example, Bakonjo and Baamba found themselves at a disadvantage in the number of school places, medical dispensaries, and positions in the district administration by comparison to the Batoro. In Sebei, Bagisu moved from the more densely populated lowlands into territory that the Sebei traditionally had regarded as their own. By 1962 they were producing twice as much of the coffee marketed in Sebei as the Sebei themselves.[73] The sub-national move-

TABLE 2

Ethnic Composition in Secondary Schools, Makerere, and the Police Force in the Late Colonial Period

Population 1959 %[a]	Ethnic Group	Secondary School Places 1960 %[b]	Ugandan African Makerere Students 1959/60 %[c]	Police Force 1961 %[d]
16.3	Baganda	29.0	46.6	3.8
8.1	Iteso	10.6	6.1	15.2
8.1	Banyankole	6.5	6.1	2.6
7.8	Basoga	6.1	6.1	4.2
7.1	Bakiga/ Bahororo	5.5	6.4	2.7
5.9	Banyaruanda	2.6	1.8	1.2
5.6	Langi	6.5	1.8	7.5
5.1	Bagisu	4.6	3.6	4.0
4.4	Acholi	7.1	4.3	15.5
3.7	Lugbara	2.6	0.4	4.5
3.2	Batoro	3.7	1.8	0.7
2.9	Banyoro	3.5	3.6	2.6
2.2	Rundi	–	0.0	–
2.0	Karamojong	–	0.4	0.5
1.9	Alur	1.2	0.4	3.5
1.7	Bagwere	1.7	2.1	1.3
1.7	Bakonjo	–	0.7	–
1.6	Japadhola (Badama)	1.4	1.4	2.2
1.4	Banyole	1.3	1.4	–
1.2	Madi	1.1	0.7	3.8
1.0	Kumam	1.2	1.4	3.7
0.7	Samia	1.8	0.7	3.1
0.6	Kakwa	0.5	0.0	1.6
0.6	Sebei	–	0.0	0.2
0.6	Bagwe	–	0.4	–
0.6	Jaluo	–	0.0	3.4

0.5	Baamba	–	0.0	–
0.4	Jonam	0.4	1.4	2.6
0.3	Suk (Pokot)	–	0.0	0.1
n.e.s.[e]	Abaluhya	–	0.4	3.1
n.e.s.	Bachope	–	0.0	0.1
n.e.s.	Bukusu (Kitosh)	–	0.0	0.3
n.e.s.	Nubian	–	0.0	0.5
n.e.s.	Okebo	–	0.4	–
3.1	Other Ethnic Groups[f]	1.1	0.0	5.3
100.0	TOTAL	100.0	100.8	99.8
(N = 6,449,558)		(N = 3,586)	(N = 281)	(N = 4,804)
	INDEX OF DISSIMILARITY	Δ[g] = 21.4	Δ = 33.1	Δ = 43.3
65.7	Bantu	66.3	81.5	29.8
14.5	Nilotic	16.6	9.3	34.8
12.7	Nilo-Hamitic	12.3	7.8	21.4
5.0	Sudanic	3.7	1.4	8.8
2.1	Others	1.1	0.0	5.3
100.0	TOTAL	100.0	100.0	100.1
	INDEX OF DISSIMILARITY	Δ = 2.7	Δ = 15.8	Δ = 36.0

[a] *Uganda Census 1959: African Population* (Statistics Branch, Ministry of Economic Affairs), 1961, p. 18. The percentages are based on the population of Ugandan Africans only.

[b] Compiled from *Annual Report of the Education Department: 1960* (Government Printer: Entebbe), 1961, pp. 27–28. The percentages are based on Ugandan Africans in the first through the fourth year of secondary school only. They omit all ethnic groups with a total of 10 or fewer pupils.

[c] Compiled from *Makerere University College Nominal Roll of Students,* 1959/60. The percentages are based on the population of Ugandan Africans only.

[d] Compiled from *Annual Report of the Uganda Police: 1961* (Government Printer: Entebbe), 1962, p. 4. The percentages include all non-gazetted African ranks, except for 253 Africans whose ethnic breakdown was not given. The table also omits the 59 Af-

ments for separate districts in both cases were strengthened by the economic inequality they observed at home.

Some degree of modernization of social structure is probably just as necessary for the creation of sub-national movements as perceived inequality among ethnic groups. People who can play the modern roles of publicizers and organizers are needed. Financial backing can come only from followers who have entered the monetary sector of the economy. Finally, it is advantageous to include men who can communicate and negotiate skillfully with central government politicians and administrators. Differences along this dimension help to explain why sub-national movements got started in certain districts, but remained moribund or nonexistent in more isolated places like Madi and Karamoja.

---

rican Gazetted Officers, who occupied 22.3 per cent of the gazetted posts.

e n.e.s.—not enumerated separately.

f This category includes a different segment of the population in each column. As there are both secondary school students (40) and police (253) who are not broken down into ethnic groups, it would be incorrect to assume that groups for which there is no entry in these columns have no members in secondary schools or the police.

g Δ is the index of dissimilarity and is used here to measure the sum of the deviations of ethnic representation in each institution from that group's percentage of the general population. A perfect fit ($\Delta = 0$) would result, if the institutional percentage distribution were identical to the ethnic distribution of the general population. The result indicating the poorest fit would have a value of $\Delta = 100$. Note that for secondary schools and the police the values of Δ are approximate, because the identity of the ethnic groups making up the residual category are not available. I wish to thank Stephen Taber for bringing this index to my attention.

F. DEVELOPMENT OF NATIONALIST PARTIES IN UGANDA AS COALITIONS OF DISTRICT POLITICAL NOTABLES RATHER THAN CENTRALIZED NATIONAL ORGANIZATIONS CONTRIBUTED TO CULTURAL SUB-NATIONALISM

Wallerstein argues that "the most important mechanism to reduce the conflict between ethnicity and national integration is the nationalist party."[74] Ugandan political parties, however, exacerbated cultural sub-nationalism up to 1966. But the contradiction is more apparent than real, because Ugandan parties were oriented toward district politics and susceptible to the appeals of ethnic movements. The national organization of the UPC controlled neither nominations of candidates for the National Assembly nor policy statements of district branches.[75] The Democratic Party (DP) also showed few signs of centralization and found it extremely difficult to impose a single approach to strategy, policy, or candidate nominations on branches or members.[76] KY, as discussed in the next section, was a pure example of cultural sub-nationalism, and only in the broadest sense a party at all.

A number of factors contributed to the failure of Ugandan parties to develop strong national organizations. In the early 1950s the colonial policy of relying on tribes led Governor Cohen to suggest that African members to the Legislative Council should be elected by district councils, because "abler representatives would be likely chosen, since it is the district which is the natural unit of public life everywhere outside Buganda; here tribal loyalty and cohesion is strong . . ."[77] In 1958 the district was made the constituency in those areas in which representatives were to be elected. By necessity, then, the district also became the "natural unit" for organization of the party.

The Uganda National Congress (UNC), predecessor to the UPC and first popular Ugandan party, made headway only where it was able to take advantage of local issues.[78] It never developed a specifically national appeal. Furthermore, as it was led by Baganda commoners, it reaped a full harvest of mistrust from both the Buganda government, to which it posed a fundamental challenge, and from other Ugandans, who feared Baganda domination. Finally, the UNC itself temporarily abandoned its efforts to gain a nationwide following, when its leaders felt the integrity of Buganda threatened during the crisis over the exile of the *Kabaka* in 1953.[79]

Low offers several additional reasons to explain the lack of political party development. The most important include (1) the lack of urgency about the nationalist struggle (from the middle 1950s no one doubted independence ultimately would be granted); (2) the small number of elections; (3) the inability of parties to find issues that would arouse the public due to the vigorous reforms undertaken by the colonial government in the 1950s; (4) the absence of a dynamic or charismatic leader; and (5) the attack on all political parties by Baganda neotraditionalists (who feared that the *Kabaka* and chiefs would necessarily lose power to commoners, if elections were held).[80]

After the 1961 elections (won by the DP on a fluke growing out of a boycott of the election by most Baganda), the DP and UPC struggled to achieve an absolute majority in the National Assembly and prepared to fight the 1962 elections. They were both forced to take up local grievances and accept deviations from the national party line. Thus, for example, both parties felt constrained to support the demands of Ankole, Bunyoro, Toro, and Busoga for full federal status.[81] The Prime Minister and leader of the DP, Benedicto Kiwanuka, agreed that Sebei should have its own district and managed to give the same impression to the Baamba and Bakonjo without actually saying so. The result was to further legitimize the politics of cultural sub-nationalism within the national arena.

The party candidates selected for the 1961 elections demonstrate the importance placed on ethnic factors by politicians, which in turn probably stimulated ethnic rivalries.[82] Only 9 out of 185 African candidates were born outside the district in which their constituencies were located. Only 18

out of 175 candidates in non-urban constituencies were members of a tribe other than the most numerous one in their respective constituencies. Most of these came from the second most numerous tribe. Seventy-five per cent of the winners and 49 per cent of the losers were born in their home constituencies. Rothchild and Rogin conclude that "ethnic and religious politics . . . dominate Uganda's voting patterns" with "tribalism" becoming even more important in the 1962 elections.[83]

G. AS INDEPENDENCE APPROACHED CULTURAL SUB-NATIONALISM INCREASED, BECAUSE MINORITY ETHNIC GROUPS FEARED THEIR RIGHTS WOULD BE ERODED WHEN THE BRITISH DEPARTED

Independence, it is popularly assumed, increases national integration, because an alien colonial administration is replaced with a local indigenous government. But the coming of independence can also arouse fears of future ill-treatment. The British had established a reputation as relatively impartial "umpires" who would protect the rights of groups under their jurisdiction. Would an African regime do the same?

In addition the departure of the alien government tended to remove one force for unity within the national state. With the British present all Africans could unite against the common enemy. With the British absent they would have to allocate resources among themselves. The situation is parallel to the problem of industrial relations in African countries. Where Africans are opposed to Europeans (usually in management-worker disputes), ethnic differences are insignificant. But in matters between Africans (for example, union elections) ethnic affiliation is important.[84] Removal of a negative force creating unity reduces integration.

One result in Uganda was an increased willingness to regard ministers and senior civil servants "as representatives of their respective tribes, whose function in Government was to safeguard and plead tribal interests in matters of appointments, distribution of development projects and social services."[85] Burke found that many MPs also tended to consider themselves "district-tribal ambassadors."[86]

Another consequence was the initiation or intensification of secessionist movements and demands for separate districts all over Uganda. The "Lost Counties" issue, which was concerned with whether the area surrendered by Bunyoro to Buganda at the beginning of the century should be returned, produced agitated pronouncements and desperate maneuvers that resulted in violence and arson. Sebei nationalists organized their followers behind the demand for a separate district. Baamba and Bakonjo leaders began to demand entrenched constitutional protection from the Batoro and, when they failed to get it, launched the Rwenzururu movement. In October 1963 a motion for a separate district in East Acholi was proposed but was defeated.[87] The Bahororo living in Ankole and the Iteso of Bukedi also demanded separate districts.[88] Perhaps an indication of events to come could have been read into the increasing demand for creation of new districts.

4. Six Cases of Cultural Sub-nationalism

A closer look at some of the movements that aroused intense passions will help to explain the dynamics of cultural sub-nationalism within a newly independent African state. A brief summary can provide a sense of what motivates people to join such movements and how the central government copes with them and with the controversies they create. Five of the six cases discussed here include three movements, and two controversies (based on somewhat less organized opposing movements). They include *Kabaka Yekka,* Sebei's drive for a separate district, Rwenzururu, the "Lost Counties," and Mbale disputes. These cases were highly salient for their participants, aroused the most public concern in Uganda, and involved a considerable proportion of the energies of the central government in coping with them. The sixth case examines the Bantu and Nilotic "coalitions," which, many claim, dominated Ugandan politics.

A. *KABAKA YEKKA*

KY is perhaps the classic case of cultural sub-nationalism. It dominated the loyalties of the overwhelming majority of Baganda, and bridged conflicts over religion, class, ideology, and modernity. Radical left-wing educated nationalists clasped hands with conservative neotraditionalists. KY drew enormous support from the traditional beliefs of Baganda, as the name, *"Kabaka* Only," indicates. It had elements of a mass movement and yet was most effective when supported by the organizational resources of the Buganda government.

Although KY was founded in June 1961 only a little more than a year before independence, its roots are much older. KY descended from a series of political organizations within Buganda which emphasized the common man's struggle against the chiefs. However, it gained its extraordinary power by uniting these opposed factions. The split in Buganda's political life developed out of a basic change in its traditional political system. Several hundred years ago the *Bataka,* or heads of clans, probably occupied the positions of greatest power within Buganda. This meant that the political system was far more decentralized and perhaps more equalitarian than it was in the 1870s when the first Europeans visited. By then the *Kabaka* had established his pre-eminent position as *Sabataka,* head of all the clans, and as head of a separate administrative hierarchy. In his latter capacity he received the personal loyalty of chiefs whom he appointed. As tax collectors, military leaders, and road builders, these chiefs became far more important than the clan heads, who retained responsibilities over land and ancestor-worship. In certain cases the *Kabaka* was required by tradition to appoint a clan head as county chief. Basically, however, there were two systems of authority, which were united in the person of the *Kabaka.*

When the British agreed in 1900 that the *Kabaka* and his higher-ranking chiefs should receive freehold land, the *Bataka* lost their rights over these areas. They put themselves forward as the protectors of ancient traditional customs of the people against the chiefs, who were attacked as opportunists. The *Bataka* first raised the issue of land rights in 1922, and directed their appeal against the chiefs to the *Kabaka*.[89] With support from both traditional custom and peasants paying rent the *Bataka* movement introduced an important populist element into Baganda politics and left open the possibility for the *Kabaka* to lead it.

From 1938 through 1949 the Sons of Kintu (organized by Ignatius Musazi) and the *Bataka* Party represented these feelings. They attacked the *Kabaka*'s government, that is, the chiefs, and appealed to the *Kabaka* to dismiss them.[90] The riots of 1945 and 1949 were inflamed by the activities of these politicians. They advocated a combination of traditionalism and democracy in the *Lukiiko* (the Buganda Parliament), then dominated by appointed chiefs. After the *Bataka* Party was proscribed by the Protectorate government, Musazi and Abu Mayanja formed the Uganda National Congress in 1952 to bring Uganda to independence. But, as mentioned above, the UNC tended to revert to a "Buganda-first" party whenever its members felt Buganda's institutions were threatened.

The position of Sir Edward Mutesa, the *Kabaka*, remained ambivalent during this period. He was not personally popular and tended to rely on the advice of his appointed chiefs and ministers. Many nationalist Baganda politicians regarded him as little more than a British agent.[91] However, the crisis of 1953 wrought a major change in the structure of authority in Buganda. Old fears over the possibility of federation of the three East African territories were stirred by a speech given by the Colonial Secretary. Unsatisfied by the Governor's reassurance that federation would not be imposed, the *Kabaka* refused to recommend the Protectorate government's proposals for a new Constitution to the *Lukiiko*. The government responded by withdrawing recognition and deporting him. One of his ministers thought that if his deportation had been delayed a few months, the *Kabaka* would have been deposed.[92]

Instead he became a hero to his people. "The identification of the *Kabaka* with Buganda nationalism was immediately and clearly displayed."[93] Traditional religious practices were adopted, and ancient praise-names for the *Kabaka* were used by the vernacular press.[94] Upon his return groups vied to give him presents and demonstrate their loyalty.[95] The *Kabaka* became an extremely powerful figure in his own right and the symbol of Baganda traditionalism.

The civil service chiefs who formed the *Kabaka's* government at Mengo (capital of Buganda) received high income from rents on official lands which went with their positions, and were heartily disliked for it. However, as KY later demonstrated, the chiefs still held enormous influence among the peasants. The Mengo government had long taken special pains to preserve Buganda's privileges and autonomy. Since 1921 leaders of the Buganda *Lukiiko* had consistently attempted to reduce the Protectorate government's supervisory role, opposed East African Federation and participation in the Legislative Council. Joining a larger political unit, it was feared, would mean that the Baganda no longer controlled their own destiny. They were even willing to forego independence for Uganda in order to protect their ethnic autonomy. "Buganda," they said, "cannot sell all her heritage for the purchase of Uganda's independence."[96]

The *Lukiiko* also opposed direct elections in 1958 and 1961 as it meant acceptance of participation in the Legislative Council (and, of course, political parties that were likely to attack the Mengo government). The 1955 Agreement in which the *Kabaka* became a constitutional monarch, and Mengo received virtual autonomy in domestic affairs, represents the high-water mark in preserving Buganda's special position. It strengthened Buganda's hand at the independence conferences in 1961 and was a major factor leading to federal status for Buganda after independence.

As independence approached and Baganda became more concerned over the protection of their unique status these two groups—chiefs and politicians—began to draw closer together. The Uganda National Movement (UNM) sprang up in 1959 to fight for independence (though it had little support outside Buganda), to oppose the Wild Committee and to boycott foreign goods and buses run by non-Africans. It was run by populist-minded Baganda politicians, but also appeared to have the backing of the *Kabaka*'s ministers. The UNM sponsored a parade of protestors dressed in bark cloth, symbol of Buganda nationalism. It was declared illegal after a few months.[97]

At the end of 1960 the *Lukiiko* declared that Buganda had decided to terminate its agreement with Great Britain and thus was independent. It turned out to be a highly symbolic, but empty, gesture. In March 1961 the *Kabaka*'s government called for a boycott of the General Elections which was over 97 per cent effective in Buganda. However, the twenty thousand people who cast their votes managed to elect Democratic Party candidates in twenty out of twenty-one constituencies. As a result Benedicto Kiwanuka, a Catholic Muganda commoner, became Uganda's first Prime Minister. To many Baganda he appeared to have a more important position than the *Kabaka,* which, given the popularity and traditional status of the latter, was unthinkable. Furthermore, as a Catholic he was unacceptable to the Protestant establishment that ran the Mengo government.

In this atmosphere KY held its first meeting in June 1961. Most of the men who founded it were wealthy Protestants with close informal ties to the *Kabaka*. It met with an immediate enthusiastic response far beyond the expectations of its sponsors. The name was adopted from the shouts of the crowd demanding that the *Kabaka* only should rule them. Politicians of all ideologies, conservative and radical, quickly joined the bandwagon, and before long it had the open support of Mengo government officials.[98] It grew rapidly throughout Buganda.

KY leaders denied that it was a political party, but it acted as one to contest the *Lukiiko* elections of February 1962.[99] These were of particular importance, as the *Lukiiko* was to choose Buganda's representatives for the National Assembly (another concession to Buganda not shared by the rest of the country). The electoral machinery of the party consisted mainly of the chiefly hierarchy,[100] completing the *rap-*

prochement between chiefs and politicians. The frankly ethnic appeal with overtones of traditional obligation was overwhelming. The party symbol was a chair that could easily be interpreted as a throne. Even though KY candidates were certain winners almost everywhere, in two thirds of the constituencies over 90 per cent of the registered voters cast a ballot. Only 9.8 per cent of those who registered and voted (mainly Banyoro in the "Lost Counties") resisted this ethnic appeal, while 80.5 per cent voted for KY.[101] Sixty-five out of the sixty-eight seats went to KY candidates.

However, KY was not a political machine and its victory at the polls removed the common goal that had cemented all factions. The *Kabaka*'s senior ministers feared that the popular support generated by the movement might be turned against them. They moved to prevent elected members or progressives from taking control. To achieve this Michael Kintu, the *Katikiro* (Prime Minister of Buganda), was elected head of the executive committee.[102] The chiefly hierarchy won all battles against reform. Most important KY decisions were made after discussion with Kintu and the *Kabaka*. The progressive and educated politicians who had joined KY began to resign, and in 1963 nine KY members of the National Assembly crossed the aisle to the UPC, claiming that this was the best way to protect Buganda's traditions.[103]

As a movement of cultural sub-nationalism KY briefly achieved a unity that had eluded Buganda for at least the past hundred years. It united populist democrats and the bureaucratic elite by drawing on the new popularity of the *Kabaka*. It was a mass movement appealing at a deep level of personal identity during a critical period for the Baganda. At the same time it employed a formidable organization— the largely indigenous governmental machinery—to direct the emotions aroused by the movement. As Richards notes, this was a case of the state taking over the party, rather than the other way round.[104] On the other hand, KY possessed little in the way of party machinery. It combined several traditional symbols and practices centering on the *Kabaka* with the political goal of ethnic autonomy for the Baganda.

"Kabaka Yekka became a movement of Buganda against the world."[105] Surprisingly, engaged in an increasingly danger-ous political battle with the UPC, KY's hold on Baganda po-litical leaders and the masses waned after two years.

B. SEBEI

Sebei sub-nationalism may have reached the same level of intensity as KY for a short period, but was less concerned with protection of traditional values and authority patterns and more with elimination of Bagisu overrule and faster eco-nomic and social development.[106] The movement was based on a single ethnic group easily distinguishable from its neigh-bors by language and customs. By comparison to KY it is a weak case of cultural sub-nationalism.

The Sebei are few in number (35,000 compared to 275,000 Bagisu living in Bugisu District in 1959) and live on Mt. Elgon and the nearby plains close to Uganda's border with Kenya. Their traditional political organization was decentral-ized. No individual could command obedience from all Sebei. The present district was a backwater county of Bugisu during the colonial period and shared to a small extent only in mod-ern development until a road was built across the mountain in the late 1940s. There were few missions, few schools, and few means of earning a cash income. Meanwhile their neigh-bors, the Bagisu, had many schools and grew high quality arabica coffee in a scheme introduced by the colonial govern-ment. The majority of teachers in Sebei primary schools were Bagisu.

Sebei political consciousness began in the 1950s and quickly intensified in response to the introduction of the Bu-gisu District council in 1956. Sebei political leaders felt that the interests of their people were being neglected by Bagisu, who controlled the Council, and that independence would only make matters worse. They complained that few Sebei were employed by the district administration or the coopera-tive union. When the central government insisted on reduc-tion of services to Bugisu to cut down a deficit created by a

District council resolution to lower tax assessments but not social services, Sebei County lost an expected ambulance and new road. The Sebei felt they were being "punished" for the Bagisu councillors' mistakes.

A branch of the UNC was formed in 1956, but the movement did not take root until 1960, when Y. K. Chemonges became its leader. He had served for fifteen years with the Kenya Police and was well known in the district. Through flamboyant behavior and his ability to articulate Sebei grievances, Chemonges became a charismatic leader unifying the Sebei for the first time.

Toward the end of 1960 Chemonges set up a road block and stopped the car of an Assistant District Commissioner. Standing on top of the car with a spear and shield, he demanded a separate district for his people. His subsequent arrest and fine aroused the Sebei. The Sebei leaders then announced that no further taxes would be paid to Bugisu District, but would be collected by the county council. No Bagisu officials were permitted to enter the county. Bagisu primary school teachers were driven out. The Bugisu District Council responded by suspending all services to the county in April 1961.

The dispute was then transferred to the national arena. Chemonges was elected to the Legislative Council in 1961 as a UPC candidate. However, the DP government under Kiwanuka agreed to make Sebei a separate district in late 1961 and Chemonges won the 1962 election as a member of the DP.[107] Young points out that the nearly identical vote totals for Chemonges and his two Bagisu opponents in the two elections, in spite of changing party labels, indicate that politics in the district revolved around the separate district issue. When the UPC/KY coalition took power, Chemonges crossed the aisle again and campaigned for the UPC candidates in the District council elections of 1963.

Sebei sub-nationalism was officially consolidated when the District council created the position of constitutional head called "Kingoo." Chemonges was the unanimous choice to fill this position, and received three votes in the election for

the Presidency of Uganda. The fruits of district status came
to Sebei in the form of a new hospital and senior secondary
school. Chemonges had sufficient influence to gain government
approval for the creation of the Sebei Elgon Co-operative
Union, which was carved out of the Bugisu Union. Not surprisingly, there was intimidation of Bagisu farmers living in
the district who refused to join the new union. Many took
refuge in Bugisu. In 1967 the Co-operative Officer reported
to the Sebei District Team that the Sebei alone cannot produce sufficient coffee to permit the Union to break even due to
heavy transportation expenses. However, members of the
Union were not prepared to accept the larger Bugisu Co-operative Union's offer to amalgamate and give ten administrative posts to Sebei Union members.[108] In addition to inflating
ethnic prestige, these new projects and the staffing of district
administration meant many jobs for the men of Sebei.

Achievement of a separate district meant satisfaction of the
major goal of Sebei sub-nationalism. Though there were continuing ethnic troubles with the large (25 per cent) minority
of Bagisu living in the district, the movement lost much of
its *raison d'être* a few years after it was founded.

Before leaving Sebei, it is worth taking a brief look at the
creation of Madi District on the Sudanese border in north-
western Uganda, because it is an example of a different pattern which hardly qualifies as any form of sub-nationalism
at all.[109] For many years the colonial government attached
Madi first to Acholi and then to West Nile District on the
grounds that it was not large enough nor sufficiently well developed to justify district status. But its lines of communication with the headquarters of both districts were poor. Thus,
it was convenient to make Madi a separate subdistrict. Later
a District Commissioner was posted there partly because a
senior administrator was needed on the border following the
Equatoria Corps revolt in 1955, and full Sudanese independence in 1956.[110] The West Nile District Council obliged the
Madi—after complaints had been voiced—by electing a Madi
as the West Nile and Madi representative in the Legislative
Council. Unlike Bugisu, West Nile did not oppose the desire

of the Madi for a separate administrative identity. However, even during the last years of colonial rule no political movement was formed to fight for Madi's autonomy and demonstrate its cultural integrity. On October 9, 1962 Madi officially became a separate district, and Madi's political life sunk back into apathy.

To judge from KY, Sebei, and Madi, the degree of intensity of opposition to the demand for autonomy appears to have been an extremely important factor in the growth and articulation of Ugandan sub-national movements. The revival of traditional culture becomes important only so long as it can serve as a weapon to help achieve modern political goals—relatively higher status, more administrative jobs, and more development projects. The development of the Rwenzururu movement also supports this proposition.

C. RWENZURURU

The Rwenzururu secession is in many ways the most spectacular example of cultural sub-nationalism in Uganda.[111] While it began shortly after the Sebei movement and for largely the same reasons, it did not result in a separate district. Frustration of its demands created splits within the movement, but one faction declared Rwenzururu an independent state and for the past seven years has collected taxes, run schools, organized an army, trained government officials, and met a government payroll, though the area it controls has steadily diminished since 1966.

"Rwenzururu" is the vernacular equivalent of Rwenzori and refers to the mountains in which the Bakonjo live and the surrounding plains inhabited by both Bakonjo and Baamba. Through the mountains runs the boundary between Uganda and the Congo (Kinshasa) which divides families and clans of both ethnic groups. The Batoro, a break-away Banyoro ethnic group, have exercised control over the area as part of Toro District (formerly Kingdom). However, the mountains have never been brought under effective administrative control, and Bwamba County (home of the Baamba) was not opened up until a road was completed through the foothills in 1938.

Both groups have a vivid sense of a traditional period free from Batoro overrule, though the Baamba were in closer contact with the Batoro through payment of tribute and later as laborers on farms run by Batoro. Many Bakonjo living in the mountains have never experienced the sovereignty of any outside group. Both Bakonjo and Baamba traditional political systems are decentralized in contrast to the Batoro, whose system tends to resemble that of the Baganda. The 1959 census reported 104,000 Bakonjo, 33,000 Baamba, and 183,-000 Batoro living in Toro Kingdom.[112] Therefore, the Baamba and Bakonjo amount to about forty per cent of the population of the district.

Like the Sebei the Baamba and Bakonjo have suffered discrimination in the development of education. However, figures collected by a Commission of Inquiry indicate that the Toro government had made an effort to develop schools in areas in which Baamba and Bakonjo predominate. At the same time the Commission felt there had been discrimination favoring Batoro in the award of bursaries and scholarships.[113]

Few Baamba and Bakonjo had been appointed chiefs at the subcounty level (six of thirty-eight in 1963) and none at the county level even though they amounted to a sizable proportion of the population. They felt that they were given inferior medical treatment and often forced to wait until Batoro were examined by the Batoro medical staff in rural dispensaries. They were aggrieved by the requirement of using Lutoro, the language of the Batoro, rather than their own. However, the most serious complaint underlying all others concerned the contemptuous attitude with which Batoro regarded the other two groups. The Batoro considered them primitive and found it inconceivable that they should share political power with them. This attitude was reinforced by the struggle of the Batoro for full federal status, which they based on the unity of their people and the pre-eminent position of their *Omukama*.

Unlike the Sebei the Baamba and Bakonjo were both a populous minority and the chief source of wealth and taxes in the district. The mountain areas are suitable for coffee, the plains on the southeast side of the mountain for cotton, and the rich volcanic soil of Bwamba for coffee, rice, sugar cane, and cocoa. There is a salt industry and a copper mine in this part of the district. The rest of Toro is not so blessed. As a result the potential for conflict between Batoro political control and growing Baamba and Bakonjo wealth rapidly increased. Batoro resistance to separatist demands could be expected to be far more severe than those of the Bagisu.

Baamba political and cultural societies were started in the 1940s by members of the tiny educated elite. Their discussions centered primarily on how to get better jobs within the Toro District administration. Later, more progressive groups began covertly to attack Batoro domination. The Bakonjo participated in an abortive rebellion against the *Omukama* in 1919 for which three men were publicly hanged. The memory of this event has remained vivid and is now cited with pride by Rwenzururu leaders. Bakonjo associational activity began in the 1950s with attempts to record the history and customs of the Bakonjo people. After the visit of a British journalist, a group called the Bakonjo Life History Research Society was formed. Its president was Isaya Mukirane, a primary school teacher, who under the pretense of investigating the customs of the people, organized branches of the society and instilled political consciousness by inveighing against the wrongs committed by the Batoro. The Bakonjo and Baamba have traditionally regarded each other as inferior. There is virtually no intermarriage between the two groups. The Baamba rarely venture into the mountains and the Bakonjo have only come down to the plains during the past two generations.

The grant of separate district status to Sebei, as well as agitation for return to Bunyoro by Banyoro in the "Lost Counties," had its effect on Baamba and Bakonjo leaders. In February 1962 after getting two places on the Toro constitutional committee (originally denied them), they demanded that the constitution for the kingdom officially recognize that all three groups were tribes in Toro. When the Batoro refused, they walked out. The following month most Baamba and Bakonjo representatives walked out of the *Rukurato* (district "parliament") after disagreement on the same point, and the leaders escalated their demands by announcing that they would accept nothing less than a separate district. The Toro government struck back by arresting Mukirane and two Baamba leaders (Yeremiya Kawamara and Petero Mupalya) on charges of violating customary law by insulting the *Omukama*.

Baamba and Bakonjo refused *en masse* to pay taxes and license fees to the Toro government and threatened Batoro living near the mountains. In August 1962 spontaneous incidents broke out when Batoro chiefs attempted to collect taxes. Meanwhile the three leaders were in Kampala waiting for their appeal to be heard and petitioning the Ugandan government to create a separate district. Following arguments over tactics and ranking of the leaders, Mukirane broke with the other two and headed for the mountains. From this time there was only the loosest connection between Baamba and Bakonjo in the movement, though in their documents they invariably purported to represent all members of both ethnic groups, and both claimed the name Rwenzururu.

While this meant separate and largely uncoordinated activity, it did not spell the end of the movement for either Baamba or Bakonjo. The Baamba continued to recognize Kawamara and Mupalya as their leaders and paid taxes directly to the Ugandan government (bypassing the Toro administration). However, other Baamba organized a guerrilla movement, operating at night, that attacked Batoro who refused to leave Bwamba County and Baamba who collaborated with the Toro government and its chiefs.

Under Mukirane's leadership many Bakonjo set up an independent Rwenzururu government in the mountains which was based on the branches of the Bakonjo Life History Research Society and to collect first "contributions" and later taxes. Mukirane soon had himself appointed King of Rwenzururu. During the early period Bakonjo support for the movement was virtually unanimous. However, the people living on the plains found themselves in a difficult security situation when the Ugandan government announced that it would not grant a separate district (virtually impossible under the 1962 Constitution). They were expected by both Uganda and Rwenzururu to pay taxes and give undivided loyalty. The more highly educated community leaders in lowland areas, most of whom had been members or chairmen of Bakonjo Life History Research Society branches, began to lose enthusiasm for a movement that intended to secede from Uganda and set up an independent nation with few trained manpower resources. They remained adamantly opposed to the Toro government, but were ready to accept either a separate district or direct rule by the Ugandan central government.

For many the declaration of an independent nation was simply a ploy to engage the attention of the Ugandan government. Mukirane, however, may have been ready to go it alone on the theory that the rewards flowing from separate district status were apt to be mutiplied by United Nations membership with the possibilities of foreign aid. An attempt was made to enlist the Banandi (Congolese Bakonjo) and to include a large portion of Kivu Province, Congo, in the Rwenzururu kingdom. This met with virtually no response as the Banandi were represented in the Congolese Parliament and had never experienced discrimination at the hands of the Batoro who live only in Uganda.

In early 1963 the central government introduced another possibility by taking over the administration of services in the Toro counties in which the disturbance was then active. They also appointed agents, many of whom had been involved in Rwenzururu activities, to carry out the functions of the chiefs. At first this policy had little effect and the agents had their homes burned and lives threatened. After a while, however, larger numbers of people tiring of the constant dangers rallied to the agents. The promise of a hundred-bed hospital in Bwamba and the grant of an amnesty by President Obote in late 1965 weakened the secession movement. Passage of the

1967 Constitution which abolished the Toro *Omukama* along with all other kings in Uganda also advanced reconciliation.

The Baamba appear to have had less heart for rebellion, less encouragement for secession from their leaders, and a far more exposed position, as they lived entirely on the plains. Their resistance became increasingly disorganized and ineffectual. Some Bakonjo, on the other hand, with intimate knowledge of the mountain paths—there are no roads in the mountains, with the exception of one security track built after the troubles began—and with the Congo border providing sanctuary, are still holding out in 1970.

Once the Batoro had been removed from Bakonjo areas, though, the fury of the movement turned onto Bakonjo who, because of their exposed position on the plains, had refused to cooperate with the mountain government. Lowlanders, often with the help of Ugandan security forces, organized forays into the mountains to burn and loot. The Rwenzururu government responded in kind. By 1969 Uganda had achieved peace and order in the lowlands and lower mountain spurs by stationing security forces throughout villages in the southernmost mountains.

Of all the organizations claiming the name Rwenzururu, the kingdom government was the best organized and demonstrated the greatest concern with developing the national consciousness and culture of the people (in actual fact limited to Bakonjo), and removing all contaminating Batoro influences. Much effort was expended in returning *Lunyarwenzururu* (Lukonjo, language of the Bakonjo) to its pristine state. The language was the required medium for teaching purposes in lower primary grades in Rwenzururu schools, in churches, and for official government communication. The history of the Bakonjo people was taught as a required subject in the schools (aside from the change in language of instruction and the addition of the local history subject, the Ugandan curriculum was followed). To celebrate independence day each year a program of traditional songs and dances would be performed. The kingdom government saw itself as fulfilling the historical mission of the Bakonjo.[114]

The kingdom government illustrates an important ambiguity typical of many African cultural sub-national movements. The rationale for the movement is cast in traditional terms and based on rights presumed once to have been possessed by the "tribe." However, the methods used to dramatize the movement's demands and to organize the members of the movement are basically modern. For example, there was no effort to set up the Rwenzururu kingdom government on the basis of traditional Bakonjo political organization. Nor was there any return to ascriptive standards of recruitment.

The government was consciously modeled on the most modern political organization available for imitation—that of Uganda. Few older men served in the government. Almost all of the officeholders were extremely young men in their twenties. (The major exceptions were Mukirane and his Prime Minister.) Traditional positions of authority or prestige counted for little (though the leading clans contributed most of the officeholders). Also, the charismatic appeal with which Mukirane held the government together seems to have been based mainly on the fact that he had more modern education and had held a more skilled position (headmaster of a primary school) than any other member of his government. Even Mukirane's creation of the position of king to head the government was intended more for tactical (and personal) reasons than as a response to tradition. The Bakonjo were accustomed to local hereditary chiefs who regard themselves as kings, but they are mainly ceremonial figures who have little power to command anyone. Mukirane argued that the Rwenzururu government "needed an *Omukama* to fight an *Omukama*," and thus the existence of a king gave the government greater legitimacy for its struggle against the Batoro in the eyes of the people.[115] As king, Mukirane behaved as if he were an executive president in a modern government.

D. THE "LOST COUNTIES" CONTROVERSY

In 1894 British and Baganda forces overran Bunyoro and drove out the *Omukama*, Kabarega.[116] Bunyoro had been

the ancient enemy of Buganda and during the religious struggles a few years earlier, many Baganda sought refuge in Bunyoro to renew their strength before making another attack.
In reward for their assistance the British agreed that Buganda
should receive all Bunyoro land south of the Kafu River.
A provision to this effect was included in the 1900 Agreement.
A considerable amount of territory was involved amounting
to all of Mubende District and parts of Singo, Bulemezi, and
Bugerere counties. The graves of the Banyoro *Omukamas*
and important shrines are located in this territory. In two
counties the Banyoro form an overwhelming majority of the
population, while in the remainder they are a small minority.

The question of return of this land has dominated politics
for the Banyoro ever since. In 1901 the successor to Kabarega resigned as *Omukama* over "persecution" of Banyoro in
the "Lost Counties." In 1921 a political organization, the
Mubende-Banyoro Committee, was formed to agitate for return of the land. Their campaign was carried out primarily
through formal appeals and petitions to various British authorities during the colonial period.

As independence approached, the Banyoro became fearful
that an independent African government would be heavily
dependent upon Baganda support and would refuse to en-
tertain any notions of changing the boundaries. A commission
appointed to consider issues that had to be resolved in
Uganda's independence Constitution proposed that a referendum be held to determine the wishes of the residents, at least
in those counties populated primarily by Banyoro. Another
commission recommended that these two counties be transferred to Bunyoro before independence, and that Mubende
town, which contained certain shrines, be declared a munici-
pality (and thus no longer under Buganda's jurisdiction).
Both Banyoro and Baganda were intransigent in their rejec-
tion of any compromise.

During the early 1960s violence supplanted petitions,
partly perhaps as a way for both sides to demonstrate the
depth of their feelings to the various commissions of inquiry.
Over two hundred incidents involving crop slashing, arson,

and threats of assault against Baganda occurred in the two counties in which Banyoro form a majority. When neither side would agree to any solution before independence, the Secretary of State for the colonies decided to put the matter into the hands of an independent Ugandan government by leaving the decision on a referendum to the National Assembly but delaying the possibility of holding it until two years had passed.

Rioting and disorder continued through 1962, but gave way to more ominous developments in 1963. The *Kabaka* established a new lodge at Ndaiga on Lake Albert in one of the counties in which the referendum was to be held, and invited Baganda ex-servicemen to take up residence there to increase the pro-Baganda vote. Bunyoro reacted by gathering and arming its ex-servicemen in Hoima, its capital. Fortunately conflict was avoided.

The national situation was sufficiently fluid to encourage desperate tactics, because the UPC had been able to form a government after the 1962 elections only through alliance with KY. This meant that the Prime Minister had to take a cautious position with respect to the referendum. At the same time, however, several MPs were leaving their parties to join the UPC. When the UPC achieved an absolute majority of MPs in 1963, it decided to press ahead with the referendum. This decision caused KY to withdraw from the governing coalition in August 1964 and set the stage for the 1966 confrontation.

In the referendum the government decided to deny the vote to the Baganda ex-servicemen who had recently moved into the area on the grounds that they were not on the 1962 voting registers in the "Lost Counties." The vote in both counties was strongly in favor of rejoining Bunyoro. The Buganda government attacked the referendum in court, claiming that the exclusion of its ex-servicemen from voting was invalid. Its case was dismissed on appeal and Buganda's battle with the central government moved on to other fronts.

What was striking about manifestations of cultural sub-nationalism in Buganda and Bunyoro in this dispute was the intransigence of both sides. The issue was defined in ethnic terms and reached a high level of intensity, because it was successful in evoking traditional affiliation as a moral obligation. Richards reports that she "met no Muganda, educated or uneducated, who was willing even to consider Bunyoro's case. . . . It is a matter of prestige."[117]

Given too much of a free rein, the dispute over the "Lost Counties" could have resulted in serious internal warfare, which in turn might have stimulated other ethnic groups to adopt similar methods in equally intensely felt disputes. It is also significant that an issue creating such concern could disappear so rapidly without raising serious alarm in Buganda to recover territory it has now "lost." However, the resolution of the controversy undoubtedly contributed to the anxiety of Baganda, who now saw their worst fears being realized. They were demonstrating their inability to control their own destiny in an independent Uganda.

E. THE MBALE CONTROVERSY

Besides the intense feelings it aroused, the controversy over the "ownership" of Mbale illustrates the different varieties of sub-nationalism that can become intertwined in a single dispute.[118] Though at an earlier time the area around the present town of Mbale at the foot of Mount Elgon in eastern Uganda was the scene of ethnic rivalry between Bagisu and Bagwere, the later controversy also pitted the sub-nationalisms of the districts of Bugisu and Bukedi against each other.

The district boundaries of Bugisu and Bukedi have been altered several times. At one point there were three districts called Bugwere, Bugisu, and Budama. In 1937 Bugwere and Bugisu were amalgamated, only to be split apart in 1954 when Bugisu was made a separate district in recognition of its greater ethnic homogeneity (two "tribes," including the Sebei) and political and economic progress. Bugwere was then rejoined to Budama to form Bukedi District. During these changes Mbale town remained the common administrative capital, though it became a separate "Territory" in 1954 belonging to neither district.

The Bagwere resented the intrusion of Bagisu into Mbale and felt humiliated by the necessity to cross a thin strip of land belonging to Bugisu District in order to enter the town. The crusade for the "return of Mbale," however, became one of the few instances in which the Bagwere were supported by the other six ethnic groups in Bukedi.

The demands of each group that Mbale be amalgamated with their district became the focus for high emotions exacerbated by having the two district administrations housed in different wings of the same building. Tempers flared in September 1962 when the car of the Bukedi Secretary-General was stopped by Bagisu tribesmen, and he was forced to flee for his life. As in the other cases examined, an urgency felt by all participants that they might fare less favorably at the hands of an independent government caused the issue to take on greater political significance. The controversy has also deepened interest in ethnic history and culture at least among the Bagisu. A research society was formed in the 1950s to collect traditions and standardize the language. Bagisu students at Makerere published a magazine concentrating on ethnic matters.

A commission of inquiry suggested a compromise altering the boundaries to give the inhabitants of Bukedi direct access to Mbale, while giving nominal title to the town to Bugisu. Under this scheme the Bukedi District administration would be moved to Tororo, which is within the district. The 1962 Constitution specifically omitted the possibility of boundary changes involving Bukedi, Bugisu, and Mbale from constitutional entrenchment for a period of two years following independence. However, no decision was made. The Ugandan government finally took action in 1967, when the new Constitution left Mbale and the strip of land surrounding it in Bugisu. The Bukedi District administration was then transferred to Tororo. Characteristic of the current state of affairs in Uganda (discussed in section 5), the decision did not spark off a resurgence of cultural sub-nationalism.

F. ANTI-BAGANDA COALITIONS AND THE BANTU AND NILOTIC GROUPINGS

Lastly there are the various coalitions of political forces in Uganda which have been interpreted as ethnic groupings. At first these were presumed to have formed as a negative reaction to Buganda's efforts to gain greater privileges and autonomy. Later they were seen as groupings formed on linguistic lines which appeared to parallel economic position (the richer south vs. the disadvantaged north). For the most part these groupings have consisted of little more than a few politicians seeking tactical advantage in a fluid situation. Few, if any, cultural ties existed to give these groups more than a transitory semblance of coherence.

For the variety of reasons discussed earlier other ethnic groups have tended to resent Buganda's special position and feared its dominance. Although this resentment was felt generally, it did not achieve political form until 1958. Prior to that Baganda had been influential in the organization of all political parties. Following the 1958 elections to the Legislative Council seven members (from seven districts) formed the Uganda People's Union (UPU).[119] The UPU attempted to channel dislike of Baganda into a political party. One specific event that gave impetus to the party was the hostility outside Buganda over statements in the Buganda *Lukiiko* that the *Kabaka* should be made king of a self-governing Uganda.[120] Another was the resistance of non-Baganda areas to Buganda's campaign against a strong unitary central government.[121] However, the party never achieved an organization outside of the Legislative Council. It remained a collection of the personal followings in each district of the politicians who formed it.[122] In March 1960 it merged with the Obote-led faction of the Uganda National Congress to become the UPC.

Two years after independence factional struggle in the Cabinet gave rise to rumors of developing Bantu and Nilotic groupings within the UPC each seeking to control the state. The ideological positions of leaders in each group seemed to be opposed. The Nilotic group was presumed to be "pro-East" (in international affairs), and in favor of more radical social policies, while the Bantu politicians favored more conservative social policies (particularly with regard to kingship) and a "pro-West" international stance. The arrest and detention of five Bantu ministers by Obote in February 1966 appeared to indicate the formation of two wide sub-national groupings.

If the confrontation of 1966 had not occurred, such groupings might have solidified into serious sub-national movements. Geertz has pointed out that post independence struggles can result in a transfer of loyalties to larger groups, as local issues are resolved in a national arena and groups seek allies to secure their positions.[123] In Uganda, however, this has not happened. Both Bantu and Nilotic areas were marked more by conflict than by political, let alone social, solidarity.[124] Other Bantu areas did not overcome their suspicion of Buganda (especially the Banyoro), and many were badly divided internally (particularly Kigezi, Ankole, and Toro). The Nilotic ethnic groups were also suspicious of one another. The Alur were not on good terms with the Lugbara (a Sudanic tribe) nor were the Acholi and Langi. Neither grouping was sufficiently coherent to overcome the pervasive factionalism that marked the politics of Ugandan sub-nationalism before 1966.

5. The Impact of the Confrontation of 1966

Single dramatic events can rarely bear the burden of social explanation placed upon them. In retrospect earlier developments often begin a process of political change which is not recognized until a climactic struggle occurs. However, the confrontation between the central government and Buganda in 1966 made a clean break with the past and set Uganda on a new course. While the conflict pitted only one sub-national group against the nation, the result was the end—up to now— of all public sub-national political activity. This outcome was highly uncertain, especially since Obote, who was probably the leading force in favor of elimination of sub-national political competition, came extremely close to losing control of the government. Thus, the events of 1966 form the basis for understanding the reasons for the later overhaul of the constitutional and parliamentary machinery and some of the problems created by the new stance taken by the central government.

With hindsight it is possible to see that the national leadership of the UPC was somewhat more interested in national unity and ready to take steps to limit sub-national movements in general and Buganda's autonomy in particular than was the DP (and certainly more so than KY). In 1960 Obote had indicated his opposition to sub-nationalism. He merged his wing of the UNC with the anti-Buganda UPU. In the same year he asserted that "African nationalism hates small states."[125] In March 1963 he stated that the tribe has "served our people as a basic political unit very well in the past. [But now] the problem of people putting the tribe above national consciousness is a problem that we must face, and an issue we must destroy."[126]

Still, the forces of fragmentation appeared to be far more powerful than those of unity as late as February 1966. By 1965 the UPC government had moved from a minority to an overwhelming majority in Parliament, through aisle-crossing by MPs, and in district councils through local elections and patronage. But a variety of factional disputes lay behind the façade of unity. In the April 1964 Gulu UPC Conference, the contest for the Secretary-Generalship of the party pitted John Kakonge, candidate of the radicals interested in policies promoting national mobilization, against Grace Ibingira, a representative of the somewhat more conservative local notables with close links to the *Kabaka*'s government.[127] Both candidates came from the Bantu area—Bunyoro and Ankole respectively. Ibingira won by two votes.

A year later a struggle for control of the UPC brought Ibingira and several followers into direct rivalry with Obote in the Cabinet and in party ranks. According to most accounts, KY members tried to take advantage of this split by infiltrating the UPC's Buganda branch (which began organizing intensively after the coalition between UPC and KY broke down).[128]

The crisis came to a head on February 4, 1966, while Obote was out of Kampala touring Lango, his home district. The Cabinet reversed an earlier decision and scheduled immediate debate on a motion brought by Daudi Ocheng (a northerner, but nonetheless a parliamentary member of KY) to set up a commission of inquiry to investigate charges of corruption against the second ranking army officer, Colonel Idi Amin. The charges which grew out of alleged gold smuggling across the Congo border implicated the Prime Minister and other members of the Cabinet (all northerners). In the debate many Cabinet ministers spoke in favor of the inquiry and that evening only one man voted against the motion—Kakonge. On February 13 a new election was held for UPC branch chairman in Buganda. Godfrey Binaisa, the Attorney-General and a supporter of Obote, was defeated by another Muganda, Dr. E. Lumu, a close associate of Ibingira. Obote's control of the UPC seemed to have ebbed away to the point where he was virtually isolated.

During this time, however, he carefully consolidated his support among political and military figures. On February 22 he struck back by having five ministers arrested during a Cabinet meeting. Two days later he announced that the Constitution was suspended. On March 2, Obote declared that all powers of government were temporarily in his hands. During this period Brigadier General Shaban Opolot, the military commander of the Uganda Army and an Itesot with links to Baganda, visited Sir Edward Mutesa, the *Kabaka*. An attempt to rally troops against Obote failed.

Several days after that Obote accused Mutesa of approaching foreign powers and discussing possible military intervention. This the *Kabaka* admitted and Obote dismissed him from his office as President of Uganda.[129] In March a commission of inquiry composed of respected jurists from outside Uganda was appointed to look into Ocheng's charges. Little substantial evidence was brought forward, though testimony did indicate an enormous increase in Colonel Amin's personal bank account. Obote testified that the money was intended for the purpose of buying supplies for Congolese rebel forces though he conceded that it was unwise for Amin to use his personal account for this purpose. The case against the accused government officials seemed to collapse. The commission's report, however, has not yet been published.

The impact of the impartial public hearings of the commission, the admissions of the *Kabaka*, the lack of public support for the arrested ministers, and the surprisingly calm atmosphere in which government officers carried out their normal duties helped to swing public opinion behind Obote once again. On April 15 the National Assembly was suddenly convened and a new Constitution was presented to the members for immediate action with no opportunity for debate. The opposition and four government members walked out. The "revolutionary" Constitution was enacted fifty-five votes to four.[130]

The 1966 Constitution kept many provisions of its predecessor, but its changes removed many of the legal provisions which encouraged expressions of sub-nationalism. Among the three major changes was the virtual elimination of autonomous powers of districts and federal states. The finances of district councils were to be more carefully supervised by the central government and the councils lost the power to appoint local civil servants. Second, the Buganda government lost a number of prerogatives including its entrenched privilege of indirectly electing its members to the National Assembly, and the right to give official lands to chiefs and Buganda ministers as perquisites of office. The *Kabaka* (and other kingdom rulers) was reduced to a ceremonial position on the same level as constitutional heads in the districts. Henceforth Buganda was to be treated as a district no different from any of the others. By severely weakening the position of civil service chiefs as well as the Mengo government's control over them, the 1966 Constitution crippled the organizational framework that had given the KY its overwhelming success in rural areas.[131]

A third important change was a significant enlargement of the powers of the head of government—as much a result of the way the Constitution was amended as the changes themselves. The largely ceremonial Presidency was merged with the office of the Prime Minister. Most of the formal powers of the new office existed in the 1962 Constitution, though the President could now legislate when Parliament was not sitting. These three changes—elimination of the independent powers of the districts and kingdoms, removal of Buganda's special privileges, and creation of a new and more powerful Presidency—provided a new legal framework that was instrumental in the decline of cultural sub-nationalism.

The Baganda reacted angrily to this sudden attack. The *Lukiiko* rejected the new Constitution and on May 20 ordered the central government to withdraw from Buganda. When three Buganda county chiefs were arrested by central government police two days later, the Baganda rioted and attacked police stations. Ex-servicemen arrived at the *Kabaka*'s palace (called the *Lubiri*), which was surrounded by Uganda Army and Special Force units. After brief, but fierce, fighting on May 24, the central government captured the palace and the *Kabaka* escaped to England where he resided until his death in 1969.

The new Constitution was intended to be no more than an interim document, as it specifically provided for the establishment of a constituent assembly at some future time. However, the government did not act until after the 1966 Constitution had been tested in the Uganda High Court. In overruling the *habeas corpus* plea of a former Buganda county chief, the court found that a revolution had taken place "that destroyed the entire legal order and was superseded by a new Constitution, and by effective government . . ."[132] For these reasons the 1966 Constitution was deemed legally valid.

With the court decision legitimizing the "revolutionary" Constitution, the government began to formulate the present "republican" Constitution. Its approach was quite different from the swift imposed solution of 1966. The proposed document was issued in June 1967 and subjected to intensive and relatively free debate for over a month by a Constituent Assembly (made up of members of Parliament).[133] In direct response to the debate the government substantially amended certain of its proposals, and after brief further discussion the Constitution was adopted on September 8. Considering the factional struggles in the country only one year before, the performance was deeply impressive. As the President said, "Uganda was probably making history in Africa by having its proposals debated so openly."[134] The very fact that the central government and the UPC felt sufficiently secure to permit open debate on the fundamental political structure of Uganda was an indication of the degree to which the events of 1966 had shifted political power from district and ethnically oriented groups to those promoting national unity. More recent events, however, indicate that deep feelings of resentment have not vanished.

The 1967 Constitution carried the changes of the previous year another step forward in a careful effort to create conditions that would reduce cultural sub-nationalism. First, the kingdoms were abolished and the kings (with the exception of the *Kabaka*) were given pensions. Constitutional heads were also eliminated. Second, Buganda was divided into four districts subject to the Minister of Regional Administrations on the same basis as all other districts.

Third, central governmental control over district administration was further tightened by leaving to the National Assembly the determination of the form district administration should take and the right to provide for appointment rather than election of members of district councils. Later events have shown that local administration is to be given very little room for initiative. The dispute over the location of a textile factory in Acholi or Lango District (discussed below) has shown that the top political officeholder in the district, the Secretary-General, cannot object to policies laid down by the ruling party and the national government. In addition stricter financial controls have been imposed on district administration expenditures, and the central government has taken over several services previously administered by local bodies.[135]

Fourth, and of great potential importance, the requirement that boundaries of constituencies of MPs be limited by district boundaries was eliminated. This raised the possibility of redrawing constituency lines so that candidates have to appeal to members of two or more ethnic groups and thus may have the opportunity to wage campaigns on issues that are less likely to arouse ethnic grievances and competition. However, a different route was actually taken in the electoral proposals issued by Obote in July 1970. Each candidate for the next National Assembly will have to run in four different constituencies each in a different ethnic area, though he would represent only his home or "basic" constituency if elected.[136] This approach achieves the same purposes in a more spectacular fashion.

The UPC party structure has also been overhauled in an effort to eliminate its earlier tendencies toward factionalism on an ethnic basis.[137] By giving the Party President (Obote) the power to appoint the other national party officials where previously they were elected, the UPC is less likely to be responsive to ethnic pressures. The new structure maintains a dual hierarchy of conference and executive at several levels (the parish, parliamentary constituency, district, and nation).[138] However, the district level is being frozen out by the absence of a district conference and by having the constituency executive maintain direct communication with the national executive.[139] Finally, the disappearance of the KY and the patronage of the *Kabaka*'s government has created a vacuum that may possibly result in active UPC organization in what was formerly Buganda.[140]

The official position of the government today (1970) is that nation-building in Uganda is based on unity and not ethnic origin. It is not surprising to discover, for example, that the question on "tribe" was quietly dropped from the 1969 census forms. Top political leaders and the party newspaper have been quite emphatic in condemning appeals to "tribalism." Much as Julius Nyerere, President of Tanzania, has used the expulsion of students from the University of Dar es Salaam to create a climate of opinion favorable to socialism, Obote is using the confrontation with Buganda in his efforts to develop a greater sense of national consciousness among Ugandans.[141]

In these ways a coordinated effort has been made by the government to attack the causes of sub-national feeling discussed in section 3. The UPC has been centralized. The importance of districts as political units has been reduced. Ethnic appeals are illegitimate. However, three significant problems greatly complicate Obote's mission.

First, most of what has been achieved has taken place at the expense of the Baganda. No one knows how deep runs their bitterness over the sudden withdrawal of their special status. It has been surprising—and perhaps a sign of hope— that after the *Lubiri* fell, the Baganda retreated into passivity. There have been relatively few violent incidents (partly perhaps because Emergency Regulations remain in effect), and virtually no demonstrations of the sort that followed the exile of the *Kabaka* in 1953.[142]

On the other hand, turning the *Bulange* (the building in which the former Buganda *Lukiiko* met) into an office building for the Ministry of Defense must have rankled most Baganda even though the central government has paid the four new districts created out of Buganda for the building. A more important indicator was the intense grief displayed by all classes of Baganda from farmers to university students upon hearing of the death of the *Kabaka* in late 1969. A month later an attempt was made to assassinate Obote at a UPC conference. That night a number of people were wounded or killed as the army maintained roadblocks throughout Kampala and Mengo. A few months later several Baganda were arrested and confessed that they had taken part in the crime.

Second, as Uganda moves toward holding new elections, various sub-national grievances, among others, are likely to surface. A variety of conflicts greatly complicated the elections for UPC constituency chairmen in 1969. In many cases a top party official had to mediate between dissatisfied factions.

Sub-national competition can no longer become an issue between political parties, however. In the wake of the assassination attempt all parties except the UPC were banned. Whether forcing all sub-national groups to campaign through a single party committed to oppose tribalism will eliminate ethnic competition will be tested by the election.

Third, to maintain a policy of totally ignoring ethnic considerations cannot overcome another cause of sub-nationalist feeling—resentment over ethnically differentiated educational and economic development. To push ahead relatively underprivileged groups may further embitter the Baganda who are often better prepared and skilled. To take the best qualified individual for the job may arouse resentment in groups previously denied opportunities for preparation. Either way, distrust is fueled by ethnic suspicions and rivalries.

To some extent the government has been able to avoid the problem by greatly expanding the resources available for distribution. By 1971 total government hospital beds are expected to increase by eighty per cent over the 1964 figure.[143] Between 1961 and 1966 senior secondary school places more than tripled, and university places almost doubled.[144] The number of government positions open to Ugandans increased enormously due to Africanization and the creation of additional jobs as a result of new development projects.[145] Thus, the government has been able to reduce feelings of deprivation by enlarging the pie.

The government has also tried to avoid accusations that it favors particular ethnic groups by stressing that new projects are located on the basis of technical criteria. As far as the location of new social services is concerned, assisting outlying areas to reach the level of development enjoyed by Buganda can be justified on this basis. Somewhat contradictorily, however, the government also stresses the importance of equal distribution of social services.[146]

This approach has not been without its problems, however, as the Acholi-Lango factory dispute illustrates. Acholi and Lango are neighboring districts populated almost entirely by

Acholi and Langi respectively. The boundary between them has been disputed for many years. The issue remained a live one and was debated in the Acholi District council in 1967.[147] One of the first demands of Langi nationalists was to call for replacement of Acholi as the language of instruction in Lango primary schools.[148]

In February 1968 the Acholi District council sent a delegation containing UPC (and one DP) members to Kampala to complain about unfair distribution of industry between the two districts.[149] Their principal complaint was that a textile factory which they claimed had been intended for an Acholi site was now to be placed in Lango. The issue was quite sensitive, since Obote comes from Lango.

The Soviet Union had agreed in 1964 to lend the money to build the factory and had carried out feasibility studies to determine the site. It appears that sites in both Acholi and Lango were under consideration. However, Lira, the capital of Lango, was ultimately chosen. The Ugandan government defended its decision on technical grounds. Lira had an adequate supply of water and other necessary facilities to service a factory. In addition Lango produces almost twice as much cotton as Acholi and thus transport costs would be lower, if the mill were sited in Lira.[150]

The government was particularly irked by the Acholi demand, since Acholi District had already received a disproportionate share of development benefits, including a new airport, senior secondary school, and farm institute. The government also took the position that the bipartisan character of the delegation indicated that its members were coming as representatives of the Acholi "tribe," and not as members of a political party. In doing so the Secretary-General and his assistant had violated party policy. As a result they were dismissed and replaced by the leaders of the other Acholi UPC faction. The Minister of Regional Administrations, James Ochola, explained that the districts must carry out central government policy and could not formulate policies of their own. In a long article in the party newspaper the allegations put forward by the Acholi District council were refuted one by one. Finally, the government argued that the District council had no business discussing a matter to be decided upon by experts in the Ministry of Planning in consultation with the Russian foreign aid team.

The incident illustrates both the intense desire of the people to gain as full a share as possible of the new resources being allocated, and the efforts of the government to reduce the sub-national feelings that such desires inevitably engender. In particular the case demonstrates the growing centralization of both the national government and the national executive of the UPC, and the attempt to put ethnic appeals outside the rules of the political game. In these ways the central government is continuing its attack on the causes of sub-nationalism. On the other hand, a year later many Acholi District councillors were still refusing to cooperate with their new Secretary-General (whom they had repudiated when he held the job some years before).[151] Whether the new policy of the government of introducing structures which deflect ethnic demands and of directly attacking all sub-national movements can succeed is still in question. Much depends on the ability of the government to maintain and enlarge its reputation for ignoring ethnic considerations, while at the same time redressing the ethnic inequities of past development.

6. Ethnic Composition of Politicians, Bureaucrats, and University Students

Since feelings of cultural sub-nationalism are still fresh in the minds of the people, the ultimate question of who controls the government underlies all others. It is in this area that the government faces the most important test of its credibility. If certain ethnic groups monopolize top government positions, development of the level of trust in the central government, which is necessary for making the adjustment from ethnic to national identity, is unlikely to take root. There is a widespread belief among Ugandans (and academics who have written about Uganda) that Bantu groups and particularly the Baganda dominate the civilian bureaucracy, while northerners and particularly Acholi and Langi dominate the top political positions, the army, and the police.

Post independence data on the army and police are not available, but these hypotheses can be tested against the figures for the higher civil service, politicians, and Makerere students, the civil servants and politicians of the next generation. By examining ethnic representation at various points in time from the late colonial period through the confrontation of 1966, it is possible to determine whether the trends that have developed favor one group over another. The breakdown into ethnic groups or "tribes" used below is based primarily on the groups to which the individuals surveyed are perceived as belonging by the general public. The tabulations are therefore subject to many of the criticisms of "tribe" discussed earlier in this chapter. However, since widespread beliefs about ethnic groups have political relevance, it is important to compare them against actual data on ethnic representation.

A. POLITICIANS

Two studies show that Baganda dominated the top positions within political parties in the last years of colonial rule. A questionnaire administered in 1956 to forty branch chairmen of the Uganda National Congress indicated that 50 per cent were Baganda, 11 per cent were from Lango, 9 per cent from Acholi, and 7 per cent from Busoga and Teso. The Central Committee of the UNC contained seventeen Baganda, one Munyoro, one Musoga, and one man with a Seychellese father and a Muganda mother.[152] A second study examined the top leadership positions of the major parties active in 1958. Out of thirty persons whose ethnic origin could be identified, twenty-five were Baganda, two were from Acholi, and one each came from Busoga, Lango, and Toro.[153]

When elections were held in most parts of Uganda for the National Assembly, control of branch leadership of the parties tended to become localized. A parallel trend resulted in most candidates for the National Assembly running in areas in which their own ethnic group predominated.[154] The most flamboyant exception was Daudi Ocheng, an Acholi, who became a landowner in Buganda, joined the KY, and defended Baganda interests in Parliament (though as a nominated, not a popularly elected, member). A few other MPs represent urban constituencies in which their ethnic group is not in the majority.

Control of policy formation in Uganda rests primarily in the hands of ministers and deputy ministers. The ethnic group of each one is well known, and their distribution has been tabulated in Table 3 (parliamentary secretaries and colonial civil servants holding ministerial positions are included). It demonstrates the extent to which the most important and most prestigious political offices have been spread among all important ethnic groups. Of all twenty groups containing one per cent of the population or more, only one fairly populous group (Banyaruanda) and one small one (Banyole) have never had representation at the ministerial level. Thus it is also not surprising to discover that the number of ministerial positions has increased until it now includes about one half the UPC members in the National Assembly.

Second, the Baganda—even after the 1966 crisis—have always been overrepresented on the basis of their share of the population. However, their overrepresentation has been declining since 1963, when the KY was allied with the UPC in the government. In 1967 the Baganda held a smaller proportion of ministerial positions than they filled in the higher civil service or in Makerere University College (see Tables 4 and 5). The most overrepresented group in the 1967 ministerial ranks were the Batoro.

Third, if ethnic groups are combined into the four main language groups in Uganda, their representation has been roughly equivalent to their share of the population since 1963. Bantu representation among ministers and deputy ministers fell below their population percentage for the first time following the arrest and detention of five of their number in February 1966. Neither the Acholi, Langi, nor the Nilotic

TABLE 3

Ethnic Composition of Ministers and Deputy Ministers[a]
(including Parliamentary Secretaries and the Director of Planning)

1959 Population %	Ethnic Group	Sept. 1959 Executive Council	Dec. 1961 DP	July 1963 UPC/KY	August 1965 UPC	March 1967 UPC
16.3	Baganda	3	7	11	7	7
8.1	Iteso	0	0	1	2	3
8.1	Banyankole	1	2	2	3	2
7.8	Basoga	1	1	2	2	1
7.1	Bakiga/	1	1	1	1	1
	Bahororo	0	0	1	1	1
5.6	Langi	0	1	2	2	2
5.1	Bagisu	0	0	1	1	1
4.4	Acholi	0	1	1	2	2
3.7	Lugbara	0	1	0	1	1
3.2	Batoro	0	1	1	3	3
2.9	Banyoro	0	0	2	2	1
2.0	Karamojong	0	0	1	1	1
1.9	Alur	0	0	0	1	1
1.7	Bagwere	0	0	1	1	0
1.7	Bakonjo	0	0	1	1	1
1.6	Japadhola (Badama)	0	1	0	1	1
1.2	Madi	0	0	1	1	1
0.7	Samia	0	0	1	1	1
16.9	Others[b]	0	0	0	0	0
100.0	TOTAL AFRICANS	6	16	30	34	31
Equivalent to 0.2	Europeans	6	4	0	0	0
Equivalent to 1.1	Asians	1	2	0	0	0
	CUMULATIVE TOTAL	13	22	30	34	31

1959 Population %	Language Groups	Sept. 1959 Executive Council	Dec. 1961 DP	July 1963 UPC/KY	August 1965 UPC	March 1967 UPC
65.7	Bantu	6(100%)	12(75%)	24(80%)	23(68%)	19(61%)
14.5	Nilotic	0(0%)	3(19%)	3(10%)	6(18%)	6(19%)
12.7	Nilo-Hamitic	0(0%)	0(0%)	2(7%)	3(9%)	4(13%)
5.0	Sudanic	0(0%)	1(6%)	1(3%)	2(6%)	2(6%)
2.1	Others	0	0	0	0	0

a *Central Government Organisation* and *Government Directory*, Nos. 12, 19, 23, 27, and 29 (Government Printer: Entebbe).
b Including Banyaruanda, Rundi, Banyole, Kumam, Kakwa, Sebei, Bagwe, Jaluo, Baamba, Jonam, Bakenyi, Suk, Labwor, and Lendu.

group as a whole, often reputed to have consolidated the top positions, are significantly overrepresented.

Finally, UPC leaders have recently been following the practice of replacing ministers who resigned with members from the same ethnic groups. Between April and July 1967, C. Obwangor (Itesot), A. Nekyon (Langi), and G. Binaisa (Muganda) resigned. Since then J. Anyoti (Kumam, a tribe closely related to the Iteso) and J. Okae (Langi) have been the only new recruits to ministerial positions.

B. CIVIL SERVANTS

The higher civil service plays just as important a role in guiding government business as top politicians. Permanent Secretaries and District Commissioners receive high salaries and much deference. It is not surprising that fears of ethnic domination in the bureaucracy have been raised from time to time.[155] Different members of Parliament have claimed either that there is a calculated policy of "northernizing" the civil service, or that there is increasing Baganda domination. The data presented in Table 4 tends to refute both of these allegations.

The higher civil service is made up of appointed officials

who control the formulation and implementation of government policies. The criteria for inclusion used here was a listing in the *Government Directory* (excluding personal secretaries and jobholders in the office of the National Assembly),
or holding a position of District Commissioner or Assistant
District Commissioner. The positions analyzed focus on the
administrative cadre, and exclude most technical officers.

The data must be approached with some caution, however.
First, no attempt has been made to give additional weight to
more sensitive posts (some of which are not even included in
the *Government Directory*). Second, the security forces—in
which members of non-Bantu ethnic groups predominate—
and the para-statal bodies have not been considered, since no
recent figures are available. Consequently, the findings of this
analysis cannot be taken as describing the whole government.
Third, the listing of posts in the *Government Directory* has
changed over the past ten years, though there is no evidence
that the changes have been influenced by ethnic considerations. Fourth, the identification of a civil servant with a particular ethnic group does not mean that he necessarily regards
that ethnic group as important for any purpose. Fifth, the
percentages for the early years (1959 and 1961) are somewhat misleading, as the total number of Africans was so small.
Thus, both percentages and absolute numbers are given in
the table.

The determination of each officer's ethnic group was made
by analyzing his name. However, since many ethnic groups
use the same names, an attempt was made to confirm the
identity of each person, by asking someone who knew him.
The Ugandan bureaucratic elite is still sufficiently small that
almost every person could be positively identified in this
manner.

Table 4 indicates that the Baganda were overrepresented
in the higher civil service by a factor fluctuating between 2
and 3 during the period between 1959 and 1967. Their percentage reached a high of 46.9 per cent in 1961 during the
first frantic phase of Africanization and then fell steadily to
35.6 per cent in 1967.[156] However, a comparison of the

changes in their percentage of representation against the changes in their absolute numbers reveals that while their proportion of higher civil servants fell by more than 10 per cent, the actual number of Baganda in this sector of the bureaucracy increased from 11 to 105. These simultaneous changes in opposite directions helped to keep the civil service insulated from the imposition of ethnic criteria. In this way Uganda's sudden late start on Africanization has paid an unexpected political dividend. The Baganda cannot claim they are being discriminated against, and others can take satisfaction in the rise of percentage of higher civil servants from their respective ethnic groups.

None of the "northern" groups has ever been significantly overrepresented, except the Acholi, who were somewhat so, in 1965. The Langi, contrary to the claims of critics of Obote, have always been somewhat underrepresented. Aside from the Baganda, in 1967 the Iteso, Batoro, Banyoro, Japadhola, Banyole, Samia, and Kakwa were the only tribes to have achieved parity or better by comparison to their share of the general population. Apart from the Rundi, no ethnic group with more than 1 per cent of the population has been totally unrepresented in the higher civil service. The sharp fall in Δ indicates that the ethnic profile of the higher civil service was coming to resemble more closely the distribution of the general population by 1963. Since that time it appears to have stabilized, though the percentages of higher civil servants from various ethnic groups have fluctuated since then. Changes in ethnic composition of secondary schools and Makerere may alter these percentages in the next few years.

If Ugandan ethnic groups are categorized in terms of the major language divisions, the arguments about northern or Bantu domination are further weakened. By 1967 Nilotic and Nilo-Hamitic speakers were very slightly underrepresented, though Sudanic speakers were more so. Without the Baganda the other Bantu ethnic groups are also underrepresented, and have been over the entire eight-year period. With the Baganda added in, the overrepresentation is relatively mild. The degree of dissimilarity with the general population fell by almost one half during this time.

For comparison a racial breakdown of the higher civil service during the years examined is included. There has been a rapid rate of Africanization (from 10.2 per cent to 67.9 per cent) which reflects Uganda's late start, while the number of European members of the bureaucracy has slipped from 84.2 per cent to 18.7 per cent. Much more surprising has been the steady increase in Asians (Indians) from 5.7 per cent to 13.4 per cent. The extreme dissimilarity between the racial composition in the bureaucracy and in the general population has been moderated somewhat, but it remains quite high.

In contrast to some other African countries, notably Nigeria, Uganda has managed to avoid heavy pressures to share bureaucratic positions on a solely ethnic basis. As a northerner asked, ". . . why should we leave [out] capable Baganda, who can render service to the nation . . . Are they not part of Uganda?"[157] In Nigeria many posts in the federal bureaucracy were either left vacant or filled under contract by expatriates, "because of the understandable desire to hold a proportion of posts open until northerners are available to fill them."[158] The consequences of these divergent policies toward representative bureaucracy may have been reflected in the tragic degree to which sub-nationalism triumphed in Nigeria during the past few years in contrast to Uganda.

C. UNIVERSITY STUDENTS

Receiving a university degree automatically secures one's entry into the upper reaches of the small Ugandan elite. It is thus a matter of intense concern to all parents that their children survive the competition for secondary school places and enter Makerere University or go abroad for further studies. There is, however, surprisingly little public discussion of the allocation of places at Makerere. It is generally assumed that merit alone is the criterion for entry, though the differential location of secondary schools and missions does give advantages to certain ethnic groups, as we have seen.

TABLE 4

Ethnic Composition of the Higher Civil Service[a]

1959 Population %	Ethnic Group	September 1959 % (N)	December 1961 % (N)	July 1963 % (N)	August 1965 % (N)	March 1967 % (N)
16.3	Baganda	40.7(11)	46.9(23)	38.1(51)	37.3(87)	35.6(105)
8.1	Iteso	3.7(1)	2.0(1)	5.2(7)	4.7(11)	8.1(24)
8.1	Banyankole	0.0(0)	4.1(2)	7.5(10)	6.9(16)	6.8(20)
7.8	Basoga	7.4(2)	4.1(2)	9.0(12)	6.0(14)	3.4(10)
7.1	Bakiga/ Bahororo	3.7(1)	10.2(5)	6.0(8)	5.2(12)	4.7(14)
5.9	Banyaruanda	11.1(3)	4.1(2)	3.7(5)	4.7(11)	4.4(13)
5.6	Langi	3.7(1)	2.0(1)	1.5(2)	3.0(7)	4.1(12)
5.1	Bagisu	0.0(0)	4.1(2)	4.5(6)	3.0(7)	2.7(8)
4.4	Acholi	7.4(2)	4.1(2)	6.7(9)	7.3(17)	4.4(13)
3.7	Lugbara	0.0(0)	2.0(1)	1.5(2)	1.3(3)	1.4(4)
3.2	Batoro	7.4(2)	6.1(3)	3.0(4)	3.4(8)	7.1(21)
2.9	Banyoro	7.4(2)	6.1(3)	5.2(7)	6.0(14)	5.1(15)
2.0	Karamojong	0.0(0)	0.0(0)	0.7(1)	0.9(2)	0.7(2)
1.9	Alur	0.0(0)	0.0(0)	0.7(1)	0.9(2)	0.7(2)
1.7	Bagwere	0.0(0)	0.0(0)	0.0(0)	0.4(1)	0.3(1)
1.7	Bakonjo	0.0(0)	0.0(0)	0.0(0)	0.4(1)	0.3(1)
1.6	Japadhola (Badama)	0.0(0)	2.0(1)	2.2(3)	0.9(2)	4.1(12)
1.4	Banyole	3.7(1)	0.0(0)	0.7(1)	1.7(4)	1.4(4)
1.2	Madi	3.7(1)	2.0(1)	1.5(2)	0.9(2)	0.3(1)
1.0	Kumam	0.0(0)	0.0(0)	0.0(0)	0.9(2)	0.7(2)
0.7	Samia	0.0(0)	0.0(0)	0.7(1)	3.0(7)	2.4(6)
0.6	Kakwa	0.0(0)	0.0(0)	0.7(1)	0.9(2)	1.4(4)
0.6	Sebei	0.0(0)	0.0(0)	0.0(0)	0.0(0)	0.3(1)
0.4	Jonam	0.0(0)	0.0(0)	0.7(1)	0.4(1)	0.0(0)
7.0	Other[b]	0.0(0)	0.0(0)	0.0(0)	0.0(0)	0.0(0)
100.0	TOTAL	99.9(27)	99.8(49)	99.8(134)	100.1(233)	100.4(295)
		$\Delta^c = 46.2$	$\Delta = 41.1$	$\Delta = 29.0$	$\Delta = 30.0$	$\Delta = 30.2$

1959 Population %	Language Groups	September 1959 % (N)	December 1961 % (N)	July 1963 % (N)	August 1965 % (N)	March 1967 % (N)
65.7	Bantu	81.5(22)	85.7(42)	78.4(105)	78.1(182)	73.9(218)
14.5	Nilotic	11.1(3)	8.2(4)	11.9(16)	12.4(29)	13.2(39)
12.7	Nilo-Hamitic	3.7(1)	2.0(1)	6.7(9)	7.3(17)	11.2(33)
5.0	Sudanic	3.7(1)	4.1(2)	2.9(4)	2.1(5)	1.7(5)
2.1	Other	0.0(0)	0.0(0)	0.0(0)	0.0(0)	0.0(0)
100.0	TOTAL	100.0(27)	100.0(49)	99.9(134)	99.9(233)	100.0(295)
		$\Delta = 15.8$	$\Delta = 20.0$	$\Delta = 12.8$	$\Delta = 12.5$	$\Delta = 8.2$

1959 Population %	Race	September 1959 % (N)	December 1961 % (N)	July 1963 % (N)	August 1965 % (N)	March 1967 % (N)
98.7	Africans	10.2(27)	19.0(49)	45.6(134)	66.8(233)	67.9(295)
0.2	Europeans	84.2(223)	73.6(190)	46.3(136)	24.1(84)	18.7(81)
1.1	Asians	5.7(15)	7.4(19)	8.2(24)	9.2(32)	13.4(58)
100.0	TOTAL	100.1(265)	100.0(258)	100.1(294)	100.1(349)	100.0(434)
		$\Delta = 88.6$	$\Delta = 79.7$	$\Delta = 53.2$	$\Delta = 32.0$	$\Delta = 30.8$

ᵃ Compiled from *Central Government Organisation* and *Government Directory*, Nos. 12, 19, 23, 27, and 29 (Government Printer: Entebbe), and from *Staff Lists*, 1959, 1961, 1963, 1965, and 1967 (Government Printer: Entebbe).

ᵇ Including Bagwe, Baamba, Jaluo, Suk, Labwor, Rundi, Bakenyi, and Lendu.

ᶜ Δ measures the degree of dissimilarity by comparison to the ethnic distribution of the general population. See Table 2.

University students of today are likely to be the top civil servants—and perhaps politicians—of tomorrow. Consequently, an examination of trends in the ethnic composition of Makerere yields a prediction about the likely profile of the higher civil service in the late 1970s.

The data on representation of ethnic groups at Makerere was compiled from the *Nominal Roll* for four different years. Since Makerere offers a three-year degree program, an overlap of students was avoided by choosing every fourth year from 1959/60 to 1968/69. Each student's ethnic group is listed, so it is possible to make an accurate determination of the numbers representing each group. The sudden increase in foreign scholarships just before independence explains why Makerere attendance fell between 1959/60 and 1962/63. As a large number of Ugandan students take their degree abroad, these figures may be a somewhat inaccurate measure of the entire class.[159]

Once again the Baganda are heavily overrepresented, though their percentage steadily falls from 46.6 per cent to 33.6 per cent over the ten-year period. While the Baganda took more than two of every five places held by Ugandan Africans in 1959/60, or almost three times their percentage of the general population, they now occupy one place in three, or double their expected share. As in the case of the higher civil service, the absolute number of Baganda at Makerere has rapidly risen, while their percentage has fallen. The rapid expansion of the University from 873 to 2011 students, and the increasing share of the places held by Ugandan Africans, has made this possible. Thus, there has been little reason to complain of discrimination.

The most overrepresented ethnic group in 1968/69 are the Samia who are present in almost triple the proportion they are found in Uganda's population. The Acholi, Batoro, Banyoro, Bagwere, and Madi are slightly overrepresented at the moment. The rest are underrepresented. However, it is clear that most ethnic groups, even the smallest ones, have had some sons or daughters who have attended university. The degree to which the ethnic composition of Makerere has reflected the distribution of the general population has steadily risen.

The major language groups have also become represented more equitably at Makerere, as the decade passed. The Bantu group remains somewhat overrepresented, though without the Baganda the remaining Bantu speakers always were underrepresented. The Nilotic, Nilo-Hamitic, and Sudanic groups remain slightly underrepresented. In terms of language groups Makerere is twice as representative of the general population in 1968/69 as it was in 1959/60.

If we ask which Makerere students are most likely to become high level civil servants, we should examine more closely the Arts and Social Science Faculties. To the extent that the British tradition of "generalists" remains an important norm of recruitment into the Ugandan public service, the administrative cadre is more likely to include men and women with degrees in political science, economics, English, and the like than those taking more technical subjects.[160]

In general the percentages of ethnic distribution of students in arts and social science subjects hover around the respective percentages of students in the University as a whole. The Baganda composed slightly over half (51.2 per cent) of arts

TABLE 5

Ethnic Composition of Ugandan Makerere Students[a]

1959 Population %	Ethnic Group	1959/60 % (N)	1962/63 % (N)	1965/66 % (N)	1968/69 % (N)
16.3	Baganda	46.6(131)	42.5(102)	36.9(206)	33.6(377)
8.1	Iteso	6.1(17)	5.0(12)	5.9(33)	7.8(88)
8.1	Banyankole	6.1(17)	8.8(21)	7.5(42)	6.2(69)
7.8	Basoga	6.1(17)	7.1(17)	7.3(41)	6.4(72)
7.1	Bakiga/	5.3(15)	7.5(18)	7.2(40)	6.5(73)
	Bahororo	1.1(3)	1.7(4)	0.9(5)	0.4(5)
5.9	Banyaruanda	1.8(5)	2.5(6)	2.0(11)	2.9(33)
5.6	Langi	1.8(5)	3.8(9)	4.8(27)	5.2(58)
5.1	Bagisu	3.6(10)	2.5(6)	2.9(16)	2.9(33)
4.4	Acholi	4.3(12)	4.2(10)	7.0(39)	5.4(61)
3.7	Lugbara	0.4(1)	0.8(2)	1.6(9)	2.2(25)
3.2	Batoro	1.8(5)	1.3(3)	2.5(14)	4.1(46)
2.9	Banyoro	3.6(10)	2.1(5)	4.3(24)	4.5(50)
2.0	Karamojong	0.4(1)	0.0(0)	0.0(0)	0.2(2)
1.9	Alur	0.4(1)	0.4(1)	0.9(5)	1.4(16)
1.7	Bagwere	2.1(6)	1.3(3)	1.4(8)	1.9(21)
1.7	Bakonjo	0.7(2)	0.4(1)	0.2(1)	0.3(3)
1.6	Japadhola (Badama)	1.4(4)	1.7(4)	1.6(9)	1.1(12)
1.4	Banyole	1.4(4)	0.8(2)	0.5(3)	0.8(9)
1.2	Madi	0.7(2)	0.4(1)	1.3(7)	1.9(21)
1.0	Kumam	1.4(4)	1.3(3)	0.9(5)	0.7(8)
0.7	Samia	0.7(2)	2.1(5)	1.4(8)	1.9(21)
0.6	Kakwa	0.0(0)	0.0(0)	0.2(1)	0.3(3)
0.6	Sebei	0.0(0)	0.0(0)	0.2(1)	0.1(1)
0.6	Bagwe	0.4(1)	0.0(0)	0.0(0)	0.2(2)
0.5	Baamba	0.0(0)	0.0(0)	0.4(2)	0.2(2)
0.4	Jonam	1.4(4)	2.1(5)	0.0(0)	0.5(6)
0.1	Labwor	0.0(0)	0.0(0)	0.0(0)	0.1(1)
–	Okebo	0.4(1)	0.0(0)	0.0(0)	0.0(0)
–	Abaluhya	0.4(1)	0.0(0)	0.0(0)	0.1(1)
–	Bari	0.0(0)	0.0(0)	0.2(1)	0.0(0)
–	Nubian	0.0(0)	0.0(0)	0.0(0)	0.2(2)
5.9	Other[b]	0.0(0)	0.0(0)	0.0(0)	0.0(0)
100.0	TOTAL UGANDAN AFRICANS	100.4(281)	100.3(240)	100.0(558)	100.0(1,121)
		Δ[c] = 33.1	Δ = 32.4	Δ = 26.6	Δ = 23.3

1959 Population %	Language Groups	1959/60 % (N)	1962/63 % (N)	1965/66 % (N)	1968/69 % (N)
65.7	Bantu	81.5(229)	80.4(193)	75.4(421)	72.9(817)
14.5	Nilotic	9.3(26)	12.1(29)	14.3(80)	13.6(153)
12.7	Nilo-Hamitic	7.8(22)	6.3(15)	7.3(41)	9.2(103)
5.0	Sudanic	1.4(4)	1.3(3)	2.9(16)	4.3(48)
2.1	Other	0.0(0)	0.0(0)	0.0(0)	0.0(0)
100.0	TOTAL UGANDAN AFRICANS	100.0(281)	100.1(240)	99.9(558)	100.0(1,121)
		Δ = 15.8	Δ = 14.7	Δ = 9.8	Δ = 7.2
	TOTAL NUMBER OF MAKERERE STUDENTS[d]	873	763	1,158	2,011

[a] Compiled from *Makerere University College Nominal Roll*.

[b] Including Rundi, Jaluo, Bakenyi, Suk, and Lendu.

[c] Δ measures the degree of dissimilarity by comparison to the distribution of the general population. See Table 2.

[d] Including students from Kenya, Tanzania, and other countries as well as non-African Ugandans.

and social science students in 1959/60, but now include about one third (34.6 per cent). Most ethnic groups have not been represented at a level consistently above or below their percentage in Makerere. The ethnic profile in these faculties is currently only very slightly more dissimilar to the ethnic distribution of the population (Δ = 25.6) than is the profile of the University as a whole. In terms of language groups for the past ten years there has been slightly higher overrepresentation of Bantu speakers at the expense of all other groups than that which existed in the University.

In summary there appears to be a trend in the ethnic profile of Makerere and the higher civil service to more closely approach that of the general population. Ethnic representation at Makerere in 1968/69 has almost achieved the degree of similarity found in secondary schools in 1960.[161] Thus, even though the ethnic profile of the higher civil service has remained at the same cumulative level of dissimilarity from the ethnic distribution of the general population since 1963, the Makerere figures suggest that it will become more representative during the 1970s.

Cultural sub-nationalism is likely to rise when resources to be allocated are scarce. Fortunately, this has not been a problem for Uganda during the first seven years of independence. Extremely rapid expansion of civil service posts due to Africanization and of places in University and secondary schools due to educational development have resulted in the accommodation of far more members of every ethnic group than ever before. At the same time the percentage of overrepresentation of the Baganda among top politicians, bureaucrats, and university students has declined. While opportunities in education and the civil service will expand much more slowly in the future, the trade licensing act, the new requirements for work permits, and particularly the sweeping nationalization measures announced in May 1970 will open up a wide variety of positions in commerce and industry previously monopolized by Asians and Europeans. Consequently, in a later period when the possibilites of expansion may not be so likely, Uganda will already have corrected some of the ethnic imbalances inherited from the colonial period.

7.   Political Development in Uganda

Are the changes that have occurred in Uganda part of its political development, or merely another chapter in its political history? Though these changes have resulted in fundamental shifts of power, they are both recent and fragile. As yet there has been no test that has revealed the degree to which major sections of the populace—particularly the Baganda—have accepted them. An army *coup* or sudden deflation of confidence for some reason could end this experiment. While it continues, however, a new political framework is slowly being developed out of the old polity with which Uganda entered into independence.

A polity becomes more politically developed as it acquires effective political organizations, which promote harmony among social groups and achieve other desired goals.[162] When the expression of social forces becomes politically unmanageable, the polity is likely to decay. Thus, the assertion of cultural sub-nationalisms is not necessarily a sign of political development or decay. The question is whether the system can meet the demands of these movements without losing the capacity to meet the other goals of running a national state.

For a little over three years after independence, Uganda operated a somewhat decentralized political system that encouraged the formation of sub-national movements and gave legitimacy to their demands. The central government, though at all times more powerful than any one of the local units, was limited in its effectiveness in pursuing goals of economic development and particularly national consciousness by local sentiment and organizations. Moreover, there was a distinct growth in sub-national appeals. By late 1965 one could say that ethnic mobilization had resulted in political decay. The confrontation of 1966 has produced a much simpler polity with few effective sub-units. The basic strategy has been to force loyalties and energies into the national arena by removing the power and rewards formerly available at local levels. To use Guenther Roth's felicitous distinction, Uganda has ceased to be governed as an "empire" and is in the process of instituting the political order of a nation-state.[163] Instead of establishing a political structure that explicitly recognizes social and cultural heterogeneity, Ugandan leaders are designing a political system in which they intend primordial ties to be politically irrelevant.

However, according to the view of some development theorists, creation of a simpler polity which is not based on already existing primordial ties is not political development at all. Zolberg points out that the central government in most African countries possesses an extremely limited domain and "on the whole the regime has little authority."[164] Henry Bienen carries this argument a step further, noting that "political development in Africa should not be confused with dramatic change at the government or party level . . ."[165]

Thus, he suggests that national authority is likely to be institutionalized only by building up organizations at the local level and through them the national organization.[166] In addition, Huntington has argued that a more complex political system can better secure and maintain the loyalties of its citizens, because of the number and variety of its sub-units.[167] Consequently, on the basis of these writers, it would seem more appropriate to build a nation by developing political structures which take ethnic and district loyalties into account rather than disregarding them.

In Uganda policies embodying this theory of political development were unsuccessfully applied in the first years following independence. Instead of satisfying the demands of sub-national groups, the extremely complex political system exacerbated them. Loyalties based on ethnic and district groups resulted in political competition that weakened national political leaders and diverted resources.

Whatever else, it is clear that Ugandan political leaders have consciously rejected this path to development. They have done so because they found no political institutions capable of restraining sub-national forces under a Constitution that gave ethnic groups legitimacy. Instead, they turned to the strongest and most institutionalized political organization in the country—the central government—in order to find a political structure that would reduce and redirect local demands. Based on sixty years of colonial development, the authority of the central government has again become the vital core of the political system. Building a nation in Uganda, if successful, will be accomplished by working from the center outwards, not from the periphery inwards.

For the moment there is little public assertion of cultural sub-nationalism in Uganda. Considering the salience of ethnic groups in politics up to 1966, this is quite remarkable. It suggests unsuspected reservoirs of authority open to the central government to achieve its intended goals. There remains, of course, a complex network of sub-national loyalties. Some of these are probably felt intensely, but none are publicly asserted in Ugandan political life today. The government can keep them quiescent only by maintaining a moderate level of trust. At the same time it must simultaneously assist less developed areas and avoid the appearance of unduly favoring any ethnic group. Whether Uganda will successfully traverse this tightrope cannot be predicted now. But a bold and creative effort to attack one of the central problems of most new states has been carried through successfully thus far.

Postscript: The ethnic policies of the military government that came to power in the *coup* of January 25, 1971, were not clearly defined before this chapter went to press. However, the new leaders seem to be placing greater stress on ethnicity in order to strengthen their short-run legitimacy. At the same time they have announced that Uganda will remain a Republic (which means that the former kingdoms will not be re-established). Thus, ethnicity remains an important consideration in Ugandan politics, but the consequences of the new policies cannot now be predicted.

NOTES

1. Clifford Geertz, "The Integrative Revolution: Primordial Sentiments and Civil Politics in the New States," in Geertz, *Old Societies and New States* (New York: Free Press, 1963), p. 111.

2. See Rupert Emerson, *Self-Determination in the Era of Decolonization* (Cambridge: Harvard Center for International Affairs, 1964).

3. Walker Connor, "Self-Determination: The New Phase," 20:1 *World Politics* 30–53 (October 1967), p. 53.

4. Guy Hunter, *The New Societies of Tropical Africa* (London: Oxford University Press, 1962), p. 295. See also Apolo Nsibambi, "Political Integration in Uganda: Problems and Prospects," 6:2 *East Africa Journal* 31–39 (February 1969).

5. Donald Rothchild and Michael Rogin, "Uganda," in Gwendolen M. Carter, *National Unity and Regionalism in Eight African States* (Ithaca: Cornell University Press, 1966), p. 337.

6. Proceedings of the Legislative Council, 34th Session, 6th Meeting, February 17, 1955, p. 131. Quoted in David Apter, *The Political Kingdom in Uganda: A Study of Bureaucratic Nationalism* (Princeton: Princeton University Press, 1967), p. 39.

7. Apter, p. 19.

8. The Buganda Agreement of 1900 was signed prior to British occupation of all parts of Uganda. Agreements were later signed with certain other groups and these are reflected in the semi-federal status given Ankole, Bunyoro, Toro (and indirectly Busoga) in the 1962 Constitution.

9. *Modernization: Protest and Change* (Englewood Cliffs: Prentice-Hall, 1966), p. 123.

10. See F. B. Welbourn, *Religion and Politics in Uganda: 1952–*

62 (Nairobi: East African Publishing House, 1965), and D. A. Low, *Political Parties in Uganda: 1949–62*, Institute of Commonwealth Studies, Commonwealth Paper No. 8 (London: Athlone Press, 1962).

11. "African Tribalism: Some Reflections on Uganda," 80:3 *Political Science Quarterly* 357–72 (September 1965), p. 367.

12. As discussed below, two ethnic coalitions, the Bantu and Nilotic, are popularly, though misleadingly, thought to have provoked the Ugandan crisis of 1966.

13. Edel, "African Tribalism," p. 368.

14. "Ethnicity and National Integration in West Africa," 1:3 *Cahiers d'études africaines* 129–39 (October 1960), p. 130.

15. *The Politics of Modernization* (Chicago: The University of Chicago Press, 1965), pp. 81–122.

16. *Dreams and Deeds: Achievement Motivation in Nigeria* (Chicago: The University of Chicago Press, 1966). LeVine offers several persuasive reasons indicating that traditional cultural patterns may still be dominant influences on present-day African adults despite sixty to a hundred years of colonial rule. See *ibid.*, p. 22.

17. An important pioneering article is Audrey Richards' discussion of cultural patterns of the Baganda in "Traditional Values and Current Political Behaviour," in Lloyd Fallers, *The King's Men: Leadership and Status in Buganda on the Eve of Independence* (London: Oxford University Press, 1964), pp. 256–335.

18. The remainder of this paragraph summarizes Michael Twaddle, "'Tribalism' in Eastern Uganda," in P. H. Gulliver, *Tradition and Transition in East Africa* (London: Routledge & Kegan Paul, 1969), pp. 334–38.

19. A. W. Southall and P. C. W. Gutkind, *Townsmen in the Making: Kampala and Its Suburbs* (Kampala: East African Institute of Social Research, 1957).

20. See Roger Scott, "Trade Unions and Ethnicity in Uganda," 1:3 *Mawazo* 42–52 (June 1968), and A. W. Southall, "The Concept of Elites and Their Formation in Uganda," in P. C. Lloyd, *The New Elites of Tropical Africa* (London: Oxford University Press, 1966), pp. 342–63.

21. Edel, "African Tribalism," pp. 367–68.

22. Audrey Richards, *Economic Development and Tribal Change* (Cambridge: Heffer & Son, 1954), pp. 161–93.

23. "Tribalism in Modern British Central Africa," 1:1 *Cahiers d'études africaines* 55–70 (January 1960), p. 55.

24. Arnold L. Epstein, *Politics in an Urban African Community* (Manchester: Manchester University Press, 1958), p. 236.

25. Wallerstein, "Ethnicity and National Integration," p. 131.

26. Discussed in Gluckman, "Tribalism in British Central Africa," p. 64.

27. Raymond Apthorpe, "Does Tribalism Really Matter?" 7:6 *Transition* 18–22 (October 1968), p. 18.

28. Twaddle, " 'Tribalism' in Eastern Uganda," p. 335.

29. *Politics in the Congo: Decolonization and Independence* (Princeton: Princeton University Press, 1965), pp. 245–46.

30. *Local Government and Politics in Uganda* (Syracuse: Syracuse University Press, 1964), p. 186.

31. Young bases his discussion on this criterion, *Politics in the Congo,* p. 234. Twaddle also accepts it. " 'Tribalism' in Eastern Uganda," p. 333.

32. Edel, "African Tribalism," p. 358.

33. *Local Government and Politics,* p. 214.

34. Burke, pp. 138 and 164.

35. "The Integrative Revolution," pp. 117–18.

36. *Ibid.,* p. 109.

37. Robert O. Byrd, "A Portrait of Leadership in a New Nation: The Case of Uganda," 69:4, *Queen's Quarterly* 521–36 (1963), pp. 523–24.

38. See Martin Doornbos, "Kumanyana and Rwenzururu: Two Responses to Ethnic Inequality," in Robert I. Rotberg and Ali A. Mazrui, *Protest and Power in Black Africa* (New York: Oxford University Press, 1970), pp. 1088–1136. In addition to ethnic considerations intense political and religious conflicts further fragmented politics in Ankole.

39. Burke, *Local Government and Politics,* pp. 149–51.

40. See Colin Leys, *Politicians and Policies: An Essay on Politics in Acholi, Uganda 1962–65* (Nairobi: East African Publishing House, 1967).

41. See Emanuel Hansen, "Busoga," in Michael Davies and Emory Bundy, *Uganda District Handbook* (forthcoming).

42. See, for example, Burke, *Local Government and Politics*, p. 181.

43. R. Cranford Pratt, "The Politics of Indirect Rule: Uganda, 1900–1955," in D. Anthony Low and Pratt, *Buganda and British Overrule* (Oxford: Oxford University Press, 1960), p. 178. Lucy Mair, on the other hand, argues that the introduction of freehold land and the division of the office of *Katikiro* into Prime Minister, Treasurer, and Chief Justice makes the use of the term "indirect rule" for the Buganda case "singularly inappropriate." "Busoga Local Government," 5:2 *Journal of Commonwealth Political Studies* 91–108 (July 1967), pp. 92–93.

44. H. B. Thomas, "Capax Imperii: The Story of Semei Kakunguru," *Uganda Journal* (1939), quoted in Mair, "Busoga Local Government," p. 93.

45. Lloyd A. Fallers, *Bantu Bureaucracy: A Century of Political Evolution among the Basoga of Uganda* (Chicago: University of Chicago Press, 1965), p. 248.

46. "The Footsteps of Uganda's Revolution," 5:10 *East Africa Journal* 7–13 (October 1968), p. 9.

47. Young found that Belgian colonial administrators used similar devices in the Congo. *Politics in the Congo*, pp. 265–66.

48. See Burke, *Local Government and Politics*, p. 218.

49. *Ibid.*, p. 59.

50. James D. Barber, *Imperial Frontier: A Study of Relationships between the British and the Pastoral Tribes of North East Uganda* (Nairobi: East African Publishing House, 1968), pp. 201–21.

51. Apter, *Political Kingdom*, p. 362.

52. Colin Leys, *Politicians and Policies*, pp. 9–10.

53. See Rothchild and Rogin, "Uganda," pp. 348–51.

54. Audrey I. Richards, "Epilogue," in Fallers, *The King's Men*, p. 379.

55. Quoted from District Council Minutes in Mair, "Busoga Local Government," p. 99.

56. *Politicians and Policies*, p. 10. Up to 1900, British officials toyed with the idea of instituting a "Kabaka" in each district to clothe British rule with what they thought was traditional legitimacy. Recognition was officially given to a "Kabaka" of Bukedi and proposals for a "Kabaka" of Acholi were put forward. D. A. Low, "The Anatomy of Administrative Origins: Uganda 1890–1902" (Kampala: East African Institute of Social Research Conference, January 1958), pp. 19–20.

57. Constitutional Heads (Elections) Act, No. 66 of 1963.

58. Paragraph 8, Constitution of Uganda (First Amendment) Act No. 61 of 1963. Edward Mutesa, *Kabaka* of Buganda, and Wilberforce Nadiope, *Kyabazinga* of Busoga, were elected President and Vice President respectively.

59. See, for example, Crawford Young, *Politics in the Congo,* p. 256.

60. For a presentation of his hypothesis comparing the Baganda to several other ethnic groups with different cultural patterns, see *The Politics of Modernization,* pp. 81–122.

61. Low, *Religion and Politics*, pp. 4–15.

62. H. C. A. Somerset, *Predicting Success in School Certificate: A Uganda Case Study* (Nairobi: East African Publishing House, 1968), pp. 18–19. The JSLE is now called the Primary Leaving Examination.

63. J. E. Goldthorpe, *An African Elite: Makerere College Students 1922–1960* (London: Oxford University Press, 1965), p. 24.

64. *Ibid.,* p. 28.

65. Compiled from data in the *Annual Report of the Education Department: 1960* (Entebbe: Government Printer, 1961), p. 46.

66. *An African Elite,* pp. 30–48, and van den Berghe, "An African Elite Revisited," 1:4 *Mawazo* 57–71 (December 1968), pp. 60–61.

67. Kenneth Ingham, *The Making of Modern Uganda* (London: George Allen & Unwin, 1958), pp. 108–9.

68. M. B. Wamala, *Where Does Uganda's Wealth Come From? From the 1900 Agreement: Report 1904–1948* (Kampala: Uganda Growers Co-operative Union, Ltd., n.d.), p. 34.

69. Lloyd Fallers, "The Modernization of Social Stratification," in Fallers, *The King's Men,* p. 148.

70. *The Economic Development of Uganda* (London: Oxford University Press, 1961), p. 13.

71. The Samia and the Jaluo were more heavily represented by comparison to their *Ugandan* population than were the Acholi. However, it is likely that a large number of each of these groups were Kenyans. In September 1964 there were 488 Kenyans serving in the Uganda Police Force. Grace Ibingira, Minister of State, 34 *Parliamentary Debates* (Entebbe: Government Printer, 1964), p. xv.

72. There are some indications that Baganda do not apply for positions in the Police Force in very large numbers. In 1967 only 104 Baganda applied to the police training school out of 47,975 applicants. Of these, 13 were accepted. In 1968, 217 Baganda applied out of 24,534, and 63 Baganda were accepted. These figures may be influenced by the Baganda reaction to the events of 1966. They were stated in Parliament by Basil Bataringaya, Minister of Internal Affairs, *Uganda Argus,* 22 February 1969, p. 3.

73. Twaddle, " 'Tribalism' in Eastern Uganda," p. 345.

74. "Ethnicity and National Integration," p. 138.

75. Cherry Gertzel, "Report from Kampala," 9:9 *Africa Report* 3–8 (October 1964), p. 7. Rothchild and Rogin, "Uganda," pp. 394–95.

76. Rothchild and Rogin, "Uganda," pp. 390–91.

77. *Correspondence Relating to the Composition of the Legislative Council in Uganda* (Entebbe: Government Printer, 1953), p. 3, quoted in Apter, *The Political Kingdom,* p. 272.

78. Apter, *The Political Kingdom,* pp. 326–28.

79. Richards, "Epilogue," p. 379.

80. *Political Parties in Uganda,* pp. 7–43.

81. *Ibid.,* p. 56.

82. Byrd, "A Portrait of Leadership," pp. 524, 531. Byrd also notes that the UPC was slightly more willing than the DP to nominate candidates outside their district of birth, pp. 532–33.

83. "Uganda," p. 384.

84. Gluckman, "Tribalism in Modern British Central Africa," p. 61. It has been argued that Buganda similarly provided a negative force integrating Uganda by stimulating other frustrated ethnic groups to unite against her. Ali A. Mazrui, "Privilege and Protest as Integrative Factors: The Case of Buganda's Status in Uganda," in Rotberg and Mazrui, *Protest and Power in Black Africa*, pp. 1072–87.

85. Obote, "Uganda's Revolution," p. 7.

86. *Local Government and Politics*, p. 229.

87. Leys, *Politicians and Policies*, p. 19n.

88. Rothchild and Rogin, "Uganda," p. 413.

89. Apter, *The Political Kingdom*, pp. 141–46.

90. *Ibid.*, pp. 203–4, 226–29, 259–60.

91. *Ibid.*, p. 279.

92. Welbourn, *Religion and Politics in Uganda*, p. 26.

93. Richards, "Traditional Values and Current Political Behaviour," p. 323.

94. *Loc. cit.* See also Welbourn, *Religion and Politics in Uganda*, pp. 42–44.

95. Apter, *The Political Kingdom*, p. 372.

96. *Termination of British Protection: A Memorandum to Her Majesty Queen Elizabeth II Submitted by Members of the Lukiiko of the Kingdom of Buganda* reproduced in Apter, *The Political Kingdom*, p. 488.

97. Richards, "Epilogue," pp. 371–72.

98. *Loc. cit.*

99. Cherry Gertzel, "How Kabaka Yekka Came to Be," 9:9 *Africa Report* 9–13 (October 1964), p. 10.

100. Welbourn, *Religion and Politics in Uganda*, p. 32. KY candidates had to get the *Kabaka*'s approval as well. *Loc. cit.*

101. *Ibid.*, p. 33. The defeat of the DP in the election demonstrated that for Catholic Baganda cultural sub-nationalism exerted a stronger pull in 1962 than did religion.

102. Gertzel, "Kabaka Yekka," p. 10.

103. *Ibid.*, p. 13. I am indebted to Ian Hancock for points made in this paragraph and general facts on KY. See also Hancock, "The Buganda Crisis of 1964," 69:275 *African Affairs* 109–23 (April 1970), pp. 114–17.

104. Richards, "Epilogue," p. 385.

105. *Ibid.*, p. 384.

106. This section is based on M. Crawford Young, "Sebei," in Michael Davies and Emory Bundy, *Uganda District Handbook* (forthcoming). See also Rothchild and Rogin, "Uganda," pp. 412–13.

107. Prior to independence a district could be formed by administrative *fiat*. Partly as a result of Sebei's political success without justification based on size, population (it is Uganda's smallest and least populous district), or economics, the 1962 Constitution made it virtually impossible to alter district boundaries. However, exceptions for Mbale and the "Lost Counties" were included.

108. Minutes of the District Team, Sebei, May 10, 1967, p. 2.

109. See Emory Bundy, "Madi," in Michael Davies and Bundy, *Uganda District Handbook* (forthcoming).

110. Personal communication from Michael Davies, formerly Assistant District Commissioner in West Nile and later in Acholi.

111. This account is based on the author's field research and on Martin Doornbos, "Kumanyana and Rwenzururu." See also Karen Alnaes, "Songs of the Rwenzururu Rebellion: The Konzo Revolt against the Toro in Western Uganda," in P. H. Gulliver, *Tradition and Transition in East Africa*, and Nelson Kasfir, "Toro: Society and Politics," 2:3 *Mawazo* 39–53 (June 1970).

112. *1968 Statistical Abstract* (Entebbe: Government Printer, 1969), p. 11.

113. *Report of the Commission of Inquiry into the Recent Disturbances amongst the Baamba and Bakonjo People of Toro* (Entebbe: Government Printer, 1962), pp. 6–11.

114. In September 1967 the official stamp was changed from "Rwenzururu–Bakonjo Baamba" to "Rwenzururu Kingdom Government," thus avoiding recognition of the fact that the Baamba never participated in the kingdom's government.

115. However, many of the officeholders in Mukirane's government were distinctly unhappy about being led by a king, but felt

they could do nothing about it without seriously weakening the movement.

116. This account is taken primarily from Burke, *Local Government and Politics,* pp. 77–85. See also Rothchild and Rogin, "Uganda," pp. 415–18, and G. F. Engholm and Ali A. Mazrui, "Violent Constitutionalism in Uganda," 2:4 *Government and Opposition* 585–99 (July–October 1967), pp. 587–89.

117. "Epilogue," p. 387.

118. This section is based on Twaddle, " 'Tribalism' in Eastern Uganda," pp. 341–42, and Burke, *Local Government and Politics,* pp. 204–8.

119. Apter, *The Political Kingdom,* pp. 346–47.

120. Low, *Political Parties,* pp. 29–30.

121. *Ibid.,* p. 43.

122. Rothchild and Rogin, "Uganda," p. 395.

123. "The Integrative Revolution," pp. 153–54.

124. M. Crawford Young, "The Obote Revolution," 11:6 *Africa Report* 8–14 (June 1966), pp. 11–12.

125. Quoted from *Uganda Argus,* February 3, 1960, by Ali A. Mazrui, "Violent Contiguity and the Politics of Retribalization in Africa," *Journal of International Affairs* (Winter 1969).

126. Rothchild and Rogin, "Uganda," p. 418.

127. André de la Rue (pseud.), "The Rise and Fall of Grace Ibingira," 5:10 *The New African* 207–8 (December 1966), p. 208.

128. Young, "The Obote Revolution," p. 13. See also Emory Bundy, "Uganda's New Constitution," 3:4 *East Africa Journal* 23–32 (June 1966), and G. F. Engholm, "Buganda's Struggle for Power," *New Society* (June 2, 1966).

129. For Obote's account of these events, see "Uganda's Revolution," pp. 12–13.

130. The 1962 Constitution was quite difficult to amend as it required a two thirds vote in the National Assembly and concurrence by all Federal Assemblies in certain changes. Obote was not likely to achieve a two thirds majority for sweeping changes with five UPC members detained and with DP and KY members in opposition.

131. Apter, *The Political Kingdom*, p. xvi.

132. Uganda v. Commissioner of Prisons, *ex parte* Matovu, *Eastern Africa Law Reports* 514–46 (1966), p. 515.

133. For a brief summary of views expressed in the debate, see Nelson Kasfir, "The 1967 Uganda Constituent Assembly Debate," 7:2 *Transition* 52–56 (October/November 1967).

134. *East African Standard*, August 5, 1967.

135. *Uganda Argus*, February 17, 1968, p. 3, and December 19, 1968, p. 9.

136. *Proposals for New Methods of Election of Representatives of the People to Parliament: Document No. 5 on the Move to the Left* (Kampala: Milton Obote Foundation, 1970).

137. The new party constitution was adopted at a conference held in June 1968.

138. Michael Davies, "Structure of the Government Party: The Uganda Peoples Congress, and Its Potential as a Means of Communication" (Kampala: Uganda Institute of Public Administration, June 1968).

139. In pointing this out, Felix Onama, Secretary-General of the UPC, noted that the new "system was intended to abolish regionalism which was encouraging differences in the party." *Uganda Argus*, April 28, 1969, p. 2.

140. A. G. G. Gingyera-Pinycwa, "Prospects for a One-Party System in Uganda," 5:10 *East Africa Journal* 15–23 (October 1968), p. 19.

141. See *His Excellency the President's Communication from the Chair of the National Assembly on 11th February 1969* (Entebbe: Government Printer, 1969).

142. Richards' explanation of similar Baganda passivity in the beginning of the 1953 crisis as a cultural pattern of slowly reacting to change until it is clear which leader is coming out on top seems to fit Baganda behavior since 1966 equally well. No genuinely popular Baganda leaders have yet emerged.

143. *Work for Progress: Uganda's Second Five Year Plan, 1966–1971* (Entebbe: Government Printer, 1966), p. 151.

144. *Ibid.*, p. 136.

145. See Table 4 and discussion in the next section.

146. For example, the twenty-two new rural hospitals "are being sited in places where hospital services are most needed, with an even distribution between regions." *Work for Progress*, p. 151.

147. See discussion in 46 *Parliamentary Debates* (Entebbe: Government Printer, 1965), pp. 1948–49, and *The People*, April 13, 1968, p. 11.

148. Young, "The Obote Revolution," p. 12.

149. This account is based on reports in *Uganda Argus* and *The People* from the middle of February through the middle of April 1968. The dispute was the subject of a parliamentary debate in February.

150. Of critical importance in the minds of politicians from both districts was the fact that the factory would ultimately provide employment for twelve hundred people.

151. *Uganda Argus*, January 13, 1969, p. 6, and January 25, 1969, p. 5.

152. Apter, *Political Kingdom*, pp. 318, 322–23. The basis on which the sample of branch chairmen was selected is not indicated. Nor is it clear whether the ethnic identity of the branch chairmen refers to their "tribal" group or the district in which they live. District residence is a poor guide to the identification of a person's ethnic group, because most districts contain several groups.

153. David A. Gugin, "Africanization of the Ugandan Public Service" (Doctoral dissertation, University of Wisconsin, Madison, 1967), p. 127. Included for examination were officeholders in the Progressive Party, the Uganda National Congress, the Democratic Party, and the United Congress Party.

154. See the discussion of Byrd's findings for 1961 parliamentary candidates in section 3.

155. See the attack on such beliefs by Felix Onama, then Minister for Internal Affairs, 36 *Parliamentary Debates*, 1964, pp. 104–11.

156. Information on the ethnic composition of 151 officers paid at superscale rates in 1964 released to Parliament by Felix Onama tends to confirm the figures of Table 4. He found a somewhat higher percentage of Baganda (44.4 per cent) and Iteso (9.3 per cent), which may reflect the different category he was using. 36 *Parliamentary Debates*, p. 108.

Gugin also examined the ethnic composition of the higher civil service. His figures for Baganda overrepresentation are consistently higher than mine, reaching a level of 66.7 per cent of African bureaucrats listed in the *Government Directory* in 1962, and 50.1 per cent of those listed in 1964. However, in both cases he collected data on only two thirds of the bureaucrats listed, and tended to assign them to ethnic categories on the basis of the district in which they were born. It is likely that this technique would overstate the Baganda contribution, since only 55 per cent of the inhabitants of the former Buganda Region are Baganda. *Africanization*, pp. 135–36.

157. Onama, 36 *Parliamentary Debates*, p. 109.

158. J. Donald Kingsley, "Bureaucracy and Political Development, with Particular Reference to Nigeria," in Joseph LaPalombara, *Bureaucracy and Political Development* (Princeton: Princeton University Press, 1963), pp. 304–5.

159. A supplementary scheme was instituted in 1961 to increase the number of foreign scholarships from 49 to 300. Not all of these were filled that year, however. *Annual Report of the Department of Education: 1961* (Entebbe: Government Printer, 1962), p. 8. In 1967/68, 2500 students were studying abroad, including 345 working for bachelor's degrees. *Education Statistics: 1967* (Kampala: Ministry of Education, 1967), Section F, Table 1.

160. Oddly, considering the current demands for technically skilled personnel, the percentage of Ugandan African Makerere students in the Arts and Social Science Faculties has risen over the past ten years from 27.8 per cent to 52.6 per cent.

161. The policy of building many new secondary schools in outlying areas during the 1960s is likely to further contribute to the representativeness of Makerere and the higher civil service during the 1970s.

162. See Samuel P. Huntington, *Political Order in Changing Societies* (New Haven: Yale University Press, 1968), pp. 8–11, and Aristide Zolberg, *Creating Political Order: The Party-States of West Africa* (Chicago: Rand McNally, 1966), p. 93.

163. "Personal Rulership, Patrimonialism and Empire-Building in the New States," 20:2 *World Politics* 194–206 (January 1968), pp. 203–4.

164. *Creating Political Order*, p. 134.

165. "What Does Political Development Mean in Africa?" 20:1 *World Politics* 128–41 (October 1967), p. 134.

166. *Ibid.*, pp. 139–41.

167. Huntington, *Political Order*, p. 18.

III
SIERRA LEONE

❖ ❖ ❖

EDITOR'S INTRODUCTORY NOTE

The history of cultural nationalism in Sierra Leone is examined with reference to the roles that political norms, institutions, and rewards play in alleviating or exacerbating ethnic group violence. In pre-independence Sierra Leone, the British colonial administration treated the Creoles as a privileged group. The Creoles, therefore, enjoyed maximum participation in governing the Colony. Protectorate peoples whose largest groups are the Temne and the Mende were ruled indirectly by chiefs. The chiefs selected by the district commissioners merely promulgated and enforced the commands of the colonial administration. The people had no real representation in the government of the Colony. The colonial administration did not foster ethnic conflict within the Protectorate.

Because of jealousy, on one hand, and, more importantly, antithetical political subcultures, on the other hand, Protectorate peoples who shared similar political norms united against the Creoles. The coalition was not permanent, however. The formation of political parties around ethnic cleavages intensified the politics of sub-nationalism. Candidates of political parties used ethnic appeals to garner support, and a situation arose in which the ethnic group out of power organized against the ethnic group in power to insure its share of political rewards or "spoils."

ETHNIC CONFLICT IN SIERRA LEONE*

By Dick Simpson

UNIVERSITY OF ILLINOIS, CHICAGO

Because conflicts between ethnic groups are potentially violent, the emotions of ethnic identity and ethnic hatred are a threat to the peace of any nation and a threat to the very existence of a newly independent nation such as Sierra Leone. This is not to say that ethnic groups are the only source of conflict—generational, ideological, military-civilian, regional, political, and interest group conflict are also likely to be present. In fact, the great danger among newly independent nations is that these other cleavages will reinforce ethnic cleavages in such a way as to make violence more likely.

Since ethnic identification cannot be eliminated in the near future, the crucial problem for countries such as Sierra Leone is to lessen the likelihood of ethnic group violence and encourage ethnic group cooperation in developing the nation. This article seeks to assess the degree of success and failure which Sierra Leone has experienced both before and since independence in her attempt to avoid ethnic group violence. In making our analysis we will want to pay particular attention to political norms, institutions, and rewards. Our assumptions (or hypotheses) are that ethnic violence is more likely to be avoided: (1) if there is general agreement upon political norms rather than separate political subcultures with antagonistic values and different "rules of the game"; (2) if political parties, and other "modern" organizations represent

* The field research from which this article was drawn was made possible by a grant from the Foreign Area Fellowship Program (1966–67). The author is grateful for this support.

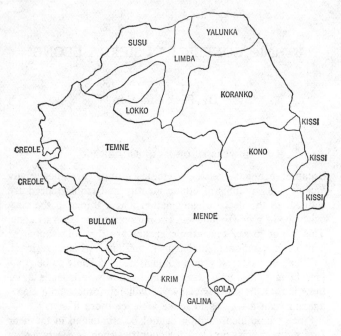

ETHNIC GROUPS IN SIERRA LEONE
Source: Arthur Porter, *Creoledom* (London: Oxford University Press, 1963), p. 14.

individuals and interests across ethnic groups rather than reinforce ethnic cleavages; and, most importantly, (3) if political rewards—wealth, prestige, services, and power—are "fairly" distributed among the various ethnic groups rather than hoarded by a single dominant group.

There are numerous ethnic groups in Sierra Leone and the map above shows the distribution of the largest ones. However, three groups, the Creoles, Mendes, and Temnes have been prominent throughout Sierra Leone's history and continue to dominate the political scene. The 42,000 Creoles who live in the Western Area are descendants of freed slaves who came to Freetown, Sierra Leone, from England and the

New World or arrived aboard slaving vessels captured by the British navy. These settlers and their descendants shared power with the British during most of the colonial period and, because of their educational advantages, still hold prominent positions in the judiciary, government administration, and private companies. As the colonial era drew to a close, the Protectorate peoples began to challenge the dominance of the Creoles. The 673,000 Mendes in the South and the 649,000 Temnes in the North gained control of the government after national elections began to be held according to the principles of "one man, one vote." Since independence the coalition of Protectorate peoples which defeated the Creoles in the struggle for political dominance has broken apart. First, the Mendes obtained effective control of the government. Their supremacy lasted until the military coups of 1967 and 1968 after which the Temnes in alliance with the Creoles gained control. Needless to say, the situation since independence has remained very unstable and the final outcome of the ethnic and political struggles remains uncertain.

In reviewing the development of Sierra Leone since the nineteenth century, this article will focus upon the colonial impact, the growth of separate subcultures among the major ethnic groups; the development of political parties during the last phase of colonial rule, the struggle for the political spoils of independence; and, finally, the ethnic conflicts which have occurred since independence. In considering this history of ethnic conflict and cooperation in Sierra Leone we shall base our analysis upon the role which political norms, institutions, and rewards have played in bringing the current ethnic crisis.

Colonial Impact

When European contact was first made along the coast of Sierra Leone they found several peoples living there. Such groups as the Limba and Loko had been there for some time, others such as the Mende had not yet come. The migration and, often, invasion by various ethnic groups of Sierra Leone tended to follow the disintegration of large Sudanic empires to the north such as Gao and Songhai. As a result of one of the early invasions the Temne were organized into a Sapis Confederation which lasted from the sixteenth until the nineteenth century. However, as the new warlords were absorbed into the general population and new peoples continued to arrive in Sierra Leone, the confederation became a weak alliance of Temne chiefdoms.

The Mende people who consisted of earlier settlers and later invaders, the last of whom arrived in the seventeenth and eighteenth centuries, were never organized as a single confederation as the Temne had been. Rather, a number of petty empires grew up in separate regions under the control of different warlords. These chiefs or warlords came to power through their own success and that of their warriors in the continuing warfare of the period. The only ties between separate Mende areas were personal alliances between chiefs and common secret societies, the most important of which was Poro.[1]

The primary result of early European contact was the slave trade. This greatly exacerbated the existing tendency of warfare and encouraged the proliferation of petty kingdoms under the overlordship of a strong warrior. Slaves in large quantity could only be obtained by raiding neighboring villages and peoples. The promise of more modern weapons and utensils, rum and tobacco, cloth and jewelry in exchange for slaves was a great temptation. As a result, the eighteenth and nineteenth centuries in Sierra Leone were ones of constant raids and counterraids. Even with the formal end to slave trade raids, the forces of war let loose by outside invasions and internal slave trade were not curtailed until the British takeover of the Protectorate.

The second stage of European contact came at the end of the eighteenth century with the founding of the Province of Freedom which later became the Colony of Sierra Leone. To the Colony's principal settlement, Freetown, came freed slaves from England, former American slaves who had fought with the British in the American Revolution and had lived for

SIERRA LEONE—Administrative Boundaries in 1896
Source: J. I. Clarke, ed., *Sierra Leone in Maps* (London: University of London Press, 1966), pp. 28–31.

years in Nova Scotia, and runaway slaves known as Maroons from Jamaica. In the nineteenth century these original settlers were joined by "recaptives" from slaving vessels brought to the Vice-Admiralty Court at Freetown. Future generations of these various peoples were known as Creoles. The British were responsible for this artificial growth of the Creole Colony on the Sierra Leone peninsula and provided the colonial government for the territory. Furthermore, from this Colony at Freetown the British slowly began more extensive contact with the rest of Sierra Leone.

Fearful that the French would claim the territory surrounding Freetown, the British in 1896 formally proclaimed that

area to be a Protectorate of the British Empire. Some five
administrative districts as shown in Map 5 were established
to be ruled by a single British district commissioner and his
staff. Administrative expenses were to be met by a house tax of
five shillings a year per house. A general rebellion against the
tax in 1898 had to be put down by force of arms. Only then
was British control of the Protectorate really established. It is
important to remember that both the Temnes and the Mendes
fought against British control in the Hut Tax War or Rebellion. While both of the principal ethnic groups were willing
to trade with the British and the Colony at Freetown, neither
wanted to be under British colonial rule.

In assessing the impact of colonial rule upon Sierra Leone
the primary questions must be to what extent the colonial
government created ethnic groups which had not previously
existed and to what extent the colonial government promoted
ethnic group conflict or hostility by its differential treatment
of various groups. It is clear that the British distinguished
between the Creoles and the indigenous peoples of Sierra
Leone. The Colony where the Creoles lived was governed
under one set of rules and the Protectorate under another.
The Creoles had representatives on advisory councils to the
Governor as early as 1811 and their own Freetown City
Council from 1893. In addition, the Creoles served as missionaries, traders, teachers, professionals, and government administrators at a time when the upcountry people did not yet
have even primary school education. In contrast to the Colony,
the Protectorate continued to be ruled by district commissioners who presided over the selection of chiefs, were a final
court of appeals, and, by means of the military force available
to them, kept the peace, collected taxes, and began the slow
process of modernization. Although the district commissioners ruled indirectly through chiefs, the people of the Protectorate did not for many years have representation in the
government and they did not hold the same high posts as the
Creoles.

Other than the distinction between the Colony and the Protectorate, the government did not directly foster ethnic group

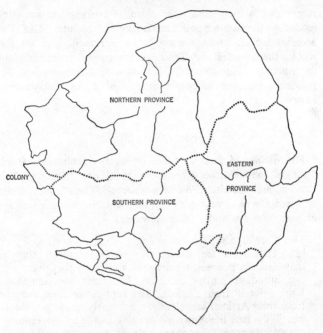

SIERRA LEONE—Administrative Boundaries in 1969
Source: J. I. Clarke, ed., *Sierra Leone in Maps* (London: University of London Press, 1966), pp. 28–31.

conflict. All the people in the Protectorate were treated in roughly the same way. The administrative divisions seen in Map 5 did not conform to and reinforce the ethnic divisions shown in Map 4. Even the later administrative divisions in Map 6 tended to divide the various groups. Thus, the Mendes are split between the Southern and Eastern provinces and many districts. However, the later divisions into provinces did tend to distinguish between the Temnes, Limbas, and Lokos living in the Northern Province and the Mendes, Konos, Kissi, and Bullom living in the other two provinces. The only major distinction between the Northern and Southern provinces during the colonial period was that the Temnes were more

staunchly Islamic and, therefore, Christian missionaries
tended to develop schools first among the Mendes. Thus the
Mendes tended to be slightly better educated. But, on the
whole, the Mendes and Temnes were treated impartially by
the colonial administration. This situation is mirrored in the
political subcultures among ethnic groups in present-day Sierra
Leone.

Political Subcultures

Historically in Sierra Leone, political subcultures can be
distinguished as either Western-oriented or traditional. The
Creoles are definitely Western-oriented. These descendants
of freed slaves developed their own culture as an amalgam
of both Western and African customs.

> The Creoles aimed at attaining a European standard of
> life. They were Christians; they wore European clothes;
> they lived in houses of European style. But they were not
> just imitation Europeans. They had their own language,
> Krio, different from English. They kept old customs brought
> from their African homelands, particularly music and danc-
> ing. They had their own companies and local government
> organized without European help in their own way.[2]

In general the Western ideals of an impartial civil service,
democratically elected officials, and public decisions through
parliamentary methods were adopted as the standards of good
government. While Creole participation in either colonial or
local government did not always meet these standards, they
remained as goals to be sought.

The different norms between Creoles (reflecting to a great
extent Western standards) and non-Creoles (reflecting standards of traditional peasant societies) are to a certain extent
the result of and are certainly reinforced by their respective
patterns of local government. The Creoles for over a hundred
years participated in colonial government. From 1811 the
Sierra Leone Council included "one unofficial member from
among the most considerable of the Protestant inhabitants."[3]

With the establishment in 1863 of a Legislative and Executive Council to advise the Governor General also came the practice of appointing at least one Creole to the Legislative Council. In 1893 the Creoles began to gain control over the capital city, Freetown, through the institution of a City Council. As the years went by this elected body was to take over more and more of the governmental functions for the city such as collecting rates (local property taxes), paving streets, and supervising schools. Many of these functions it shared with the colonial government but the City Council nonetheless gave the Creole citizens of Freetown a voice in their local government in much the same way as citizens of London had a voice in theirs. Finally, with the adoption of a new Constitution in 1924 Creoles obtained the right to *elect* three representatives to the Legislative Council.

In the part of the Colony outside of Freetown, Creoles have a somewhat different form of local government. In their villages they have headmen who serve functions similar to headmen in the more traditional villages upcountry. They are thus not unfamiliar with the paternalistic government of the Mende and Temne and, in fact, these tribes have their own headmen in Freetown who are charged with collecting taxes for the government, adjudicating minor problems, and helping newcomers adjust to the city among members of their own ethnic group. Despite this exposure to paternalistic government in the Creole villages and with other ethnic groups in Freetown, the Creole ideal remained Western, democratic government as exemplified by their elected City Council and elected representatives in the colonial government.

The upcountry peoples differ from the Creoles in their perceptions and patterns of government. Since the tribal wars of the seventeenth and eighteenth centuries, they have been organized into chiefdoms containing several villages under the protection of a chief. Among both the Mendes and Temnes these chiefs are restricted in their autocratic rule by custom, by subordinate officials, by secret societies or ritual officials, and by colonial administrators. After the arrival of the British administrators the chiefdom remained the local unit of government in the Protectorate in contrast to the development of the City Council for the Creoles.

The political norms or "rules of the game" are similar for both Mendes and Temnes but different from those of the Creoles. Traditional African politics is based upon the family rather than upon the individual citizen and voluntary associations of Western politics. When we consider the family as a model of government, we note that it is the head of the family who is responsible for providing food and insuring, in so far as possible, that the family prospers. He assigns tasks and dispenses whatever wealth or surplus is available. Members of the family are expected to show him and other elders proper deference and to work as directed on the family farm. In turn, he is expected to exhibit the proper paternalistic concern for the family and to rule as wisely as his abilities allow. So it is with the traditional political leaders. They are expected to make decisions for the village or chiefdom as a father would for his family. They are expected to perform their duties conscientiously and to conduct themselves in manner befitting their position of authority. In return, they are respected and obeyed by those they rule.

From the basic principles of the family model of government which is followed in the Protectorate we can deduce several norms or "rules of the game" which affect the selection of political leaders and the making of political decisions.[4] Rules generally affecting political recruitment to leadership positions among both the Mendes and the Temnes are the following:

(1) To be a full-fledged citizen with the right to participate in the councils of government one must have passed his initiation into adulthood, married, and become the head of his own family.

(2) To become an influential or "big man" in the community one must exhibit the proper behavior:

    a. A "big man" should be friendly with everyone.
    b. A "big man" should be liberal in distributing gifts.

c. A "big man" should judge disputes and palvers without bias.

d. A "big man" should be fearless.

e. A "big man" should faithfully keep customary laws.

(3) To become a chief or hold some other political office one must be a member of a family which has a "right" to hold such an office and be approved by the elders.

Thus, in both Mende and Temne chiefdoms one gains his citizenship by initiation and marriage. A boy becomes a man when he passes his initiation into the Poro Secret Society and a girl becomes a woman when she is accepted into the Bundu Society. These ceremonies, which come after puberty, previously lasted several years and included training in customary law and various crafts. Until the ceremonies are completed one does not have the right to marry. Even after one formally becomes an adult, he does not attain "citizenship" with both respect and a role in the traditional political system until he becomes the head of a family. The explanation which Jomo Kenyatta gave for the Kikuyu of Kenya also holds for the horticulturalists of Sierra Leone:

> Marriage, and especially parenthood, gives a man his full share in the common happiness and qualifies him to think for the common good . . . It is not until he has a family growing up that he has a chance to show his capacity for wise administration and for dealing intelligently and justly, with other people and what he can do in the family group he is expected to do on a large scale in the interests of the community as a whole. Among his equals in age, a man may be selected as a leader or spokesman by reason of his innate gifts and understanding . . . If so, he will be marked out by the elders as one who will play an important part in public affairs later on, but not until he has passed successive age grades and acquired the experience of life which will qualify him to take full responsibility in tribal matters. By that time he is probably the leader of almost a miniature tribe of his own relatives, as well as his age-grade, and his family life will give evidence of his ability in government.[5]

Becoming an adult and even the head of a household is not enough to make someone a "big man" although they are necessary prerequisites. In addition, one has to accumulate the appropriate resources and behave in the accepted way. The primary resources that one needs are status and wealth. The expected behavior includes generosity, sociability, courage, and the ability to settle disputes. When influentials in Kenema and Makeni, Sierra Leone, were asked to vote on the characteristics most important to political recruitment they answered as follows:

TABLE 1

Vote by Influentials of Kenema and Makeni on Characteristics Important in Political Recruitment

	Characteristic	*Votes*
1.	Generosity	48
2.	Popularity	26
3.	Ability to settle disputes	25
4.	Ability to speak in public	21
5.	Money	20
6.	Family ties	18
7.	Being born in the town	14
8.	Political party activity	11
9.	Education	10
10.	Occupation	8
11.	Age	3
	POSSIBLE VOTE	58

Being recognized as an influential because of one's success as a household head and one's generosity, wisdom, or popularity is still a step removed from holding political office. The more important positions also require that the candidate come from a family which held the post before and that he be selected by the other household heads and elders for the position.

Turning to "rules of the game" affecting community decision-making in traditional society, we find the following:

(1) Most "arrangements" are made by the political leaders and afterwards announced to the people. However,

  a. Leaders must be willing to listen to the opinions and problems of the people even if they don't grant all requests.

  b. Major decisions such as taxation which directly affect all the people must involve consultation of the citizens before a final decision can be made.

(2) Political leaders may use their positions to do special favors for friends and family as long as they also advocate projects which benefit all the people.

(3) Even if a leader has the power, he should not be harsh or despotic. He should not exact heavy taxes, take other men's wives or wealth, nor give excessive punishments.

These norms provide the framework for a paternalistic "politics of arrangements," in which the political leaders or elders have the right to make decisions for the benefit of the entire community. But citizens have a right to voice their opinions and must be consulted on certain crucial decisions. Moreover, customary law demands that the leaders behave honorably. If they become too corrupt or despotic, they may be deposed.

Even after the establishment of colonial government by the British, local government among the Mendes and Temnes remained paternalistic. The colonial administrators would order the chief to collect a tax or introduce a new crop. The chief, in turn, would call his chiefdom officials together and tell them of the task which they would then carry out. Most decisions were thus made, not by the people, but by either the colonial administrators or by the chief. *When more modern tasks such as fostering citizen participation or providing government services were introduced into the Protectorate, it was also necessary to introduce new institutions such as district and town councils because these more modern tasks could not be accomplished by the traditional chiefdom government.* Yet the traditional norms of paternalism and "politics by arrangement" continue in spite of the new institutions and, in fact, promote corruption and other problems which greatly undermine the effectiveness of these institutions.

From this brief analysis of the political norms and local government institutions among the various ethnic groups we may conclude that the Creoles and Protectorate peoples have antithetical political subcultures. It is, therefore, not surprising that there should be conflict between them over which group and which set of rules would govern the country after independence. On the other hand, the political cultures of the Mendes and Temnes are on the whole relatively compatible. Therefore, a different explanation will have to be found for their clashes. Similarly, while the colonial government might conceivably be blamed for the ethnic hostility between Creoles and Protectorate peoples, the hostility between Mendes and Temnes must have at least in part different roots. Their hostility grew primarily in the period immediately after independence because of the unequal distribution of power and rewards by the political parties.

Development of Political Parties

Between the proclamation of the Protectorate in 1896 and World War II the British concerned themselves first with establishing their administrative system of "indirect rule." After that was achieved they improved the communications and transportation between the Protectorate and Freetown, encouraged missionaries to begin schools and clinics, and attempted minor reforms in chiefdom government. In 1906 the Bo School was built to educate the sons and nominees of chiefs in the hope that they would become enlightened chiefs of the future. In the 1920s the custom allowing chiefs to exact tribute and "forced labor" on their farms was replaced by regularized taxation. In the 1930s the colonial administration began chiefdom treasuries and required all fees and fines previously paid directly to the chief (and often pocketed by him) to be paid to a treasury clerk who, in turn, paid fixed salaries to all chiefdom officials. It was hoped that such reforms would eliminate corruption and despotism from chiefdom government. In this respect they were only partially successful.

After World War II the goals of the colonial government became those of positive preparation for eventual independence which included both greater participation in the government by the people and rapid social and economic improvements throughout the Protectorate. In 1946, district councils were introduced, followed in later years by a Protectorate Assembly and greater African representation in the national government. While proto-political groups had existed in Freetown since the late nineteenth century,[6] real political parties did not develop until there were national political offices with sufficient power to be worth fighting for. When parties did come into existence, they developed around ethnic cleavages. The Creoles formed a political party to protect their favored position in the colonial administration and the Protectorate peoples formed their own political party to wrest power from the Creoles.

The first of the two parties to emerge was the National Council of the Colony of Sierra Leone (NC) which was founded in August 1950 to represent the Creoles. It had dual purposes. At first, it attempted to elect members to the Legislative Council, but after it became clear that they would not be successful in gaining control of the government, the leaders of the National Council utilized obstructionist tactics to delay the transfer of power into the hands of the Protectorate majority:

> . . . it [the National Council] contested in court the legality of the 1951 Constitution which gave the protectorate majority representation in the legislature; it dispatched memorials and deputations to the Secretary of State for the Colonies and to the British Council; it opposed nearly all acts of the SLPP [Sierra Leone People's Party] government, regardless of their worth.[7]

In opposition to the NC the Sierra Leone People's Party (SLPP) emerged to represent the Protectorate. It was founded in April 1951 as a merger of the People's Party, the Protectorate Educational Progressive Union, and the Sierra Leone Organization Society. This merger created a formal coalition between the traditional elite of paramount chiefs and the modern Protectorate elite comprised of school teachers, doctors, lawyers, and trade unionists. Although the Mendes tended to hold most of the leadership positions, the party drew its members and leaders from most ethnic groups in the Protectorate. The SLPP was, of course, quick to exploit their advantage as representatives of the more numerous group. As John Cartwright has succinctly described the situation, "The extension of the franchise, coupled with the SLPP leaders' willingness to use the cry of 'Protectorate solidarity' as an election weapon against the Creoles, made the prospect of an independent electoral position for the latter hopeless."[8] Thus, the SLPP flourished on the notion that power for the Protectorate people could be obtained through the electoral process.

The SLPP became the dominant party in Sierra Leone for sixteen years despite its loose organization, its dependence upon traditional officials,[9] its small membership (only about 80,000 in 1960),[10] and its less than overwhelming electoral results. For instance, in the 1951 election in which seven members of the Legislative Council were to be directly elected from the Colony and fourteen were to be indirectly elected in the Protectorate (one from each of twelve district councils and two from the Protectorate Assembly) the SLPP won only two of the directly elected seats and only four of those indirectly elected.[11] The National Council won four of the directly elected seats and two of the independently elected members of the Legislative Council also supported the NC. The reason that the SLPP was able to form the government was that when the other members of the Council had to choose between supporting the NC and the SLPP, all but two chose the SLPP. After all, the SLPP promised to better the lot of the Protectorate peoples while the NC seemed to favor maintenance of the power of the Creoles. Since a majority of Council members came from the Protectorate, the outcome of a contest between a Protectorate and a Creole party had to be the ultimate victory of the Protectorate party.

A brief inspection of the membership of the 1951 Legislative Council reveals that the class origins included both the professional (modern) and chiefly (traditional) elite. The twenty-one elected African members had the occupations listed below:

TABLE 2

**Occupations of Elected African Members of the
1951 Legislative Council[a]**

Number	Occupation
8	Paramount Chiefs
2	Doctors
2	Lawyers
1	University Professor
2	Businessmen
2	Retired Civil Servants
1	Minister
1	Ex-Trade Union Official
1	Retired Baker
1	Ex-Tribal Authority Employee
21	ELECTED AFRICAN MEMBERS

[a] Porter, "Social Background of Political Decision-Makers in Sierra Leone," *Sierra Leone Studies*, n.s. No. 13 (June 1960), pp. 4–5.

This class and occupational background remained similar throughout the period of SLPP rule. Thus, Martin Kilson in analyzing the 1960 Legislature found twenty-one professionals, twelve businessmen, twelve chiefs, and seven clerks and former civil servants.[12] The SLPP's success can clearly be attributed to its ability to unite the traditional and modern elites of the Protectorate as well as to its ability to unite the Protectorate people in opposition to the Creoles.

The appeal of the SLPP was so great that the NC soon disappeared altogether to be replaced by the United Progres-

sive Party (UPP) which, because it was only a more liberal
Creole party with weak and temporary Protectorate alliances,
was no more successful than its predecessor. In the 1957 election there were to be thirty-nine elected members (fourteen
from the Colony and twenty-five from the Protectorate),
twelve indirectly elected paramount chiefs (one from each
district), two nominated members, and four ex-officio members of the new Legislature called the House of Representatives. Of the elected seats the SLPP won eighteen, the UPP
won nine, and independent candidates, twelve.[13] Once again
the SLPP failed to win a clear majority of the elected seats
but by winning over the independents and eleven of the paramount chiefs it was able to form the majority in the Legislature. The fragile nature of SLPP dominance was revealed
in its inability to fully organize the Protectorate and win
office through its own efforts. As Martin Kilson pointed
out in an earlier article on Sierra Leone politics:

> Thus the party that has been the majority party in Sierra
> Leone for the past decade has never actually gained a ma-
> jority of votes over opposition parties and independents.
> Rather, the SLPP has become the governing party through
> a process of mergers with independents (most of whom
> were always basically SLPP-oriented) and chiefs within the
> legislature.[14]

Nonetheless, it is clear that SLPP was the mechanism by
which the general oligarchy of traditional and modern elites
ruled the country. After each election, those candidates
elected independently of party labels did not hesitate to declare that their sympathies lay with SLPP.

There was a brief period from 1958 to 1960 when the
principal cleavage manifested in Sierra Leone politics moved
from ethnic divisions to generation and class conflicts. In 1958
the People's National Party (PNP) was created as a result
of a clash between Albert Margai and Milton Margai. Sir
Milton Margai, who had been the leader of the SLPP since
its founding in 1951, was committed to a policy of gradual
nationalism with eventual independence to be achieved under

his continuing leadership. Albert, who favored a more militant brand of nationalism, challenged Sir Milton's leadership in the SLPP Executive Committee. The fight over a resolution on election of the party leader along with a dispute over the appointment of cabinet ministers and general disagreement on government policies caused Albert Margai to join with Siaka Stevens to form the PNP. The PNP, although basically a Protectorate party, tended to attract a younger, more urban, only partially educated constituency. Despite some electoral success in the District Council elections, the PNP soon disappeared from the political scene. It and the other opposition parties joined the SLPP in a United National Front in March 1960 in order to prepare for a Constitutional Conference in London and the achievement of independence.

The Constitutional Conference was successful and on June 12, 1961, Sierra Leone received her independence. However, political opposition and ethnic conflict continued. Siaka Stevens withdrew from the United Front over his unmet demand that new elections be held before independence and because of his own political ambitions.[15] He proceeded to form first an Elections-Before-Independence Movement which was soon transformed into a new political party, the All People's Congress (APC). The APC was a coalition of former PNP members, dissident members of the SLPP, and some members of other minor opposition parties and began as an extension of the same ideological, class, and generational faction which had been present in the PNP under even more radical leadership.

> The APC's leaders represented the entry of a new stratum into Sierra Leone's political elite. Unlike the wealthy business and professional men who had led other parties, most of them were relatively small-scale traders or wage workers with limited formal education and few connections with traditional ruling families.[16]

Despite its new strata of leaders, the APC gradually became identified not primarily as an anti-elite party but as an anti-Mende party. This view of the APC seemed to be borne out in election results. In the hard-fought election of 1962 the SLPP won twenty-eight of the sixty-two ordinary seats in the House of Representatives and the APC won sixteen.[17] The APC successfully won twelve of the eighteen Northern seats but was unable to obtain many votes in the Mende areas.[18]

After the 1962 election the SLPP became ever more dominated by the Mendes and the APC became an alliance of Creoles and Northern tribal groups. With the death of Sir Milton Margai in 1965 this trend became even more pronounced. The Governor General quickly appointed Sir Milton's brother Albert as the new Prime Minister. This appointment was challenged by several non-Mende members of the cabinet who argued that (1) the proper constitutional and democratic procedure was not followed in appointing Albert Margai and (2) to appoint another Southerner, Christian, and member of the Margai family did not give the other groups (ethnic, religious, and family) fair representation. The objecting cabinet members were not reappointed to the cabinet and the new SLPP government began to be criticized vigorously by various dissatisfied elements in the country.

The Protectorate which had once been united in its opposition to the Creoles, having defeated them in political combat and having gained control of the government, now itself became divided. As the SLPP had once organized against the Creoles, the APC now organized against the Mendes. Once again the ethnic groups out of power were organizing against the group in power for a share in the political spoils and rewards. This fragmentation of the Protectorate into hostile ethnic groups was to cause the downfall of the Margai-SLPP government in the election and military coup of 1967. However, the process was speeded by Albert Margai's particularly inept rule. Albert's proposal of a one-party state and a republican government were seen not as progressive changes but as attempts by Albert to gain for himself dictatorial powers. The interference in local political affairs such as chiefdom elections cost the government its popularity even within the SLPP itself. Finally, the abundant evidence of corruption on the part of cabinet ministers, lesser governmental officials, and even the Prime Minister further undermined the power and prestige of the government. The amazing thing about Sir Albert Margai was that despite the large majority of SLPP members in the House of Representatives, the history of SLPP rule under his brother's leadership, and the natural appeal which he might be expected to have for the younger elements of the country because of his role as the former leader of the PNP, he consistently undercut his own base of power in the very attempt to make his position more secure. His policies, his interference in local politics, and his corruption undercut support he might have had from intellectuals, professionals, chiefdom officials, and even some members of his own party. The ease with which his government could be attacked did much to unify the opposition elements behind the leadership of the APC.

The primary point remains, however, that throughout the first period of party government (1952–67) the political parties used ethnic appeals and did battle in support of ethnic interests. Rather than bring people together on the basis of their occupation, class interests, organizational affiliations, or political beliefs, the parties tended to depend upon more fundamental family and ethnic identity to garner support. Party membership as Sklar pointed out in his study of Nigeria was primarily "communal" and not a matter of individual choice:

> Ideally communal participation implies that the individual member or supporter regards the party as an extension of a social order [ethnic or religious] into which he has been born and to which he attributes spiritual or mystical significance. In his mind and in the minds of others with whom he habitually associates, the party is endowed with the values of that traditional order. Adhesion to the party is virtually automatic for members of the communal group . . .[19]

In Sierra Leone, as in Nigeria, the parties tended to be communal in their origin and appeal. One consequence of this was that the parties remained very weak and relied heavily upon the existing traditional elite to provide contact with the

voters. What is worse, the reinforcement rather than diminu-
tion of the importance of ethnic identities in national politics
inevitably led to greater ethnic hostility and conflict than
might otherwise have been the case.

The selection of candidates, the manner of campaigning,
the method of appealing to the voters for support were all
reflections of the dependence upon the traditional society and
traditional officials. The political parties usually selected their
candidates from among the men who wanted (and possessed
the necessary wealth) to run anyway rather than seeking out
the best qualified candidates for public office. Campaigns were
not run by large staffs and did not involve large numbers of
precinct workers in order to reach the voters. Rather the parties and their candidates tended to rely throughout the Protectorate upon traditional officials to contact the people.
D. R. J. Scott described campaigns in the 1957 election as
follows:

> The usual pattern of early campaigning, according to can-
> didates' accounts, was for them to go round the several
> chiefdom towns and the more important villages, visiting
> chiefs—to one or more of whom the candidate was very
> likely to be related—and the village sub-chiefs, who in the
> opinion of some were more influential, exchanging cus-
> tomary greetings and asking the people to be gathered,
> usually in the open-sided court-house or *barri*. There the
> visitor would recount to the public his local origins or in-
> terest—and the king of arguments appeared to be that one
> had built a permanent house in the area a respectable num-
> ber of years ago and kept it in good repair—and would
> ask for the favour of the listeners' votes. Few grounds seem
> to have been suggested in most places other than the gen-
> eral plea that "I am the best man for speak to Govern-
> ment."[20]

Even the younger, more radical parties such as the APC did
not vary this process outside of the larger towns. Since the
appeal as a candidate had to be to traditional leaders and
illiterate villagers on the basis of local origin, interest in the
area, and ability to gain a portion of the political rewards for

the area, successful candidates invariably came from the same ethnic group as the majority of their constituents and 84 per cent of them in the 1957 election also had chiefly kinship ties.[21] Such candidates and electoral contests between weak political parties intensified rather than reduced the appeal to communal and ethnic interests.

Less study has been devoted to voluntary organizations, other than political parties, such as the trade unions, cooperatives, youth groups, women's organizations, and churches. But the immediate effect of these and many lesser organizations in Sierra Leone upon ethnic identity seems minimal. Either the so-called national organizations really only exist in Freetown and maybe in the provincial captials or the real contact with the organization is so local, as in the case of the farm cooperatives, that ties with other sections of the country are of little importance to the average member. The result is that while many of the voluntary organizations are not manifestations of ethnic and sectional loyalties, they are not strong or important enough to form an alternative social base for political parties. Until a firm national identity can be established and strong interest groups can draw members from across ethnic lines into effective participation we can expect to see the continuation of ethnic conflict.

Distribution of Rewards

For both the individual and a group there are many different types of political rewards which are important—material wealth, social prestige, governmental services, political power, and favorable laws which allow one to achieve his goals in other areas of life. Governments are never absolutely neutral. Some men always have greater control over and receive more of these rewards than others in the same society. Knowing who receives them and why is important in understanding the operation of any political system.

In studying the distribution of rewards in Sierra Leone we must begin with the colonial government. The intent of Euro-

pean colonialism was that the "natives" should receive the
blessings of peace, civilization, and Christianity while the
"mother country" should receive the advantages of trade
through the discovery and export of valuable raw materials
and the development of a further market for manufactured
goods. The top officials in the hierarchy of colonial administration were Europeans. Thus, they received the highest salaries, the most social prestige, and the greatest political power
within the government. The other groups which received a
major share of rewards during the colonial period were the
Creoles and paramount chiefs. It is thus not surprising that
both Creoles and Europeans were killed in the Protectorate in
the Hut Tax War of 1898 or that the riots in the North during
1955 and 1956 were directed against the chiefs. If rewards
are distributed unfairly then violence, particularly the uncon-
trolled violence of riots, will often be directed against members of the groups that are seen as the oppressors even if the
individual members who are attacked are not personally responsible for the situation.

In terms of our analysis of ethnic conflict in Sierra Leone
our concern is with the difference in the position of the Creoles and Protectorate people in the colonial period. As Arthur
Porter in his book *Creoledom* points out, 1850–1939 was a
period of Creole ascendancy.[22] For most of this time their
social, political, and economic power was second only to the
British. They held high positions in the administration, commerce, professions, and legislative bodies. They had the highest level of education available in the country. Until 1920 all
Sierra Leone students at Fourah Bay College were from the
Colony and only with the extension of teacher-training in the
1940s did any sizable number of students come from the
Protectorate.[23] The graduates of Fourah Bay were the lawyers, doctors, higher civil servants, teachers, and ministers of
the colonial period and thus most of the people holding such
positions were either British or Creoles. The Creoles slowly
began to lose their exclusive share of the rewards, however.
During the 1880s Syrians and Lebanese began to arrive in
Sierra Leone. By 1912 they had control of most of the up-

country trade while European firms gained control of whole-sale trade and major stores in Freetown. As a result, the Creoles lost their prominence in commerce. In 1899 experiments in Freetown isolated the mosquito as the carrier of malaria, and preventive techniques to avoid the disease were soon developed. After this discovery many more Europeans came to Sierra Leone. Europeans soon began replacing Creoles in the higher posts in the administration and the Creoles once again lost positions of authority and honor which they had previously held. The final defeat of their exclusive status in Sierra Leone came with the political defeat at the hands of the SLPP and the achievement of independence under Protectorate rather than Creole leadership.

In gaining political power the Protectorate people also gained control over government scholarships and expenditures in education. They quickly sought to widen educational opportunities and thus eliminate the basis of Creole predominance in the professions. In considering the distribution of education in Sierra Leone, Martin Kilson found that 57.6 per cent of the children from the Colony (mostly Creole) attended school while only 3.25 per cent of the Protectorate children did so in 1938. By 1948, 55 per cent of the Colony's children were in school and still only 4 per cent of the children from the Protectorate were enrolled.[24] By the time of the 1963 census the situation had changed somewhat. The Creoles still possessed more education than other peoples but the spread of education to the Protectorate was greater (see Table 3).

Seeing the position and advantages of the Creoles before independence, it is understandable that the hostility and jealousy of the Protectorate peoples could be sufficient to crystallize a Protectorate party such as the SLPP and bring that party victory. But what about after independence? Were political rewards equally distributed then? No, they were not. Although the distribution was considerably more equal than the colonial period, there were still inequities. We have already pointed out that the first two prime ministers were brothers and thus representative of the same tribal family and religion. The cabinet represented more elements of the

TABLE 3

Highest Level of Education Completed
for the Population 5 Years of Age and Over[a]

Level Completed	All Sierra Leoneans	Western Area	% of Total
Some Primary	135,441	46,794	35%
Secondary 1–3 Years	23,273	13,026	56%
Secondary 4 Years and Over	12,773	8,950	70%
Some University	2,171	1,470	68%
Teacher Training	1,689	294	17%
TOTAL POPULATION 5 & OVER	1,803,020	166,512	9%

[a] Sierra Leone, *1963 Population Census of Sierra Leone* (Freetown, Central Statistics Office, 1965), Vol. II, Table 8.

country but after the purge of opponents by Albert Margai in 1965 this became less true. While the House of Representatives represented all ethnic groups, the North was considerably underrepresented according to John Cartwright's calculations based on the 1963 census:

TABLE 4

Parliamentary Seats and Population in Sierra
Leone, by District (Excluding Paramount Chiefs)[a]

District	Population ('63)	Seats ('62)	Seats by Pop.	Net Change Required
Bo	209,754	8	6	−2
Benthe	73,245	4	2	−2
Meyamba	167,425	4	5	+1
Pujehun	84,869	3	2	−1
Kailahun	150,263	3	4	+1
Kenema	227,428	6	6	0
Kono	167,915	4	5	+1

Bembali	198,776	4	6	+2
Kambia	137,806	3	4	+1
Keinadugu	129,061	2	3	+1
Port Loke	247,463	5	8	+3
Tenkelili	184,460	4	5	+1
Freetown	127,917	6	4	−2
Rural Area	67,106	6	2	−4

[a] John Cartwright, "The Development of Political Parties in Sierra Leone" (unpublished Ph.D. dissertation, University of Toronto, 1967), Chapter 6.

The Mendes' and Creoles' districts were overrepresented in the House of Representatives while the Temnes' district was underrepresented.[25] In the later years of the SLPP government it was charged that the distribution of public projects and public funds mirrored the unrepresentativeness of the government—that is, that the Southern and Eastern provinces benefited much more than the Northern Province. Because the national capital was in Freetown that city also prospered. The truth of these charges must remain for future researchers to investigate. Nonetheless, the Mendes appear to have received more of the political rewards than the Temnes during the period following independence. This situation laid the foundation for intensive conflict between the political parties which in turn led to ethnic violence.

Election and Military Coup of 1967

Ethnic tensions reinforced by political parties and unequally distributed political spoils came to a head in 1967. In 1962 the APC had forcefully contested the election and since then had continued to expand its base of support. By 1967 there was justifiable fear among supporters of the government that it would be turned out of power and a similar fear among government opponents that they would be cheated out of an electoral victory despite their support from a majority of the people. Nonetheless, the government continued with the plan to hold elections. Then on February 8, 1967, Sir Albert Margai announced that an army plot to assassinate him had been uncovered. Following this announcement eight army officers and five noncommissioned officers, all of them either Creoles or Temnes, were arrested or discharged and the Guinean army in accordance with the antisubversion pact just concluded between the two countries moved up to the Sierra Leone border to assist in putting down possible revolt. According to at least one account, this "coup" was primarily "a pre-election stunt" and possibly "a means of immobilising possible opponents to a military takeover of the sort that occurred after Stevens' appointment."[26] Whatever else the arrests did, they demonstrated the government's fear of a takeover and the fact that only Creole and Temne officers were arrested indicated the ethnic nature of the potential conflict.

National elections were held as scheduled on March 17, 1967. They seem to have been more or less fairly conducted except for the disqualifying of several opposition party nominees.[27] But the government radio was careful always to report the results as if the SLPP were leading. In fact, the APC had won 32 seats; the SLPP, 28; Independents, 6; and 12 seats continued to be reserved for paramount chiefs.[28] Fired up by false election reports in the media and charges of election fraud, a riot broke out between the Foulahs supporting the SLPP and APC supporters in Freetown on March 20. About fifty people had to be taken to the hospital for treatment and one hundred Foulahs were arrested.[29]

Despite or because of the unrest, Governor General Sir Henry Boston summoned APC leader Siaka Stevens to be sworn in as the new Prime Minister on the afternoon of the twenty-first. At this point Brigadier David Lansana decided to intervene with the army and he arrested both Stevens and the Governor General. He said that he was acting to prevent the breakdown of law and order and the violation of the Constitution. Many others, and particularly the army officers who were later to depose Brigadier Lansana, believed that Lansana was really acting in order to keep Albert Margai in power. The disorders and threat of popular uprising increased after

Lansana's coup. Over the next two days roadblocks were set up by both the military and APC supporters, a curfew was imposed and several people were killed in struggles between the police and crowds.

On March 23 Lansana was arrested by a number of his own officers who, in effect, staged a counter-coup. The officers did not turn the government back to civilians, however, because they believed the elections and riots which followed indicated a tribal and ethnic conflict which the political parties could not control.

The military stepped into the fray at a point where ethnic tensions were great and, in the military's opinion, beyond the point where electoral politics could contain them. Certainly many other motives including the personal desire to hold power motivated first Brigadier Lansana and then the other officers to stage their coups. But without the ethnic conflict being so directly manifested in the election results and in the riots the military would have had much less excuse to interfere.

When the counter-coup occurred an interim military government known as the National Reformation Council (NRC) was established. This government ruled for thirteen months before being ousted by still another coup led by army sergeants and privates. During the period of NRC rule political parties were outlawed as were both national and local elected bodies such as the House of Representatives and district councils. The NRC attempted to rule by ignoring ethnic differences, by eliminating the political arena where ethnic conflict had been the most explosive, and by returning to the colonial pattern of government which stressed the pre-eminence of government administrators and paramount chiefs.

On April 18, 1968, sergeants and privates staged the third coup and on April 26 Siaka Stevens was sworn in as Prime Minister at the head of a coalition government. The original cabinet contained members of both parties as well as independents. But this was not sufficient to reunite the country and the situation has deteriorated. Election petitions challeng-

ing the right of twenty-six SLPP Members of Parliament to
their seats were successful and by-elections for those seats
were called for November 1968. If all of the APC challengers
had been successful in unseating the SLPP candidates, the
SLPP would have lost its power even as an opposition party
and disappeared from the political scene or switched to more
violent tactics. The final outcome of the by-elections left the
SLPP with twelve seats (20 per cent of all elected seats).
While this number probably does not represent the actual
support for the SLPP, it allows the party to form a legitimate
opposition and an alternative to the APC.

Unfortunately, violence has continued in Sierra Leone.
Many of the by-elections had to be postponed until March
because of riots in Mende country—particularly in Bo and
Kenema. These conflicts were related to the hostility between
the political parties and between Northerners and Mendes.
Riots also occurred at Njala University in reaction to "Creole
domination" of the university administration. In the iron ore
mining areas of Sierra Leone disputes broke out between
Mendes and Temnes which caused workers to flee back to
their home provinces. In the diamond areas much fighting
has occurred between "foreigners" and inhabitants. In
March 1970 major disorders broke out in Freetown around
party meetings preparing for City Council elections. A state
of emergency has been declared by the government numerous
times in the last decade in an attempt to deal with various
disorders and potential disorders. These various clashes have
been resolved with a minimum of bloodshed but they are a
visible warning that Nigeria's fate could happen to Sierra
Leone. The "tribalism" and ethnic nature of the conflicts
mean they are more difficult to stop permanently than non-
ethnic conflicts would be.

As a final bad omen, the SLPP members have all been
purged from the APC-dominated cabinet. Thus, the unequal
and unfair distribution of rewards which occurred under Albert Margai has been exactly reversed in the Stevens' government. The SLPP has fewer members in the National Legislature than it deserves and no cabinet ministers at all. Not

surprisingly, a letter from the current leader of the SLPP, Mr. Salia Jusu-Sheriff, to the magazine *West Africa* is filled with the same indignation that opposition newspapers employed in the Margai period:

> Since the return of civilian rule the APC has maintained and increased its hold on this country by violence, detention without trial, arrests and detentions under a state of emergency, suspension of Paramount Chiefs, removal of court presidents, and their replacement by APC agents, fabrication of evidence, threats and intimidation.[30]

From another series of resignations from the cabinet in the fall of 1970, a new party, the United Democratic Party, has been formed by dissatisfied leaders within the APC. The effect of this new party is yet to be determined although it has been formally banned and several of its leaders jailed. But, in general, the entrenched hostility between political parties coupled with the unstable ethnic situation, attacks against paramount chiefs in the North, distrust of foreigners in Freetown and the diamond mining areas, growing labor unrest, the fluctuating economy and a series of unresolved and divisive issues like a change to republican form of government makes the situation in Sierra Leone particularly dangerous. All of these problems raise the question whether Sierra Leone can yet maintain a stable, parliamentary government or whether ethnic hatred and political conflicts will become too great to control.

Ethnicity and Future Development

We have seen how differences in political subcultures can make national integration more difficult and political conflict more intense as in the case of the struggle for supremacy with the advent of independence in Sierra Leone. However, this problem is slowly disappearing as upcountry towns introduce the Protectorate people to Western culture and cause them to modify traditional standards. Experience with new forms of local government such as town councils speeds the process as does the existence of a national House of Representatives and parliamentary government. Therefore, over the next few decades it is to be expected that a national political culture—mixing both African and Western traditions—should evolve and spread throughout the country. As this common political culture comes to be accepted the conflict between the Creoles and the Protectorate peoples should abate considerably. In fact, their current alliance with the APC may be taken as evidence that the Creole-Protectorate split is already beginning to disappear.

We have also seen that the worst ethnic conflicts in Sierra Leone have been generated, not by different political norms, but by weak and ethnically oriented political institutions and by the consistently uneven and unfair distribution of political rewards to different political parties and sections of the country. It is unfortunate that political parties in Sierra Leone have always depended heavily upon their ethnic appeal to gain votes. This has meant that the very institutions which should have been the most useful in organizing the people and in alleviating ethnic and sectional hostility have actually exacerbated these conflicts. We can expect ethnic conflicts to continue until the political parties and other voluntary organizations become truly national in scope and begin to draw their members from across ethnic divisions.

Even if a common political culture and completely modern political parties were to evolve in Sierra Leone, the potential for large-scale ethnic violence would remain until the party in power is willing to distribute political rewards fairly. Each ethnic group, for practical if not for moral reason, is entitled to its share of cabinet ministers, Members of Parliament, and government projects in its chiefdoms and towns. Of the governments that have held power in Sierra Leone to date only that of Sir Milton Margai has come even close to dividing the spoils of government in a way acceptable to the various groups. Certainly, if civil war is to be avoided and the goals of economic development and social progress are to be attained, then the Stevens government must do a far better job in this regard than has been done in the past and than it has given any evidence of desiring to do in its few months in office.

Finally, in the transition period while political parties still represent ethnic and sectional interests it is extremely important that political leaders become more tolerant of their opponents. They must learn to accept political defeat when it occurs without attempting to employ either military coups or violent revolutions to gain control of the government. What is more, they must learn not to maltreat their opponents when they are victorious—particularly as these men are probably the only legitimate spokesmen for their ethnic groups. Legitimately elected officials of both parties must cooperate if the national government is to be both strong and stable. Members of both the government and opposition parties must be allowed to play their proper roles in the governmental process if the political system is to be healthy enough to dissipate ethnic hostility and channel the efforts of *all* people toward the development of the nation.

Sierra Leone is one of the few nations in Africa in which a military regime has voluntarily returned the government to civilian leadership again. Whether this experiment will be successful or end in civil war as in Nigeria or become the first of a long cycle of coups and dictatorships such as those in Latin America will depend upon the ability of the government to keep ethnic conflict within the limits of the political system and slowly to eliminate it. Unless ethnic conflict is curbed now it will hamper all future development in Sierra Leone. If ethnic cooperation prevails, then both economic and political development can proceed.

NOTES

1. No really comprehensive history and analysis of the development of upcountry Sierra Leone during the period prior to the formation of the Protectorate in 1896 has been written. However, some books and articles which give some account of this development are the following: Christopher Fyfe, *A History of Sierra Leone* (London: Oxford University Press, 1962); Christopher Fyfe, *A Short History of Sierra Leone* (London: Longmans, Green, 1962); Ade Ijagbemi, "The Temne: Traditions of Origin and Early History to 1787" (unpublished Ph.D. dissertation, University of Edinburgh, 1967); Peter Kup, *A History of Sierra Leone, 1400–1787* (Cambridge: Cambridge University Press, 1961); Kenneth Little, *The Mende of Sierra Leone* (London: Routledge & Kegan Paul, 1951); Kenneth Little, "The Political Functions of Poro," *Africa,* XXXV, No. 4 (October 1965), pp. 349–65 and XXXVI, No. 1 (January 1966), pp. 62–71; Walter Rodney, "A Reconsideration of the Mende Invasion of Sierra Leone," *Journal of African History,* V, No. 2 (June 1967), pp. 219–46; and numerous articles by various authors in *Sierra Leone Studies.*

2. Christopher Fyfe, *A Short History* . . . , p. 92.

3. A. T. Porter, "The Social Background of Political Decision-Makers in Sierra Leone," *Sierra Leone Studies,* n.s. No. 13 (June 1960), pp. 4–5.

4. These rules of the game were derived from the ethnographic literature on these tribes and through interviews with leaders in towns within the Mende and Temne areas. The rules were tested through sample surveys in Kenema and Makeni, Sierra Leone. Cf. Dick Simpson, "The Political Evolution of Two African Towns" (unpublished Ph.D. dissertation, Indiana University, Bloomington, 1968), Chapter 8.

5. Jomo Kenyatta, *Facing Mount Kenya* (New York: Vintage Books, 1962), p. 303. (First published in 1938: London, Secker & Warburg.)

6. For more information about the political groups before World War II see Martin Kilson, *Political Change in a West African State* (Cambridge: Harvard University Press, 1966), pp. 219–25.

7. Martin Kilson, "Sierra Leone," *Political Parties and National Integration in Tropical Africa*, ed. by James Coleman and Carl Rosberg, Jr. (Berkeley: University of California Press, 1964), pp. 96–97.

8. John Cartwright, "Shifting Forces in Sierra Leone," *Africa Report*, XIII, No. 9 (December 1968), p. 26.

9. Kilson, *Political Change . . .*, esp. Chapters 15 and 16.

10. Kilson, "Sierra Leone," p. 104.

11. Kilson, "Sierra Leone," p. 113. For a more complete discussion of the 1951 election see Laminah Sankoh, "Politics for the People," *Sierra Leone Inheritance*, ed. by Christopher Fyfe (London: Oxford University Press, 1964), pp. 329–35.

12. Kilson, "Sierra Leone," p. 99.

13. Kilson, "Sierra Leone," p. 113.

14. Kilson, "Sierra Leone," p. 114.

15. Kilson, *Political Change . . .*, p. 272.

16. Cartwright, "Shifting Forces . . .," p. 27.

17. Hella Pick, "Near Upset in Sierra Leone," *Africa Report*, VII, No. 6 (June 1962), pp. 4 and 23.

18. Cartwright, "Shifting Forces . . .," p. 27.

19. Richard Sklar, *Nigerian Political Parties* (Princeton: Princeton University Press, 1963), p. 475.

20. D. R. J. Scott, "Sierra Leone," *Five Elections in Africa*, ed. by William Mackenzie and Kenneth Robinson (Oxford: Clarendon Press, 1960), p. 224.

21. Kilson, *Political Change . . .*, p. 233.

22. Arthur Porter, *Creoledom* (London: Oxford University Press, 1963), Chapter 5.

23. P. E. H. Hair, "An Analysis of the Register of Fourah Bay College, 1827–1950," *Sierra Leone Studies*, n.s. No. 7 (December 1956), pp. 155–60.

24. This information was contained in a footnote and was taken from government reports on education in 1938 and 1948. Kilson, "Sierra Leone," p. 101.

25. When Kilson first looked at the tribal affiliations of Sierra Leonean legislators of 1960, he concluded that they were relatively representative according to the population estimates of that time. Mendes had 35 per cent of the legislators, Temnes 23 per cent, and Creoles 22 per cent. The 1963 census, however, revealed that the Mendes actually constituted 31 per cent of the total population, the Temnes 30 per cent, and the Creoles about 2 per cent. Thus, even the 1960 House of Representatives underrepresented the Temnes in comparison to the Mendes and Creoles. See Kilson, "Sierra Leone," p. 100.

26. "Sierra Leone: What Really Happened," *Africa Confidential,* No. 7 (March 31, 1967), p. 2.

27. There were charges of stuffing the ballot box in Freetown and of irregularities in the Mende areas. However, the APC won anyway in Freetown and the SLPP won most of the re-elections in contested areas of the Southern and Eastern provinces.

28. "News in Brief," *Africa Report,* XIII, No. 1 (January 1968), p. 47.

29. "Sierra Leone: The Election and the Coup," *West Africa,* No. 2601 (April 8, 1967), p. 477.

30. Salia Jusu-Sheriff, M.P., "Letters to the Editor," *West Africa,* No. 2713 (May 31, 1969), p. 615.

IV
CONGO-KINSHASA

❖ ❖ ❖

EDITOR'S INTRODUCTORY NOTE

For purposes of analysis Congo can be divided into fourteen cultural regions with diverse political structures. Ethnicity, then, would appear to be an overwhelming barrier to national integration. However, ethnic identities and antagonisms, which were produced or modified during the colonial period, have a relatively short history. Ethnic labels were learned by the Belgians and applied to various peoples. Such labels were used to unify or divide a people and to distinguish favored ethnic groups from the less "desirable" allies. For example, missionaries received a state subsidy and were assigned a specific zone within Congo. They themselves decided the *linguae francae* to be used as the media of instruction within the zones as well as the locations of schools. Often these decisions were made on the basis of the initial perception of a particular people. It is understandable that some Congolese would accept an ethnic label or speak a certain language in order to obtain an education. The educational policy of the colonial administration also helped to forge grievances which made traditional enmity operational in Congolese politics. Those ethnic groups with limited access to educational opportunity were handicapped in job competition and held positions in the lowest social stratum. The peoples of less economically developed regions migrated to the cities where their sense of deprivation was heightened. When the underprivileged also felt excluded from political power, ethnicity became a real factor in Congolese politics. Voluntary associations based on ethnic ties were organized both in the cities and in the countryside. As the demand for independence heightened, many of these voluntary associations became political parties each vying for its perceived legitimate share of power. Some groups exhibited separatist tendencies while other parties espoused Congolese unity. The common denominator in all political platforms, however, was a desire to promote the interests of particular interest groups.

With Belgium's announcement of Congolese independence in 1959, a number of Congolese elite members attempted to link the various ethnic groupings by means of political parties. The most successful attempt was Patrice Lumumba's MNC whose goal was a national single party. Because the MNC was ethnic by default, its efforts failed. The years immediately following independence were chaotic in Congo. Six provinces of the colonial administration were fragmented into twenty-one provinces under a federal structure. Popular grievances once again fanned ethnic enmities, and rebellion spread from province to province. The Arme Populaire de Libération, the rebel army, attempted to unify the country by force. Although the peasants were sympathetic to the goal of the rebels—to rid Congo of exploitative politicians—they regarded them as "strangers." Thus, ethnicity was more salient in Congolese politics than political issues.

In 1965 Joseph Desire Mobutu seized power through a military coup. He immediately initiated a program to alleviate ethnic sub-nationalism. The fragmented provincial structure was merged into eight depoliticized provinces which lacked their own legislatures and governments. The governors, career civil servants, were appointed to posts outside their home areas and were rotated frequently. Provincial police were nationalized, and Lumumba, a symbol of national unity, was rehabilitated. While blocking the formation of ethnic political parties Mobutu launched a single party, the Mouvement Populaire de la Révolution. He also tried to preserve ethnic balance in the national government.

Before Mobutu's attempt to integrate Congo can be declared successful, however, he faces some difficult tasks. He must supplant symbols of ethnicity with symbols of national unity. Differential modernization of ethnic groups is still acute. Therefore, he must respond meaningfully to grievances and attempt to equalize opportunity. Until the MPR is developed into a viable communication channel from the mass to the political elite, integration of Congo may be a temporary phenomenon.

CONGO-KINSHASA—Northern Limit of Bantu Languages

CONGO-KINSHASA

By Thomas Turner

UNIVERSITÉ LIBRE DU CONGO, RÉPUBLIQUE
DÉMOCRATIQUE DU CONGO

Indigenous Cultures and Political Institutions

The political evolution of the Congo-Kinshasa, like that of other countries, has been strongly conditioned by its physical and human geography. A dominant geographic trait is its vastness: with 905,000 square miles the Congo is three times as large as Nigeria; among all African states, only the Sudan is larger. However, only twenty million people live in this area.

Some 250 peoples (cultural communities, often called "tribes") have been identified in the Congo.[1] Writers in the colonial period, and more recently Lemarchand and others, have emphasized the "unique" ethnic diversity of the Congo.[2] However, one must distinguish the number of peoples from the diversity of these peoples.

In linguistic terms, 75 to 80 per cent of the Congolese speak Bantu languages, thus languages which are very similar. (The remainder speak what were formerly called "Sudanic" languages, and are now classified as belonging to the Adamawa-East family of the Niger-Congo bloc of languages, and the Central and Eastern Sudanese families of the Chari-Nile bloc.)[3]

Perhaps more important, Vansina has now demonstrated the "underlying unity of the Congolese cultures."[4] Within this fundamental unity, presumably the product not only of common origins but of frequent contacts among the Congolese peoples, one can distinguish four main subdivisions, corresponding to geographical regions: the northern savanna,

CONGO-KINSHASA
Source: Roger Anstey, *King Leopold's Legacy* (London: Oxford
University Press, 1966).

the equatorial forest, the southern savanna, and the region
of the lakes. The physical geography of these regions had
important political consequences, for the forests impeded communications, and only in the savanna or along the lakes did
large-scale kingdoms develop.[5]

Of all the Congolese peoples, only the various pygmy
groups (of which the total population is probably less than
fifty thousand) had no distinguishable political structures.
Among all the others, except the Ngbaka or Ngwaka and
related people of Équateur Province, one could find chiefs,
that is, leaders playing a defined political role, enjoying certain privileges, and possessing symbols of office. Truly com-

plex structures such as those of the Kongo, Yaka, Kuba, Luba (all of the southern savanna), or Shi (of the lakes) were rare. For the most part, there were "chiefs of the land" heading several villages. Occasionally, there was a political chief with a court with central officials and judges, and several "chiefs of the land" subordinate to him. The power of the rulers was sacred in the large states and elsewhere in the southern savanna. In contrast, the power of the Zande and Mangbetu rulers of the northern savanna was based on force, for the subjects, and on the shared history of the conquest, for the elite.[6]

A number of the symbols of kingship or chiefship are found throughout the Congo basin: some of these, notably leopard skins, have been used as resources by modern politicians.

Colonial Overrule and Social Change

The establishment of colonial rule over the Congo deprived the various Congolese societies of most of their functions of defense and law enforcement, and many of their educational functions. These societies were no longer complete in themselves.[7] They had become part of social or political fields similar to the fields Gluckman described in South Africa:

The Rand mines and the African tribe which supplies their labour are both parts of a single social field; . . . the administrator who represents a government ruling over settlers and Africans, and the chief who rules over only a tribe whose members are in constant relations with settlers and with Government are both parts of a single body . . .[8]

The members of the various formerly independent Congolese societies began to interact with each other, but especially with the three hierarchies which made up Belgian colonial rule. These three were the colonial administration, the Catholic Church, and large corporations. Each of the three had an impact upon the Congolese that was far greater than that of their counterparts upon the populations of most other African colonies:

1. By the time of independence there were 10,000 Belgian civil servants in the administration, magistrature, and army. No Congolese, rural or urban, could have failed to perceive that he was being administered. In the urban centers this is hardly surprising, but what differentiated the Belgian system from others in Africa was the extent of its occupation and organization of the countryside . . .[9]

2. In 1958, it was estimated that the Congo counted 5,317,785 Christians, 80 per cent of whom were Roman Catholics. At the end of the colonial era, the Catholics maintained 669 mission posts, manned by nearly 6000 European missionaries . . .[10]

3. The final element in the trinity of power, the large companies, was no less remarkable in the scale of its operation . . . The equatorial forest zone of the central basin became the site of the immense plantations of oil palm and rubber of the Lever group and the *Société Générale*. Large scale in the 1920s, but these, once started, operated on a labor-intensive basis which made their impact enormous. The mining operations were largely concentrated in the eastern half of the country . . . Rare were the areas, such as the Kwango district, where there was not at least one major enterprise, either plantation or mining, which dominated the zone around it . . .[11]

Verhaegen observes that the lack of enthusiasm with which the Belgian population accepted King Léopold's legacy, the Congo Independent State,

is reflected in the relative passivity of the government, which abandoned to the Catholic Church and to the capitalist corporations a large share in the direction of the colonial enterprise, and contented itself with controlling and maintaining the social order thus created.[12]

Thus, while the Catholic missions received a state subsidy from 1906 onward (as did the Protestant missions after 1945), the government established zones within which each missionary order was to work, and designated certain languages as official *linguae francae*. The missions in fact made major decisions themselves as to which areas within their zone to provide with schools, and what should be the rate of expansion of educational opportunities. Such decisions were made on the basis of the initial perception of a particular people (as friendly or hostile to Europeans, as intelligent or otherwise, etc.), as modified by subsequent experience. While indigenous culture may have played some part in determining the response of the various peoples, the opportunities offered them in the form of schools, jobs, and markets were at least as influential in determining which ones modernized fastest.

The typical pattern of development in African colonies involved one or two large cities on the coast, draining a vast hinterland which became less modernized the deeper one penetrated. (Senegal, Ivory Coast, Ghana, Tanganyika are all examples.) In contrast, the pattern of development in the Congo was multipolar. There are several reasons for this: the location of the mines, the vast size of the Colony, the falls on the lower Congo River. In the Congo, rural exodus took place not toward the coast but toward the economic centers in the interior. Similarly, nationalist politics spread outward from each major town to its hinterland.[13]

If one mapped all communications linkages between individuals in the Congo in the 1950s, a pattern of four major social fields would emerge: (1) the Lower Congo, centering on Léopoldville (now known as Kinshasa), culturally rather homogeneous, more influenced by European culture than the rest of the country; (2) Orientale Province, centering on Stanleyville (now Kisangani), a region of agriculture and mining; (3) the Copperbelt of South Katanga, around Élisabethville (now Lubumbashi); Central Kasai, around Luluabourg, caught between the gravitational pulls of Léopoldville and South Katanga. Huge intermediate regions were poorly integrated into this pattern.[14]

The most important transportation linkages between these fields were, first, the river and rail connection between Léopoldville and Élisabethville, passing through Luluabourg, and second, the river connection between Léopoldville and Stanleyville. At the time of independence (and even at the time of writing) there was not a unified transport system, in that Katanga's primary link to the world economy was the railroad through Angola.

By 1956 there were nearly one million wage-earners in the Congo.[15] This rapid economic development was paralleled by extremely rapid urbanization. Léopoldville and Élisabethville had reached 26,622 and 22,858 respectively, by 1935, and 332,230 and 131,184 by 1956. The immigrants came mostly from within the same province, although there were important interprovincial migrations into Léopoldville (the "Bangala" coming down the river from Équateur) and into Élisabethville and the other Copperbelt towns (Luba and other Kasaians coming down the B.C.K. railroad).[16]

Of the institutions connecting the various regional social-political fields, the administration and the companies were entirely European on the upper levels. Africans mixed on a Congo-wide scale only in the *Force Publique* or army (sergeant and below), the Catholic clergy, and (after 1954) the university student bodies. In addition to these, several other modern elites can be identified among the pre-independence Congolese: public-sector clerks, private-sector clerks, and even a few African businessmen (although commerce was mainly in the hands of Belgians, Portuguese, Greeks, and Indians). Of the elite categories, probably the most important for an understanding of politics are the clerks, from whose rank came most of the 1960 politicians; noncommissioned officers, and commissioned military officers; and university students.

The ethnic composition of the clerk and student elites was largely the consequence of missionary educational policies (only loosely coordinated). In contrast, the colonial government had a deliberate policy of ethnic integration within the *Force Publique:*

The *Force Publique* was the first major avenue to modernity for the Congolese; in its early years, its acculturative impact was of great importance . . . Even before the missions, the army was able through its iron discipline and the complete removal of the recruit from his traditional moorings to create a group of persons sharply distinct from the rest of the population. In the early years of this century, many of the earliest nontraditional towns were composed of former soldiers who refused to return to their own clan . . .[17]

From the "Batetela mutinies" of 1895, 1897, and 1900 (see below), the Belgians drew the lesson that the army had to be ethnically integrated down to the squad level. Following another mutiny in Luluabourg in 1944, an inquiry indicated that there had been carelessness in the application of the scrambling principle, and it was reiterated that at least four ethnic groups had to be represented in each platoon. A specific warning was issued regarding recruits from the cities, where broad "supertribal" identities were arising.[18]

In the early years, two factors conditioned *Force Publique* recruitment. First was the communications network. Until the end of the campaign against Arab slave traders, in 1894, the Independent State really had access only to the population of the Lower Congo and of the regions along the Congo River as far as Stanleyville. The second factor was the notion of "martial races": the Belgians decided that certain peoples, including the Bangala, the Zande, and the Tetela, were both fierce and quick to learn, and thus made good soldiers. The consequences of these two factors can be seen in Table 1, which demonstrates disproportionate provincial recruitment figures for 1892–1914. In subsequent years, equal numbers were recruited from every part of the Congo, but there is reason to believe that the initial overrepresentation of certain groups led to a tradition of military service among them, and hence to a tendency on their part to re-enlist for a second seven-year term and become sergeants. Vansina suggests that research would reveal that the noncommissioned officers of the terminal colonial period were heavily Bangala, Tetela, and Luba-Kasai.[19]

Belgian colonial policy did not emphasize the buttressing of traditional authority with educational opportunity or economic privilege. Two experiments in setting up schools for sons of chiefs—a typical device of indirect rule—ran into heavy opposition from Church sources and had to be abandoned.

> There was no deliberate policy of excluding chiefs from education, but their location in rural areas has meant that their offspring have perhaps had a disadvantage in comparison with the sons of the modern, urban-dwelling elite.
> Second, although the chiefs invested as heads of *circonscriptions* did receive a salary and a cut in the head tax and were authorized to continue collecting some of their traditional tribute, they were not in general prosperous, even by African standards . . . In the earlier period, there was considerable Belgian distrust of the really important paramount chiefs . . . In the very last years of colonial administration, when the paramount chiefs began to appear as bastions of moderation to be balanced against the burgeoning demands of the modern elites in the cities, attitudes underwent a sharp reversal in many colonial quarters. This was reflected in . . . interest in improving the prestige of the chiefs . . .[20]

Only a few members of the traditional elite have occupied leading positions in contemporary Congolese society for "purely ascriptive reasons," according to Young, but traditional elements (real or simulated) have contributed to modern status in many cases. A study conducted in Élisabethville showed that among both educated and illiterate respondents the traditional element in prestige was highly significant. Young suggests that the responses would have been similar in other cities with populations drawn from areas where highly structured chiefdoms survived, e.g., in Bukavu. However, in cities such as Stanleyville or Léopoldville, with populations which lack such chiefdoms, traditional prestige was less important.[21]

During the early postwar years, educated Congolese shared the assumptions of the Europeans that "elite satisfaction was the central issue in colonial society . . . (and) that any early change in the Congo's colonial status, however desirable, was impossible . . ."[22] As a result, a prolonged conflict raged over the recognition of and granting privileges to "civilized" Congolese. However, from 1956 onward the attention of the educated Congolese was focused on the issue of participation. The linking up of elite demands (for participation, and eventually for a transfer of power) with mass grievances (which typically concerned alienation of land and compulsory cultivation of certain crops) took place quite suddenly after 1956. The formation of parties was not so much a question of each ethnic group throwing up leaders, as of members of the elite lining up support from their respective groups.[23] This process will be discussed in detail as it unfolded in the most important political field, that centering on Léopoldville, then more briefly as it occurred in Katanga, Central Kasai, and in Sankuru-Maniema, in 1959–60, and as it occurred again in Kwilu, Central Kivu, North Katanga, and Sankuru-Maniema during the rebellions of 1964–65.[24]

The Léopoldville Political Field

The movement for liberation of the Congo from colonial rule first acquired momentum in Léopoldville in the mid-1950s. It is a matter of great consequence that the pace was set by the Kongo (Bakongo) people, and that anticolonial activity among the Kongo took the form of ethnic sub-nationalism.

A central element in Kongo sub-nationalism was the belief that all the Kongo were descended from the inhabitants of the Kingdom of Kongo, which had Christian kings from 1500 onward, but had been destroyed by the slave trade, and divided by the French, Belgians, and Portuguese.

The belief of the Kongo that they all descend from the Kingdom of Kongo is a myth. The Kingdom included six provinces, three of which lay in what is now Congo-Kinshasa. The remainder, including the capital, San Salvador, lay in Angola. North of the Congo River, in what are now Congo-Kinshasa and Congo-Brazzaville, were a number of other kingdoms, linguistically and culturally related to the Kingdom of Kongo, but politically independent.[25]

The Kingdom of Kongo ceased to exist on a large scale by the eighteenth century although a vestigial core continued thereafter. By the twentieth century, however, the descendants of the populations of the various kingdoms all considered themselves Kongo. The French sociologist Georges Balandier wrote that there was no one in the remotest village of the Kongo country who could not recite the tale of San Salvador, where all Kongo came from and still had relatives to receive them.[26]

The spread of this myth of the Kingdom of Kongo seems to be due mainly to early European visitors picking up the contentions of the Kings of Kongo which claimed that neighboring kings were their vassals. Later this myth was transmitted to the Kongo by the missionaries through their schools.

Léopoldville was founded just upriver from the Kongo area, but from the early days Kongo constituted a major part of the town's population, and they came to consider it their town.

The imposition of colonial rule worked great hardship upon the Kongo, who were forced to supply porters in great numbers. All goods for Léopoldville and the interior, and all rubber and ivory being exported, had to be carried on the back of Kongo porters for three hundred miles of hilly terrain, between Matadi (the port) and Léopoldville, until the railroad was completed in 1898. Soon thereafter, sleeping sickness decimated the Kongo; this was attributed to the Europeans. In 1914 the Kongo across the border in Portuguese Angola revolted; those of the Belgian Congo did not dare to join in because they felt that the Belgians were too strong to be challenged in this way.

Against this background, the prophet Simon Kimbangu arose. Kimbangu, a former Protestant cathechist, claimed to have been given a message by God to ensure the salvation of his people. After thousands of Kongo began making their pilgrimage to Kimbangu's village, and signs of overt civil disobedience began, the Belgians arrested Kimbangu, sentenced him to death, then (following commutation of his sentence by King Albert in late 1921) imprisoned him for life in

Élisabethville, where he died in 1952. Kimbanguist activity continued after the removal of the prophet, and Kimbanguist symbols figured along with those relating to the former Kingdom of Kongo, in nationalist literature of the 1950s.[27]

The early Protestant and Catholic missionaries recorded various dialects of the Kongo language for use in their schools;[28] they also included the history (myth) of the Kingdom of Kongo in their schoolbooks. The Jesuit missionary, Father Joseph van Wing, produced a classic ethnographic study of the Mpangu (the people of the former Mpangu Province of the Kingdom of Kongo), entitled *Études Bakongo*, in which he argued that the lands to the north of the river had been part of the kingdom.[29] Van Wing's book circulated widely among the Kongo, contaminating the oral history "remembered" by the chiefs and elders. His book and his lectures at the Jesuit secondary school at Kisantu were influential in arousing a sense of appreciation of Kongo culture and a sense of Kongo unity among the members of the educated Kongo elite.

The major "ethnic group" competing with the Kongo in the Léopoldville political field was the "Bangala." This group was based on a myth of a different sort: it was almost entirely a product of colonial rule.

Stanley, the first foreign traveler along the Congo River, reported encountering the Bangala, "the Ashanti of the Congo," who were "unquestionably a very superior tribe." He was impressed by the energy with which the Bangala pursued him in their canoes, and by the dread in which they were held by their neighbors. However, Stanley noted that the Bangala inhabited only a string of villages extending ten miles along the Congo River, near what became Nouvelle Anvers.[30]

On the basis of Stanley's report, Coquilhat was set down among the "Bangala" in 1883, to establish a station of the Congo Independent State. Coquilhat was told by a village chief at his station, Mata Buike, that the latter was head on "one of the most vast states in equatorial Congo." That Coquilhat believed this tale is indicated by his estimate that there

were 110,000 Bangala. Although Coquilhat was told later by
Mata Buike that the latter was not a Bangala at all, but that
the name referred to peoples downstream, Coquilhat's estimate was perpetuated by other writers.[31]

Some of the first Congolese members of the *Force Publique*
(supplementing, then replacing, the earlier Zanaibaris, Nigerians, and others) were recruited by Coquilhat from around
his post. These "Bangala" were considered by the Belgians to
be quick learners, and better soldiers than the Kongo.

Probably because of the reports of Stanley and Coquilhat
as to the intelligence of the Bangala, several of the first missionary posts in Équateur were founded in what was thought
to be Bangala country. In 1889 the Scheutist Fathers founded
Nouvelle Anvers; soon they had a flourishing *colonie scolaire*
inhabited by 250 young liberated slaves.[32]

The extension of the Bangala ethnic category from the
handful of villages described by Stanley to a vast area of the
Northern Congo was due to administrators and missionaries
mistaking a *lingua franca* for the mother tongue of peoples
of Équateur. Guthrie described the rise of the *lingua franca*
as follows:

> . . . although it has been extensively used by Europeans,
> the language seems to have arisen spontaneously among
> the Natives. The river provides a natural highway for those
> who live along the banks of the main waterway or of its
> tributaries, but tribal feuds and conflicts made contacts rare
> until the coming of the white men. As soon as State agents
> and traders began to throw together people of different
> tribes, and European domination became sufficiently strong
> to render safe intercourse between the previous hostile,
> there arose the need for a simple form of language ade-
> quate for conversation among people whose tribal lan-
> guages were quite distinct.[33]

According to the Baptist missionary Weeks, the two thousand
or more African soldiers, workers, and women at Nouvelle
Anvers station conversed with one another by means of this
lingua franca. Some of the inhabitants of the villages near the
station picked up the *lingua franca*, "and the white men

hearing the natives talking this lingo jumped to the conclusion that it was their own tongue in which they were conversing and thus called it the Bangala language, and by that name it was generally known on the Upper Congo."[34]

Arguing for the standardization and enrichment of this *lingua franca* and its use as a medium of instruction, another Baptist missionary observed in 1903 that:

> already thousands have been born to the State forces to whom "Bangala" is the only mother tongue they know; and that thousands of the workers, drawn from the different tribes of the Congo basin, are forgetting their parent speech, and whilst they speak the "Bangala" with amazing fluency, their range of thought and idea, limited enough before, is now confined to the narrow circle of physical need and supply.[35]

The Baptists and other missionary groups each adopted forms of Bangala or Lingala for use in their schools. One form, "Ngala Uele," was used by Protestant missionaries in the far Northeastern Congo. It is unclear whether the *lingua franca* had spread to the Uele region via the Uele River and/or some other tributary of the Congo; what is clear is that some of the peoples of Uele do not even speak Bantu mother tongues. Extensive *Force Publique* recruitment occurred in Uele in the years of the Congo Independent State (see Table 1) and Uele soldiers identified themselves as Bangala in some contexts, at least to distinguish themselves from Swahili speakers.[36]

Large numbers of upriver people settled in Léopoldville, where they were referred to as Bangala by the Kongo. The label came to be accepted by all but the Mongo, and those from Kwango and Kwilu districts and Kasai Province.

Although both Kikongo and Lingala had been transcribed in various versions, a unified Lingala had been produced whereas four versions of Kikongo were still in use. As a result, Lingala began to be used increasingly, not only as a language of administration but as a language of instruction, to the detriment of Kikongo. Moreover, the Belgians appeared to the Kongo to take a clear stand against them by choosing both postwar *chefs de cité* at Léopoldville from among the Bangala.[37] Thus, when the Kongo ex-seminarian Edmond Nzeza-Nlandu moved to Léopoldville and founded the Association for the Maintenance, the Unity and the Expansion of the Kikongo Language, known by the acronym ABAKO, the response of the Kongo of Léopoldville was enthusiastic. According to Nzeza-Nlandu, his motives in founding the ABAKO included both a genuine attachment to Kongo culture (of which he had gained a deeper appreciation and knowledge through frequent contacts with Father Van Wing), and an anticipation of the advantages that would ensue from a strong organization when political competition was permitted in the cities. The ABAKO apparently acquired a number of its early activists by absorbing a quiescent cultural organization, *Renaissance Bakongo,* which had been founded by former students of the Jesuits (including Van Wing) at Kisantu.

By 1953 the ABAKO had extended its activities to the city of Thysville. In the same year, in response to the charge that the leadership was dominated by the Ntandu subgroup of the Kongo, Nzeza-Nlandu invited a Yombe, Joseph Kasa-Vubu, to join the central committee. (Kasa-Vubu had distinguished himself earlier by delivering an address on "the rights of the first occupant," i.e., the Africans who had lost their independence to the Europeans, to a meeting of the UNISCO, a discussion group which had emerged from several alumni associations.) Once the ABAKO had received official recognition from the Belgian authorities, as a cultural organization, it undertook to spread its influence from Léopoldville, Matadi, and Thysville to rural areas, and to establish organizational linkages with cooperatives, youth groups, students' associations, etc.[38]

Although the problems of the Kongo of the cities did not directly concern those of the hinterland, the sense of external threat from both the colonizer and his alleged ally, the Bangala, was gradually transmitted. The myth of the Kingdom of Kongo, divided up by the colonialists, served as a vehicle for this transmission. Sharpening pressure on land, especially in Mayombe where extensive concessions had been made to European forestry, oil palm, and cattle ranching enterprises, provided rural grievance which fused readily with the protest message of the urban elite.[39]

In 1955 competition between the ABAKO and its counterpart "cultural" organization, the *Liboka-lya-Bangala,* was centered on the office of *Chef de cité* in Léopoldville, which had fallen vacant. In 1956, however, Professor A. A. J. van Bilsen published a proposal for decolonization of the Congo over a thirty-year period, and immediately the attention of the Kongo and Bangala elites shifted to the issue of transfer of power. A group of *évolués,* mainly Bangala, associated with the Catholic journal *Conscience Africaine* issued a manifesto, moderate in tone but firm in its insistence upon the right of Congolese to be consulted on the country's future, and upon the necessity for Congolese unity:

> We demand in the most explicit terms to be directly involved in the elaboration of the 30-year plan now under discussion. Without this participation, such a plan could not have our consent . . .
>
> National union is necessary because all the population of the Congo must become aware above all of its national character and its unity . . . this leads us to take a position on the introduction into the Congo of political parties from Belgium. Our position is clear; these parties are an ill, and they are useless . . . Political parties respond to no need in the present political and administrative structure of the Congo; we have neither a Parliament, nor elections . . .[40]

ABAKO regarded this manifesto, with its call for "national union" and its attack at political parties, as a threat to itself. The counterattack came in the form of a counter-manifesto, far more uncompromising in its tone and radical in its objectives:

> Rather than postponing emancipation for another thirty years, we should be granted self-government today . . .

On "national union," ABAKO declared:

> Because this veritable union of the Congolese peoples can

be realized only by means of political evolution, this evolution . . . must first begin from the base of what exists.
This means that the historically, ethnically and linguistically
united or related groups should organize to form so many
political parties.[41]

In January 1957, Kasa-Vubu told the ABAKO General Assembly that,

> to speak of mis-understanding between our fellow citizens
> from the Upper Congo and ourselves, is nonsense.

He described at length the traditional hospitality of the Kongo,
then added:

> But if the stranger, thus admitted, does not respect the
> rights of the inhabitants, the council of elders could decide
> to repatriate him, after giving him a chance to speak on
> his own behalf.[42]

A few days later, in response to what they considered "a prov-
ocation directed against the tribes of the Upper Congo," the
leaders of the *Liboka-lya-Bangala* released an open letter to
the Governor General, protesting against the "dangerous regionalism" of the Kongo:

> Conscious of our responsibilities, and in view of the Ba-
> kongo's increasing tendency to vilify the other tribes, we
> have decided to raise the most vehement protests against
> the attitude of their leaders . . . Their ideal aims at foster-
> ing the belief that we, the Bangala, are intruders in Léo-
> poldville, which according to the Directing Committee of
> the Abako, is the land of the Bakongo . . . By spreading
> such groundless rumors, we fear that the Abako will end
> up deceiving the public and influencing the administra-
> tion.[43]

ABAKO responded to the open letter with an assertion that
"Léopoldville, Brazzaville, the Lac Léopold area, Angola, and
Pointe Noire were an integral part of the ancient Kongo Kingdom, a state that was divided in 1885, at the Berlin Conference, among France, Belgium, and Portugal."[44] Two weeks
later, the *Agence Dia,* a Catholic press agency in Léopold-

ville, published an article refuting the ABAKO position. The article asserted that the Léopoldville area, initially the property of the Tyo (Bateke), was gradually occupied by the Bangala, the Mongo and Libinza, whereas the Kongo allegedly "avoided all contacts with the whites." Until recently, the Kongo "suffered from an inferiority complex toward the Bangala," and the mass of the Kongo population still did. For this reason, the article concluded, the "fanaticism" and "revolutionary outlook" of ABAKO were directed mainly against the Bangala.[45] ABAKO in turn reacted strongly to these charges; sources ranging from the Belgian historian Mgr. Cuvelier to the French sociologist Balandier were cited in support of its position. The Catholic Church was charged with applying a policy of "divide and rule."[46]

In December 1957, elections were held to select councillors and burgomasters for some of the communes of Léopoldville. ABAKO won a sweeping victory, taking 130 of 170 councillors' seats and 8 of 10 burgomasters' posts. This result reflects in part the superior organization of ABAKO, and the higher level of ethnic awareness among the Kongo. However, ABAKO apparently had undertaken negotiations with Yaka leaders earlier in 1957, according to Young, and "the great disparity . . . between the number of voters from (Kwango) district and the number of its own candidates elected suggests that a large number of these ballots went to ABAKO candidates."[47] Weiss suggests that Kwilu peoples tended to vote ABAKO as well.[48]

After these elections, ABAKO converted itself into a political party. The Bangala leader Jean Bolikango established the *Fédération des Bangala,* then attempted to broaden his base of support by grouping this and other ethnic and regional associations of Léopoldville into the *Interfédérale;* The *Interfédérale* clearly was intended as an anti-Kongo front.[49]

In January 1959, however, massive riots broke out in Léopoldville, "When a scheduled ABAKO meeting had to be postponed because administrative authorization was refused. For a brief period, the explosion mobilized virtually the entire population of the city."[50] The colonial administration reacted hesitantly in restoring order. In contrast, the government in Brussels overreacted, the Belgian King declaring that,

> We are today resolved to lead the Congolese populations, without fatal delays but also without precipitate haste, to independence in prosperity and peace.[51]

From that moment, the race to independence was on; several hundred political parties were founded in the coming months. In Léopoldville, the *Interfédérale* was dismembered by the centrifugal force created by the members of the Congolese elites seeking the support of their respective ethnic or regional groups.[52] The administration tried to make the ABAKO leaders scapegoats for the riots, and jailed them. The result of course was to make martyrs of them. The administration also expelled several thousand unemployed persons from Léopoldville, which had the effect of politicizing the countryside without reducing the level of nationalist activity in the capital.

PSA vs. ABAKO in the Léopoldville Political Field

In addition to the Kongo area (Lower Congo and Cataractes districts), Léopoldville Province included one other relatively prosperous and densely populated rural area, Kwilu District. (It also included two less prosperous, less populous areas, the districts of Kwango and Lac Léopold II.) The main rival of ABAKO in 1959–60 was the Kwilu-based *Parti Solidaire Africain*.

To understand the nature of the PSA, one must first examine the human geography of Kwilu, an area of extreme ethnic complexity. The two most numerous peoples of Kwilu, the Mbun and the Pende, together constitute less than half the population of the district. The six most numerous groups together make up only about 80 per cent.

The peoples of Kwilu belong to two distinct cultural regions and speak languages belonging to two different zones:

(1) The Yans (Bayanzi), Ding (Badzing or Badinga), and Mbun (Bambunda) belong to Vansina's "Lower Kasai" cultural region (and speak languages of Guthrie's Zone B).

(2) The Suku, Pende, and Mbala belong to the "Kwango-Kasai" cultural region, and speak either a dialect of Kongo (Suku) or a language of the same zone (Guthrie's H).

However, the distinction between the two cultural regions has not proved very salient to modern politics, perhaps because peoples of the two regions had lived together for many years.

Between Kwilu and the Kongo area lay Kwango District. Kwango was inhabited largely by peoples of the Yaka subgroup of the "Kwango-Kasai" cultural region: Yaka, Suku, Pelende, Holo. Of these, the Yaka were dominant.[53]

Since Kwango was very poor (it was one of the few districts in the entire Congo with no major European agricultural, mining, or industrial investment), the Yaka migrated in large numbers to Léopoldville, where their competition with the Kongo (who were ahead of them on the employment ladder) seems to have revived historical enmity between the two peoples.

Kwilu was more developed economically than Kwango; several large European companies dominated the palm products industry, and employed large numbers of Kwiluites, especially Pende. In 1931 the exactions of the companies precipitated a large-scale revolt among the Pende; memories of this revolt and its repression remained fresh even in the 1960s. Employment opportunities were greater in Kwilu. Consequently, emigration from Kwilu to Léopoldville was not very common. Representatives of the many small Kwilu peoples tended to gather together in Léopoldville, both because of their close association in Kwilu, and because of their small numbers in the capital.

Within Kwilu, again, it is possible to distinguish a less prosperous, less developed region in the north, including Banningville and the area east along the river. According to Henri Nicolai, writing in the 1950s, the peoples of northern Kwilu (Yans, Ding, Ngoli, etc.) resented the Mbun, who had displayed achievement-motivation comparable to that of the Luba/Kasai, immigrating in large numbers to the river towns of northern Kwilu and getting the best jobs there.[54]

The Kwilu elite founded a political party, the *Parti Solidaire Africain,* in 1959. This was a response not only to the Belgian governmental announcement that independence would be forthcoming, but to a more immediate challenge, ABAKO's announcement of a plan for the creation of a Republic of Central Kongo, which would include not only the two predominately Kongo districts but also Kwango, Kwilu, and the city of Léopoldville:

> From the point of view of the Kwango-Kwilu leaders in Léopoldville . . . there was grave danger that the ABAKO with the appeal of its history of militancy, success at challenging Belgian power and obtaining grassroots support, and its plan for a separate republic, would obtain the support of the Kwango-Kwilu masses without giving the elite from the region any part in the leadership of the party or future government.

This fear had a basis in fact, in that Kwango-Kwilu residents of Léopoldville had supported ABAKO in 1957. However, in their efforts to exclude ABAKO from Kwango-Kwilu, the leaders from the latter districts had one important advantage:

> the Bakongo were somewhat resented by other ethnic groups in Léopoldville; they had received a high proportion of the better jobs, had won a substantial victory during the 1957 communal elections, and were said to affect superior airs and often contempt for other groups . . .[55]

Accordingly, a number of elite members from Kwilu (and to a lesser extent from Kwango) founded the African Solidarity Party (PSA). Although a national (Congo-wide) party in aspiration, the PSA did not extend its influence beyond Léopoldville Province. For this reason, it had a peculiar structure: its "national" organs were located in Léopoldville but its electoral stronghold (and source of funds in the form of dues) in Kikwit, capital of Kwilu District. The core of the provincial leadership came from a pre-existing elite group in Kikwit, the Association of Former Pupils of the Jesuit Fathers (ASAP), whereas the core of the national leadership came from the welfare organization, *Fédération Kwango-Kwiloise,* composed of people from Kwango who had split off from the *Fédération* "with the beginning of proto-political activity in Léopold-ville."[56] Later, they formed their own party, LUKA, which affiliated to the "moderate" (pro-Belgian, pro-chief) Congo-wide party, PNP. For the Yaka elite, the PSA represented a threat similar to that ABAKO had represented to the Kwango-Kwilu elite as a whole; there was danger that the Yaka masses would support the PSA without the Yaka elite's receiving a fair share in the party leadership. Accordingly, the Yaka elite formed LUKA, which relied on the symbol of the Yaka King, the Kiamfu, and received strong support from Yaka voters. About the same time, the Yans elite of northern Kwilu founded an ethnic party, ABAZI, apparently with the encour-agement of ABAKO. ABAZI received strong support from Yans voters, and some support from the closely related Ding.

From mid-1959 (when the Belgians rejected the ABAKO plan for a Republic of Central Kongo), ABAKO and PSA had come to accept each other's domination of the Kongo areas and Kwilu, respectively, and the PSA had accepted the inevitability of some form of federalism. The two parties thus were able to form alliance against the Belgians (and against both the pre-Belgian parties and the unitarist parties, of which the major example was the MNC/Lumumba). This alliance declared a policy of noncooperation, boycotting sector and commune elections in late 1959. Because of this policy, and the deportations from Léopoldville, the administration pro-gressively lost control of the Kongo countryside between Léo-poldville, and Matadi, and of central Kwilu. (A similar situa-tion arose in several areas of the eastern Congo, rural strong-holds of the MNC/Lumumba. It seems likely that in these cases as in that of the Kongo and Kwilu countryside, violence spread to the countryside following urban riots, and involved a fusion of urban nationalism and rural grievances.)[57]

In the 1960 elections, ABAKO won a sweeping victory in the Kongo areas, but took only thirty-three seats in the pro-vincial assembly, to thirty-five for the PSA. Faced with this result, the autonomist tendency of ABAKO came to the sur-face again. The thirty-three ABAKO Assembly members declared unanimously their support for the formation of a Kongo provincial government, in the framework of a federal Congo. The proposed province of Central Kongo was to have Léopoldville as its capital.

They elected Gaston Diomi "provincial president." Diomi announced that he would resign in favor of Kasa-Vubu, were the latter not elected President of the Congo. A few days later, Kasa-Vubu was in fact elected President of the Congo, and Diomi and four other ABAKO members joined the Léopoldville provincial government headed by Cleophas Kamitatu of PSA. However, the idea of a separate Kongo Province remained alive and surfaced again in 1961. (Similarly ABAZI, complaining of intimidation of its supporters by the PSA during the May 1960 elections, announced the formation of a "North Kwilu provincial government.")[58]

ABAKO and PSA both experienced splits in 1960. During the Brussels Round Table (see below), ABAKO Vice President Daniel Kanza refused to go along with Kasa-Vubu's (temporary) walkout, and instead advocated a gradual independence. Afterward, Kanza openly criticized Kasa-Vubu for acting dictatorially, not consulting other officers. The feud seems to have been personal in part, involving the fact that Kanza was Protestant, Kasa-Vubu Catholic. This feud, and the resultant establishment of a dissident ABAKO/Kanza, represented a threat to ABAKO in that Kanza's home area, Manianga, had a regional sense of grievance. (Manianga had no history of unity: it included both the one section of the former Kingdom of Kongo which extended north of the Congo River, other Kongo-speaking chiefdoms, and even part of the Tyo or Teke Kingdom. Nonetheless, because it had combined economic underdevelopment with a high level of literacy, Manianga had developed a sense of regional identity and grievance.) Apparently to offset the Kanza threat, Vital Moanda of Manianga was made a top leader of ABAKO; he became Governor of Central Kongo Province in 1962. Prior to the establishment of the separate Kongo Province, President Kamitatu of Léopoldville Province attempted to exploit the grievances of Manianga by dealing directly with

Manianga leaders, bypassing the central organs of ABAKO.[59]
The split in PSA was more serious, involving more nearly
equal fragments. The resultant PSA/Gizenga and PSA/
Kamitatu represented a number of roughly coinciding cleavages:

1. national vs. provincial leaders of the PSA;
2. Marxist vs. Christian socialist;
3. Pende and Mbun leaders vs. those from smaller groups
(lumped together as "Mbala"), i.e., eastern Kwilu groups
vs. central Kwilu groups from the Kikwit area.[60]

The Political Field of Central Kasai
(Luluabourg Area)

The decolonization period in Luluabourg and in Kasai
Province in general was dominated by the fierce rivalry between the Lulua and the Luba-Kasai. However, this rivalry
is of colonial origin.

Both Luba and Lulua speak dialects of the Luba-Kasai
language. At the time of first contact with Europeans, both
identified themselves as Luba.

As with Stanley and the Bangala, the story of the Luba and
Lulua begins with European explorers, in this case the Ger-
mans Pogge and Von Wissmann. In his book *Im Innern
Afrikas*, Von Wissmann reported very favorably upon the intelligence and receptivity of people whom he called "Baluba";
these were the people now called Lulua. In his second book,
Through Equatorial Africa, Von Wissmann apologized for
the confusion:

> I am sorry that in my work *Im Innern Afrikas*, the
> Bashilange have always been called Baluba . . .[61]

Throughout the second book, Von Wissmann used the term
"Bashilange" to refer to the people now known as Lulua (e.g.,
on page 38, where he referred to Bashilange as living along
the Lulua River). Ironically, in view of their subsequent reputation as the great modernizers, Von Wissmann found the

people now known as Luba-Kasai to be much less enterprising
than the Bashilange or Lulua:

> The Baluba have remarkably little inclination to improve
> their arms and utensils . . . everything showed rudeness
> and an entire want of a sense of beauty . . .[62]

Von Wissmann was impressed not only by the Lulua in general
but by their "most powerful chief," Mukenge Kalamba.[63]
At the time the Europeans arrived, Kalamba was in the process of extending his domination over neighboring chiefs.
Wissmann established the Independent State post of Luluabourg near Kalamba's court, and backed Kalamba in his
expansion, in an effort to ensure that future administrators
at Luluabourg would have to deal with only one "upperchief"
of the Bashilange or Lulua.[64]

Wissmann's policy proved self-defeating. By 1891, State
officials reported that Kalamba was attempting to make
himself absolute ruler of Central Kasai. The first armed clash,
which ended in defeat for Kalamba, dates from that year.
In 1895 Kalamba attempted to profit from a revolt of the Independent State garrison at Luluabourg (the so-called "Batetela mutiny"). But he was again defeated and he died in
exile (elsewhere in Kasai) in 1898. Kalamba's adopted son
Tshimangu continued to lead periodic attacks against State
forces. Despite these difficulties, in 1915 the Belgians made
Tshimangu paramount chief of all Lulua of the Luluabourg
area (except for those chiefs who had been recognized by the
Belgians while Tshimangu was in exile). As recently as 1932,
one of Tshimangu's sons (recognized as chief of the Bena
Kashie, a Lulua subgroup) was relegated to Banana, in the
Lower Congo, for armed opposition to Belgian rule.[65]

While the Lulua were proving very troublesome, the Europeans were accumulating a considerable population of dis-
placed Africans at Luluabourg and other posts; this process
began under Wissmann, who explained:

> I repeatedly accepted presents and payments, even if con-
> sisting in slaves: in the first place, because this is African

custom, and secondly, because the refusal of a present would be considered an insult; moreover, the slaves would have a much better lot with me or with the Lubuku (the Lulua of Kalanda) than with the savage natives. There were a large number of such captives at Luluabourg, who had to work a certain time for the station, for which they received clothes and maintenance. After a time, which depended on the work they had done, they received full wages and were free. After being ransomed, they mostly built their villages near the protecting station, and seldom made use of their permission to return home.[66]

A visitor to Lusambo, Kasai, in 1908 reported an "enormous" African population. In addition to a number of separate ethnic villages grouped around the post, there was "a very large population of natives belonging to no particular village who are generally termed Baluba by the white men of the Kasai, but who in reality belong to that tribe no more than to any other."[67]

Because many so-called Luba settled close to the posts and missions, their children constituted the first pupils of the mission schools, and continued to constitute a majority. Thus, the clerks hired by European administrators and businessmen from among the graduates of these schools of necessity were largely Luba.

Perhaps because of some social characteristic of the Luba,[68] and perhaps because they had heard they would be favorably received by the European, Luba from Southern Kasai continued to migrate to European centers. By 1930, Luba immigrants constituted the majority of the population not only of the growing town of Luluabourg but also of its environs. The administration organized these Luba into homogeneous *chefferies* (units headed by chiefs), and in some cases shifted Lulua villages away from the environs of the town. Luluabourg grew into a major commercial center after 1945, and especially after 1950, when it was made provincial capital. The bulk of the new population was Luba, including not only rural people, but some who had worked in the mines of Southern Katanga, and wanted to return "home" without returning to village life. In 1952 the *cité indigène* (African quarter) of Luluabourg was 57 per cent Luba and only 26 per cent Lulua. In some surrounding areas, the Luba majority was still greater.[69]

In the early 1950s, the geographers Nicolai and Jacques found that the area along the Bas-Congo-Katanga Railroad was considerably more developed than the remainder of Kasai Province. This development they attributed to the activity of Luba who had come to the area since the arrival of the Europeans and especially since the 1920s. These Luba dominated both commercial agriculture and administrative jobs. However, as of the early 1950s, relations of the Luba with the earlier inhabitants seemed to present no special difficulties.[70]

It must be stressed that the Luba and Lulua both were relatively favored groups, in terms of education and social position. However, the Lulua modernized somewhat later, and as they did so they ran into Luba teachers and personnel officers. A frequent charge in Luluabourg was that the Luba teachers were blocking the advancement of Lulua children in the schools. Whether or not this charge was true, what is important is that it was believed.[71]

Similarly, when Lulua attempted to move into the area along the railroad in order to profit from the opportunities for commercial agriculture, they were rebuffed by the Luba. Yet, as the Lulua could see, new Luba continued to move into the area: for example, the population of Tshikaji sector increased by nearly 50 per cent between 1954 and 1958, due to Luba immigration.[72]

From 1925, when "pacification" of the Lulua areas was completed, until the Second World War, administrative reports rarely mention signs of discontent. Starting in 1945–46, however, protests began in Luluabourg (and in other towns) over rising prices. These protests were quieted around 1950, when economic conditions improved. However, by 1954, administrative reports indicated a new form of unrest:

A tense situation exists between the Lulua and Luba populations of Demba territory as a result of the awakening of Lulua consciousness, under the influence of *évolué* elements.[73]

The awakening of Lulua consciousness can be attributed to the formation of the *Association Lulua-Frères*. This association was set up in 1952, with the backing of Chief Kalamba Mangole Sylvestre, grandson of the earlier Kalamba, and with the apparent encouragement of the colonial administration.[74] It quickly became the best disciplined and best organized of all Congolese ethnic associations. Unlike ABAKO, for example, it was as much rural as it was urban, meaning that rural grievances (especially land pressures) and urban grievances (such as job discrimination) were linked from the beginning. Within about a year of its founding, *Lulua-Frères* had forty sections, not only in Kasai but throughout the Congo and even in Angola, Northern Rhodesia, Burundi, and Congo/Brazzaville. In Élisabethville, the appearance of the dynamic *Lulua-Frères* split the existing federation of Kasaians, leaving the latter mainly to the Luba/Kasai.[75]

By 1958, when Luba/Kasai were prominent among the leaders of anticolonial agitation, the Belgians must have been especially happy with their foresight in backing *Lulua-Frères*.

Had (the administration) not gotten M. Émile Mulumba, Vice President of the *Association Lulua-Frères,* to make— in the presence of, and with the approval of, paramount chief Kalamba—a declaration which must have run very pleasantly in the ears of the Belgian functionaries: "We need not struggle for independence since the Belgians have promised it to us."[76]

It is natural that the Lulua would be unenthusiastic about early independence, because the Luba were in better position than they to provide the educated political leaders, administrators, and technicians for an independent Congo, thereby converting their advantage into a permanent one.

As with ABAKO, the first communal election in Luluabourg in 1958 served as the occasion for *Lulua-Frères* to become overtly political. The administration counseled *Lulua-*

Frères on electoral procedures and even helped select candidates. With this aid and by virtue of their discipline, the Lulua minority won a majority of seats on the Communal Council, and they captured both African burgomaster posts.[77] The Luba then spurned an offer to cooperate with the new Lulua burgomasters, and instead established an ethnic organization of their own, the *Mouvement Solidaire Muluba*.

In April 1959, when the first congress of Congolese political parties was held in Luluabourg, Patrice Lumumba apparently attempted a reconciliation of Luba and Lulua; he arranged that Albert Kalonji (of the MNC), a Luba/Kasai, and Alphonse Ilunga, Lulua president of the *Union Congolaise* (political party deriving from *Lulua-Frères*) shake hands on the podium. The following month, however, Chief Kalamba demanded that the administration maneuver to head off a reconciliation;[78] whether or not he is correct as regards the administration role he surely is correct as to the effect of the declaration.

In July 1959, the MNC split, the dissident wing being called the MNC/Kalonji after Albert Kalonji who became its most vocal leader and was elected president. As the MNC/Kalonji was strongly anti-Lumumba, this split laid the groundwork for Lumumba's organizing an anti-Luba alliance of the Lulua, Tetela (his own ethnic group), Songye, and other peoples of Kasai.

Also in July, Luba leaders obtained a copy of a report by Assistant District Commissioner A. Dequenne, addressed to the Governor of Kasai, advocating a massive repatriation of Luba from Lulua lands. The report asserted that there is "uncontestably" a Lulua ethnic group, in whose territory the city of Luluabourg is located. Recognition of Kalamba as chief or "titled representative" of the Lulua was urged.

> Furthermore, the Lulua wish to remove all political rights from the Luba, whom they consider to be "strangers." Their goal obviously is to avoid a defeat at the next election. One could partly satisfy their wish in regulating the right to vote of the inhabitants of the town (Luluabourg) and the surrounding zone. One could set down, for ex-

ample, that only those having resided there effectively and regularly for at least ten years would have the right to vote . . .

A second conditon would be the obligation that any resident desiring to vote or stand for office declare that he belongs to the Lulua people.[79]

Chomé observes that neither the declarations of Chief Kalamba nor the discovery of the Dequenne report led to violence. Not until the administration rounded up leading Luba politicians, most notably Albert Kalonji (on charges of inciting to violence and to racial, i.e., anti-Belgian, hatred), did violence occur, and even then, according to Chomé, it was directed mainly against Europeans. Nicolai presents a different version, according to which one of the Lulua burgomasters had to be protected against a possible Luba attack, and in return Chief Kalamba approved the measures taken by the administration and threatened to intervene against the rioters.[80]

When large-scale violence did break out, it was in the form of attacks by Lulua against the Luba living among them, following the *release* of the arrested Luba leaders. (Chomé and Nicolai credit different individual acts of violence with setting off the spark.) During the week of October 12, 1959, at least thirty deaths were reported. Groups of Lulua armed with machetes and hunting rifles attacked Luba villages. In at least one case, Lulua also attacked a village of Songye living in Lulua country.[81]

By December a full-scale exodus of fifty thousand Luba from Luluabourg and environs had begun. By July 1960 the exodus from Luluabourg was nearly complete, but the process was just beginning in other parts of Kasai. From 1958 to 1963 the population of the Luba homeland in South Kasai increased fourfold, from 332,620 to 1,348,030.[82]

The secession of South Kasai seems an inevitable result of the anti-Luba alliance. On June 3, 1960, Lumumba had formed a *front commun* of all non-Luba provincial deputies in Kasai. The Provincial Constitution required that the Luba be given three provincial ministries, in proportion to their strength in the provincial assembly, but the posts given them were of minor importance. On June 14 the Luba leaders decided formally to secede from Kasai Province. On August 8 the "Mining Province" of South Kasai was proclaimed. There followed a campaign of the Congolese army against the breakaway province; however, with the support of separatist Katanga and of European mining interests, the Luba leaders gradually established a functioning regime in the severely overcrowded province. In March 1961, Kalonji (who had gradually forced out his rivals) had himself crowned Mulopwe (King) of South Kasai; the title Mulopwe was derived from the Luba Kingdom of northwest Katanga, and had no antecedents in Kasai.[83]

The Political Field of Katanga

Superficially, Katanga political competition in the terminal colonial period seems unique, due to the presence of a large European settler community, mainly associated with mining. However, closer inspection shows patterns of conflict similar to those in Léopoldville and Luluabourg.

Katanga had been the site of three large precolonial states: (1) the Luba Kingdom, centered in what was to become northwest Katanga, (2) the Lunda Kingdom, in southwest Katanga, and (3) the Yeke Kingdom (founded in the nineteenth century by Nuamwezi warrior-traders from what is now Tanzania), in Eastern Katanga.[84] Katanga was sparsely populated, a condition which was aggravated by harsh labor recruitment methods of the early twentieth century, with the result that by the 1920s labor recruiters began going farther afield, notable to what became Kasai Province. The new mining towns, Élisabethville, Jadotville, Kolwezi, and others, began filling up with "strangers" from outside Katanga, predominantly Luba from Kasai, who were particularly receptive to European influences and social change (see above). In both commercial and clerical jobs in Katanga towns, the Luba/Kasai were workedly more numerous than the Katangans.[85]

Awareness of the social disparity between "strangers" and Katangans grew in the postwar years. In 1957, when world copper prices dropped 50 per cent, the resultant unemployment hit the lowest stratum of workers, mainly Katangans, the hardest. In the same year, communal elections were held in Élisabethville and Jadotville. The results were the contrary of those in Léopoldville: in both Katanga cities the "strangers" won because they were better organized. The four African communes in Élisabethville designated non-Katangan burgomasters, two of them Luba/Kasai. Suspicion of favoritism toward Kasaians by the new burgomasters was widespread, especially as regards allocation of public housing and residence permits.

In response to the threat of entrenched stranger domination, Katangans organized the Confederation of Tribal Associations of Katanga, known as CONAKAT. A statement of reasons for the founding of CONAKAT showed marked similarities to the ABAKO position according to which the Bangala strangers were allies of the Belgians:

> (1) To show the settlers that Katanga was not a desert before the arrival of the Europeans and that this province could not serve as an outlet to certain settlers who have dreamed of making the region a zone of massive European settlement . . .
> (2) To combat the policy of the companies who have recruited a large part of their labor force from outside the province. This policy has handicapped Katanga tribes in their material and intellectual development, owing to the fact that most good schools are found only in the industrial centers . . .
> (3) To avoid any repetition of the results of the municipal elections of 1957.[86]

In May 1959, as parties were being formed and alliances being forged throughout the Congo, CONAKAT took its first position on the issue of transfer of power, demanding an "autonomous and federated state" of Katanga, to be controlled by native Katangans. This demand is very similar to that of the ABAKO, but in the different political context of

Katanga it had different consequences: it meant that CONA-
KAT became an attractive partner for the settlers political interests. The settlers had abandoned their hopes of a
Rhodesian-style white-run state, and needed African allies.
For the CONAKAT, European financial support was invalu-
able if they were to overcome the organizational headstart
of other groups. In July 1959 the settler movement, *Union
Katangaise,* was admitted to membership in CONAKAT. During 1959 the Katangan political groupings became part of the
overall Congolese network of alliances:

> The Conakat thus developed a political program tinged
> with separatism and adopted an alliance tainted with what
> seemed to other political groups to be the perpetuation of
> European domination under a new guise. The strangers re-
> acted to the growing xenophobia of the Conakat by an in-
> creased interest in the Lumumbist unitary theses . . .[87]

However, the shift to provincial and national competition in
1960 meant that the Luba/Kasai and other strangers, with
no rural backing in Katanga, were no longer major contend-
ers for power. The major competition for the CONAKAT
now came from the Association of Baluba of Katanga, or
BALUBAKAT, based on the Luba populations of Northern
Katanga. BALUBAKAT had belonged to CONAKAT, but
left because of fears of ethnic chauvinism on the part of the
CONAKAT leaders (mainly Lunda and Yeke of Southern
Katanga), and fears of settler and company influences on
CONAKAT.

The north-south polarity was not quite complete; CONA-
KAT and BALUBAKAT each had an "ally behind enemy
lines." CONAKAT had committed itself to reinforcing the
power of chiefs, which won its support from several important Luba chiefs in Northern Katanga. BALUBAKAT
formed a "cartel" or alliance with the ATCAR, an ethnic
party of the Cokwe, traditional rivals of the Lunda in Southwest Katanga.

These competing alliances placed the Luba/Kasai strangers
in quandary. They initially supported the BALUBAKAT, a

policy which made sense both ethnically (the Luba of Kasai are related to those of Katanga) and politically, since the CONAKAT was a common enemy. However, the BALUBA-KAT had allied itself to Lumumba's MNC, whereas back in Kasai, Lumumba had formed an anti-Luba coalition aimed at expelling the Luba/Kasai from areas to which they had migrated under colonial rule (see above).[88]

The elections' results in 1960 were very close: in the national elections, CONAKAT took 8 seats, BALUBAKAT 6, ATCAR 1, with one independent, while in the provincial elections, CONAKAT took 25, the BALUBAKAT Cartel 22, independents 13. BALUBAKAT and its allies received a plurality of votes cast, but its appeal against alleged irregularities was rejected, and all the independents in the Provincial Assembly sided with CONAKAT, enabling the latter to form a government without BALUBAKAT participation.

In Léopoldville, however, CONAKAT fared less well. There were two CONAKAT ministers in Lumumba's enormous cabinet (28 ministers, 10 secretaries of state), both with relatively insignificant ministries. In contrast, Jason Sendwe, head of BALUBAKAT, was named central government High Commissioner for Katanga, a post of ill-defined but potentially considerable powers. (He never assumed this post.) Tshombe, head of CONAKAT, was outraged and declared that CONAKAT had been duped and considered itself free of any obligation to support a government "in the hands of extremists."

The secession of Katanga followed, a secession made possible by the mutiny of the Congolese army, five days after independence. A detailed discussion of the secession and reincorporation of Katanga would exceed the limits of this article.[89] Of direct interest, however, is the fact that the downfall of the Katanga regime was due not only to its failure to obtain international recognition but also to the irreducible BALUBAKAT opposition in North Katanga.[90] In the days following the secession, urgent efforts were made to secure the support of all or part of the BALUBAKAT Cartel. Of the ten ministers in the CONAKAT government, two were

Luba/Katanga but of CONAKAT persuasion. Tshombe offered the BALUBAKAT five ministries. For a short time the BALUBAKAT hesitated; on July 21, representatives of Sendwe submitted to Tshombe a list of proposed ministerial candidates, but without specifying whether they accepted the secession. However, six days later the BALUBAKAT denounced the secession and announced it had refused Tshombe's offers. By August the first reports of dissidence in Luba areas on Northern Katanga began to appear; in September, with the Lumumba threat removed, the young Katanga gendarmerie launched its first "pacification" sorties against what was by then a widespread revolt.

In January 1961, BALUBAKAT leaders in Stanleyville proclaimed that a separate province of North Katanga had been created, in Luba/Cokwe areas, devoted to a unitary Congo. Sporadic fighting continued in North Katanga throughout the period of secession. This counter-secession and Tshombe's attempt to suppress it by force greatly weakened the "self-determination" argument of the CONAKAT regime.

The Intermediate Zone of Sankuru-Maniema[91]

The cases we have discussed until now have involved a major center: Léopoldville, Luluabourg, Élisabethville (with Jadotville and Kolwezi). In contrast, Sankuru and Maniema districts constitute an intermediate zone, far from the major centers, interacting to some extent with each of these centers.

Sankuru District lies in the northern portion of East Kasai Province (i.e., the northeast corner of the former Kasai Province). It is separated from Maniema District by the Lomami River. Maniema constitutes the western half of Kivu Province. Our justification for discussing the two together is that the Tetela (Batetela) who make up the majority of the population of Sankuru are also numerous in Maniema, where they are known as Kusu (Bakusu, Wakusu).[92]

Besides the fact that the Tetela of Maniema are known as Kusu, there is an additional ambiguity in this ethnic label.

Often, the label Tetela applies only to those of the savanna region of Sankuru and to the minority of people of savanna origin (known as Sambala) living in the forest region. The people of forest origin are known as Hamba (Bahamba, Ahamba).[93]

The fact that no Tetela ethnic party emerged in 1959–60 seems due in part to the ambiguities of the Tetela ethnic label (who did it include?) and in part to the marginal position of Sankuru-Maniema in the Congolese communications network.

The two labels Tetela and Kusu go back to the earliest written reports of visits to Sankuru-Maniema. The earliest visitor who has left a written record, the Afro-Arab trader Tippu Tib, reported that the chief Kasongo Rushie and his family, who lived near the Lomami River (but apparently east of it, in what is now Maniema) headed the largest clan of the WaTetera (Tetela) and "all the WaTetera and WaKusu were their people."[94]

In 1876 Stanley arrived in Maniema, and was told by an "Arab" in the entourage of Tippu Tib of a trip he and other "Arabs" had made across the Lualaba into the land of the Kusu, who were very fierce.[95] However, the Arabs crossed the Lualaba near the junction of the Ulindi, thus their Kusu lived far north of the Tetela-Kusu. That the label Kusu is sometimes applied to other peoples as well underscores the ambiguity of the ethnic labels of the area.

From Stanley onward, Europeans consistently described the Tetela-Kusu as fierce and hostile. Von Wissmann, for example, observed that the Tetela were "notorious everywhere for their fierceness."[96] This stereotype clearly has influenced European policy in Sankuru-Maniema, just as did the stereotypes of the Bangala and Luba. Stanley's initial description was greatly reinforced during the 1880s and 1890s by the slave-raiding carried out by some Tetela-Kusu (the Sambala) in the service of Tippu Tib and other "Arabs," then by a series of revolts in which some of these people took part.

Writers of the period of the 1890s show little consistency in their use of the labels Tetela and Kusu. Von Wissmann distinguished the "Batetela of Kassonga Lushia" (Tippu Tib's "Kasongo Rushie") from the "Wakussu, who are part of the Wasongora or Bassonga," located to the east of the former. Hinde, in contrast, called the Kusu a "tribe" of the Tetela.[97]

Gradually, however, the label Kusu became generalized for the Tetela of Maniema, and the label Tetela for the Tetela of Sankuru (with the ambiguities noted above). The fact that the Lomami has remained a provincial boundary through most of the redrafting of the Congo map since the 1880s, doubtless contributed to the stabilization of the use of two labels applied to the same people.

A century ago the Tetela of Sankuru and Maniema were relatively homogeneous in cultural and social terms.[98] Considerable cultural and social differentiation has occurred since then. Due to differences in degree of exposure to the East African Swahili-Islamic culture introduced by Tippu Tib and other "Arabs," and to Western, Christian culture, introduced by the Europeans, considerable cultural and social differentiation has occurred.

Tippu Tib's slave and ivory trading state introduced Islam and Swahili to Maniema. Local Africans, especially Tetela-Kusu, began to adopt East African types of houses, dress, and diet (based on rice). Although the "Arabs" lost out in competition with the Congo Independent State, the processes of change begun in this period survived them. Communities of Muslims of *Ngwana* survived in Kasongo, Kindu, Stanleyville, and other towns along the Lualaba. (*Ngwana*, Swahili for "free man," was a new identity pattern which cut across previous linguistic and cultural boundaries; some Mgwana were Tetela-Kusu, others Bangubangu, Vira, etc.) The Congolese dialect of Swahili (Kingwana) became the *lingua franca* not only of Maniema but of much of the Eastern Congo.

Another consequence of Tippu Tib's abortive state-building in the Eastern Congo was social stratification among the Tetela and their neighbors, separating rulers from rules. Tippu Tib had made Ngongo Leteta (a Songye) his representative on the Lomami, and by 1889 Ngongo had become overlord of several Tetela and Songye settlements and was raiding for slaves and ivory over much of what is now East Kasai Province. Following defeats by the Congo State forces in 1890 and 1892, Ngongo went over to the State, only to be executed that same year for plotting to assassinate the commander of the State forces, Khanis.[99] The reactions to Ngongo's death made it clear that stratification had already begun: the population of the area Ngongo had ruled rose up and killed many of his followers, and Ngongo's six-hundred-man bodyguard, "angry at their power being broken, . . . vowed vengeance against the white man and the rest of Gono's people, whom they had ruled with brutal severity."[100]

The bodyguard was transferred to Luluabourg, where it was incorporated into the *Force Publique,* as were some other men who had served under Ngongo. Subsequently, some of these men (bodyguard and others) took part in a series of revolts, which were identified by the Belgians as "Batetela mutinies." This identification was not apt. The revolts were instigated by the former followers of Ngongo who included Songye, Luba, etc., as well as Tetela. Tetela and other Congolese then joined in.[101]

Barden wrote in the 1940s that "perhaps there never has been a man more hated by the Batetela people than Ngongo Lutete . . . His power extended throughout the Lomami valley, and people are still living there today who were mutilated by his orders . . ." In contrast, Lemarchand wrote in the 1960s that the "Batetela chief Ngongo Lutete (is) remembered today by his people as the former ally of the Free State who became its victim as well."[102] Neither of these generalizations does justice to the complexity of the situation: some Tetela associate themselves with their forebears who were followers of Ngongo, whereas others associate themselves with Ngongo's victims.[103]

Ngongo's successor Lupaka was used by the Congo Independent State to bring under its authority a vast area, east to the Lualaba, north to the Tshuapa, and west to Lac Léopold II. Lupaka had a total force of about six hundred men, trained by former noncoms of the *Force Publique* and mostly armed with modern rifles. His method was to send a small platoon of armed auxiliaries to subdue a particular area; once this had been done Lupaka would leave one of his lieutenants there, with the latter's "acolytes," with the responsibility for maintaining order and collecting taxes. In this way, communities of Sambala (Basambala, Asambala) were built up in the midst of the dominated population.[104]

Later, the Belgian authorities regrouped the Sambala, mainly around the administrative centers;[105] a consequence, presumably unintended, of this regroupment was that the Sambala received a disproportionate share of the educational and economic advantages. The regrouping probably was as important to their subsequent modernization as was their exposure to "Arab" cultural influence.

Among the Tetela, the schools not only contributed to linguistic nationalism ("pantribalism") by dispensing standardized language and history, but also contributed to disunity in that their activities tended to reinforce the cleavage between Sankuru and Maniema. Moreover, it gave certain Tetela subgroups on each side of the river a considerable lead over others in terms of education.

Catholic and Protestant missionaries began working among the Tetela just prior to the First World War. For the Catholics, the Lomami constituted the border between two Apostolic Vicariates: Sankuru was entrusted to the Scheutist Fathers, Maniema to the Holy Ghost Fathers. Tshumbe, first Scheutist station in Tetela country, was founded in 1910; others followed at Lodja, Lubefu, and Katako Kombe.[106] Subsequently, Sankuru was turned over to the Passionist Fathers; the Scheutists had used the Luba-Kasai language as medium of instruction, but the Passionists turned to Otetela, apparently in response to the Protestant challenge.[107]

The Holy Ghost Fathers established their first stations at Kindu (1907) and Kongol (1909), end points of the second section of the C.F.L. railway. More stations were founded at Lubunda, Malela, and Kibombo, all on the rail line. These stations are all in ethnically mixed areas; Swahili was used as medium of instruction.[108]

For the Protestants, Tetela country on both sides of the Lomami constituted a single missionary field, responsibility for which was taken up by an American group, the Methodist Episcopal Church, South. The first Methodist missionaries arrived in Kasai in 1912; the Presbyterians at Luebo suggested Tetela country as a promising field (perhaps taking into account the fact that Scheutists had just moved into the area), and supplied Tetela Christians from around Luebo to act as interpreters. The first mission was established at Wenbo-Nyama, Sankuru, in 1914. In 1921 they established a second station, across the Lomami at Tunda. Later come Minga, Lodja, Katako Kombe, Kindu, and Lomela. The Methodists used Otetela in Sankuru from the beginning, but found that Swahili was necessary in Maniema because the populations were mixed.[109]

Another Protestant body, the "North Sankuru Mission," worked among the non-Tetela of northwest Sankuru. The NSM attempted to establish a station among the Nkutshu of Kole in 1929 but failed because of violent opposition from the local people who had recently revolted against Belgian rule. They finally established a station at Kole in 1937. By 1954 the NSM had made a substantial number of converts at its Loto station, but only a very few at Kole. The NSM used Otetela as the medium of instruction at both these stations; that would make it particularly likely that the Tetela-speaking Sambala were overrepresented among the educated, at the expense of the local Nkutshu and Yela.[110]

The 1956 census indicated that in Maniema, Kindu *territoire* had a substantial lead in the number of people with post-primary education and that Kibombo *territoire* lagged behind the rest of the district. In Sankuru, Lubefu led, and Lodja lagged behind in the same manner.[111]

The Methodists considered all the Tetela-speakers of Sankuru and Maniema to be members of a single Tetela community, essentially similar in language and culture. In contrast, the Catholics tended to use subgroup labels: they referred to the savanna Tetela of Sankuru as "Batetela" and the forest Tetela of Sankuru as "Ahamba."[112] (It seems pos-

sible that his Protestant schooling influenced Patrice Lumumba to undertake the regrouping of the Tetela and Kusu
in a single movement.)

Since the Tetela had begun to receive Western education
at a fairly early date (relative to most peoples of Kasai and
Kivu provinces), they were able to provide members for the
nascent white-collar elite. Raucq reports that in north Sankuru (i.e., north of Lusambo) the Tetela (by which he means
Sambala, or Sambala plus savanna Tetela) have played a role
similar to that of the Luba in Kasai as a whole: wherever
towns or other centers grew up under colonial rule, Tetela
were found filling the jobs of *commis* and *vendeurs*. Together
with the Kusu of Maniema, they covered all of Maniema with
a network of *commis* and minor functionaries, even in the
rural areas.[113] However, in Sankuru, but not in Maniema,
the Tetela took a back seat to the Luba, who had received
education somewhat earlier, and had the better jobs.

The urbanization of the Tetela had several important
characteristics. First, although educated Tetela were fairly
common in the towns, there was little mass migration. Second,
because of the intermediate position of Sankuru, Tetela
tended to migrate in various directions to various cities, rather
than concentrating in one or two.

Lux attributed the low level of migration from north Sankuru to the sparsity of the population, the economic self-
sufficiency of most of the area, and the low level of development of much of the forest portion, where the population
remained semi-nomadic.[114] Also of importance is the low
level of urbanization in and near Tetela country. Kindu and
Lusambo had fewer than twenty thousand people each in the
1950s and no other town in the area had as many as ten thousand.[115]

The transportation network tended to pull the Sankuru-
Maniema region apart, rather than to unify it. Northwest
Sankuru, around Kole, was isolated even in terms of roads.
Lodja, Lomela, and Lusambo were connected to Léopold-
ville via the Lukenie, Lomela, and Sankuru rivers, respectively,
which meant that migrants to Léopoldville from northern,

central, and southern Sankuru arrived separately rather than being mixed together as might have occurred had there been a single route. In contrast, Maniema did lie on a major transport axis, the river and rail link north to Stanleyville (and south to Katanga). Along this route the Islamized Kusu (Ngwana) were an important reference group. The fact that the various Tetela subgroups tended to get drawn into different migration patterns, and hence into different urban "supertribal" groupings, reinforced existing cleavages such as that between Tetela of Sankuru and Tetela-Kusu of Maniema and Lomami, and between forest and savanna Tetela of Sankuru. Also of importance in terms of subsequent political activity was the fact that these Tetela were in markedly differing positions in the patterns of social stratification in the various cities; in a few instances they were dominant but in most they were in secondary positions.

In Luluabourg in the 1950s, Tetela were a small minority (2.7 per cent of the population, as compared to 56 per cent Luba-Kasai, 25 per cent Lulua, 5.8 per cent Lunta, and 4 per cent Songye). The majority of all Tetela (including children) had been born in Luluabourg, but the majority of adults had been born in the Katako Kombe area. No other part of Kasai north of the Sankuru River was represented by more than a handful of people. The Tetela were by far the most educated ethnic group in Luluabourg, on an average; however, in absolute numbers, educated Tetela were far fewer than Luba.[116] Many of these Tetela had worked in Lusambo before the provincial capital was shifted. In Luluabourg even more than in Lusambo, their upward mobility seems to have been blocked by the Luba.

In Léopoldville, the Tetelas seem to have been organized in two ethnic associations: Tetela of Sankuru in the *Fédération des Batetela,* and Tetela-Kusu of Maniema in the *Fédération du Kivu-Maniema.*[117]

Tetela-Kusu have been in Élisabethville in small numbers since the early days. The first ethnic associations recognized by the authorities, in 1926, included both the *Compagnie des Batetela* and another body for "Kusu," suggesting that the two considered themselves to be separate groups.[118] They tended to remain separate because Tetela and Kusu arrived by different routes and at different periods. The *Union Minière du Haut Katanga* recruited in Maniema in 1926–38, but stopped because of high mortality rates.[119] The same company recruited heavily in Sankuru in 1936–41. During this period approximately two thirds of the sixteen thousand workers recruited came from Sankuru. (It is unclear how many of these were Tetela, how many Luba or Songye.)[120]

Although Tetela may have been fairly numerous at the UMHK by the 1940s (UMHK did not keep records of ethnic origin, so it is impossible to be sure), they were few in the *Centre extra-coutumier* (African sector of the city). In 1956, there were 109 Kusu and 191 Tetela adult males in the C.E.C. The forest zone of Sankuru (Lodja, Lomela, and Kole *territoires*) was almost unrepresented. Despite their small numbers, Tetela and Kusu supplied a number of elite members in South Katanga. Paul Kimwanga, a Kusu, was first subchief of the C.E.C. of Élisabethville. Pascal Luanghy, a Tetela-Kusu from Maniema, was a member of the council of the C.E.C. of Élisabethville, then *bourgmestre* of Albert commune, Élisabethville. Victor Lundula, a Tetela from Sankuru, was *bourgmestre* of Kinkulu commune, Jadotville.[121]

In Stanleyville the categories of Kusu and *Arabises* (or Ngwana) overlapped to a large extent. In their 1956 account, Pons, et al., assigned the *Arabises* to their respective "tribes," e.g., Kusu, Kono, with the result that Kusu was the second largest ethnic category, at 10 per cent. In his 1962 book, in contrast, Pons restructured the same 1953 data so as to preserve *Arabise* as a separate category, comprising 11.8 per cent of the population. The *Arabises* were relatively prestigious in Stanleyville in 1953, when Pons's data was gathered. They were referred to as "the rulers here before the Europeans." However, the "clever" Lokele, with their reputation for getting on, were even more prestigious.[122] Many of the Kusu lived in the *village des Arabises,* outside the city of Stanleyville, and in a former *Arabise* village which had been absorbed into the Belge II quarter of the city. In Belge I, lo-

cated close to the center of Stanleyville and considered relatively "civilized" and fashionable, there were large numbers
of Kusu (along with Lokele and Boa) but not in ethnic clusters.[123] In short, the *Arabises* and/or Kusu were relatively
well represented in the upper levels of Stanleyville's social
stratification, but not the best represented, that position being
held by the Lokele.

Tetela and Kusu were separate categories in Stanleyville,
as is shown by the fact that there were both an *Association
des Bakusu,* recognized by the administration, and an unrec-
ognized *Mutuelle des Batetela,* as of 1953.[124] This seems to
reflect the fact that it had recently become possible for Tetela
to come to Stanleyville from Sankuru by road, rather than
Kindu and up the river.

In Kindu, in contrast, the Tetela-Kusu seem to have been
dominant in the elite, thanks to the educational advantage
they received from the early founding of mission schools in
Kindu, Tunda, etc., and especially from the founding of an
École des candidats-commis in 1929.[125] This educational advantage led to Tetela-Kusu dominance not only in Maniema
but elsewhere in Kuvu as well. In Bukavu, the provincial
capital, Tetela-Kusu were numerous in the administration but
relatively few in the working force.[126]

In 1959–60, the Tetela-Kusu gave overwhelming support
to the *Mouvement National Congolais* which was led by Patrice Lumumba. Lumumba's goal was the establishment of a
national, i.e., Congo-wide single party.[127] This goal could be
explained with reference to Lumumba's membership in the
clerical elite or "rising class" of the Congo. This class has a
tendency to promote regional or national unity at the expense
both of localism and of class distinctions.[128] However, there
would remain the question of why Lumumba and his colleagues aspired to found a Congo-wide party, rather than a
regional single party such as ABAKO. Here it could be argued that the economic interests of Sankuru and Maniema
were determinants. These districts depended on links to the
rest of the Congo for their prospects of economic development. Such arguments would not be incorrect, but they would

be incomplete. To complete the answer, one must take into account the characteristics of the Tetela ethnic group, which restricted the uses to which it could be put as a political resource. First of all, the Tetela numbered only a few hundred thousand, their homeland was divided between three provinces, and their elite members were scattered. A Tetela ethnic party would have had only a marginal impact on Congo-wide or even province-wide events. On the other hand, as one element in a national party, the Tetela could furnish to a Tetela politician a source of support in most parts of the country.[129]

Also of importance is the fact that the Tetela found themselves in markedly different situations in the two provinces where most of them lived, situations which suggested radically different strategies of party-building. In Kasai, the Tetela (like the Lulua, Songye, Kuba, and others) were underdogs to the Luba. From the viewpoint of the underdogs, the Luba appeared to have profited from Belgian rule by gaining an advantageous position, upon which they could capitalize after independence. They were overrepresented in the clerical elite; ethnic polarization was already a fact in Kasai, due to the presence of the militantly anti-Luba *Association Lulua-Frères*. These circumstances dictated to the Tetela elite a strategy of forming an ethnic party of Tetela and related Mongo of northern Kasai (Nkutshu, Kengese, etc.), then entering an anti-Luba coalition with the other ethnic parties. In contrast, the situation in Kivu Province, where the Kusu were the leading elite element, recommended a strategy of forming as broad a party as possible and attempting to avoid ethnic polarization. These two contradictory strategies could best be reconciled within the framework of a nominally non-ethnic party.

The difficulties represented by the ambiguity of the Tetela ethnic label and by the differing strategies dictated in the two main provincial arenas were reflected in the Congress held in Lodja in March 1960, attended by representatives of Tetela-Kusu ethnic associations from fourteen localities (including Léopoldville, Luluabourg, Élisabethville, Usumbura, Bukavu,

Katako-Kombe, and Lodja). The Congress tended to be dominated by educated Tetela from the savanna zone of Sankuru; the bureau elected by the Congress included four savanna Tetela from Sankuru (one of whom represented the forest town of Lodja), and one Kusu from Maniema (Pascal Luanghy).[130]

The Congress decided not to set up an ethnic party, but rather to support the majority party in the area, which was of course the MNC-Lumumba. It also decided to adopt a new ethnic label, "Ankutshu-Anamongo," to apply to all Tetela-Kusu. This awkward label represented a compromise. The report of the Congress indicated that the label "Ana-Mongo" (Sons of Mongo) had been adopted by majority vote, but the chiefs from Maniema protested against this decision, saying that if the label "Ankutshu" were not adopted they would return home, and refuse to cooperate with the others.[131]

Support for the "Ana-Mongo" label was to be expected from évolué elements, familiar with the pan-Mongo idea propagated by the Flemish administrators and missionaries Van der Kerken, Hulstaert, et al. The resistance of the chiefs of Maniema suggests that the idea was an imported one. However, there was also a tactical aspect. For Lumumba, the Mongo label would have been attractive as a basis for a larger electoral coalition, notable among the Mongo of Équateur, Orientale, and Léopoldville provinces. The resistance of Maniema delegates to the Mongo label may have reflected concern that it would stress differences between the Tetela-Kusu and the other peoples of Maniema, e.g., Binja, Bangubangu, with whom they had close relations.

The sweeping victory of the MNC-L in Sankuru (all four National Assembly seats, 14–15 in the Kasai Provincial Assembly) concealed the emergence of a split within the ranks of the Tetela, a split which cannot be understood without reference to the ambiguity of the Tetela ethnic definition. As mentioned above, that label sometimes included only Tetela of the savanna, including the Sambala minority living in the forest but of savanna origin.

In 1960 the Lodja politicians, feeling neglected by the dominant savanna group, organized a counter-group calling itself *Asa-Ekonda* (forest people) and distinguishing itself from the *Ase-Eswe* (savanna people, including the Sambala). This distinction corresponds to that between Tetela and Hamba, except that the *Ase-Ekonda* included not only forest Tetela but their Mongo neighbors as well. (Nkutshu, Yela, Mbuli, etc.)

In March 1960, about the time of the Lodja Congress, the *Association des Atetela de Lodja* (Lodja people living in Léopoldville) allegedly asked André Diumasumbu, one of the very few Ekonda with a higher education, to defend Ekonda interests. Diumasumbu convened a Congress of Ekonda "intellectuals" which approved a list of Ekonda candidates for the national and provincial elections of May. However, the Ekonda leaders apparently decided the time was too short to launch a party of their own. Instead they agreed to support the MNC-L provided that they received a fair share of the candidatures. A number of Ekonda were in fact given places on the MNC-L lists—Diumasumbu was elected to the Chamber of Deputies—but the Ekonda complained afterwards that they had been slighted.[132] In Maniema, the MNC-L won a sweeping victory, and showed some strength elsewhere in Kivu, especially through its alliances.

Linking of the Regional Political Fields

Until the late 1950s, the regional political fields had been linked mainly by the European organizations: State, Church, companies.[133] Following the Belgian government announcement of January 1959, a number of Congolese elite members attempted to link the various regional fields by means of political parties. Most of these attempts were abortive. Both the PSA and the MNC-Kalonji were intended to be Congo-wide, but became regional or ethnic by default. The most successful attempt at a Congo-wide party was that of the MNC-Lumumba.

The results of the May 1960 elections indicate the low level of linkage between regional fields. Only the MNC-Lumumba

and the "moderate" (pro-Belgian) PNP won seats in the
Chamber of Deputies from more than one province. Half
the seats went to ethnic parties, or regional parties with
definite ethnic overtones.[134] The MNC-L won 33 of the 137
seats, picking up an additional eight seats through alliances
with minor parties in Kasai (through the anti-Luba front).
In addition to sweeping Sankuru and Maniema, the MNC-L
did well both at Stanleyville and in Orientale Province in
general; the latter results seem attributable to the extreme
ethnic heterogeneity of both Stanleyville and Orientale, which
favored a non-ethnic party, and to the "martyrdom" which
Lumumba had achieved by being imprisoned after riots at
Stanleyville in 1959.

PSA and ABAKO, with 13 and 12 seats respectively, were
the second and third largest parties. The PNP had 15, if the
votes of its ethnic affiliates in Léopoldville and Équateur
provinces (LUKA, MEDERCO, *Association Ngwaka*) are
combined with those for the PNP *per se*. CEREA's total of
10 is misleading in that that party's factions were virtually
independent by that time.[135]

Lumumba's lack of a majority has been attributed to the
short time the MNC-L had to organize. It would seem to reflect also the consequence of acquiring allies on the basis of
local enmities; that is, each ally brought along an opponent.

The immediate cause of the chaos which followed Congolese independence was a mutiny of the army (former *Force
Publique*), which had been considered the most truly national Congolese institution. The alleged Congo-wide, national
orientation of the *Force Publique* had been eroded in the
terminal colonial period as leaders of the political parties,
fearful of the possible use of the *Force Publique* against
them, had sought to forestall this possibility by establishing
close relations with the (Congolese) noncommissioned officers. Each politician apparently concentrated on members of
his own ethnic group; for example, by 1959 Kasa-Vubu could
count on the support of adjutant Kokolo, a Kongo who became a colonel after independence.

PROVINCES OF THE CONGO AS OF 1963
Source: Congo 1964 (Brussels: CRISP, 1965).

By 1960 there was a growing malaise among the troops concerning the slowness of the Africanization program (which would have produced the first Congolese officers by 1963). The soldiers blamed the nationalist leaders for failing to give them a fair share of the benefits of independence; Lumumba, who was responsible for defense in the pre-independence Executive College, was a particular target of their resentment. The mutiny of July 1960 seems to have been spontaneous; Belgian intervention, supposedly to protect Belgian nationals, caused the mutiny to spread.[136]

In 1961–62, the various Congolese factions—ranging from the Katanga secessionists to the unitarist heirs of Lumumba —came to agree upon the need for new provinces and a federal structure.[137] Some regional and/or ethnic groupings actively sought new provinces; those which were less enthusiastic found themselves left with smaller provinces when other areas had opted out. For example, in Léopoldville Province, the secession of Central Kongo, Kwango, and Lac Léopold II left Kwilu as a separate province despite the unitarist orientation of its PSA leaders. In Kasai, the secession of South Kasai (the Luba area) was followed by the disintegration of the remainder of the province into four pieces, as the anti-Luba coalition had lost its *raison-d'être*. In all, there were twenty-one new provinces in place of the six inherited from the colonial regime.

The 1960 elections, the ousting of the Lumumba government, and the splitting up of the six original provinces each produced winners and losers among the Congolese politicians and their followers. Similarly, the disruption of the Congolese economy affected some parts of the country much more than others. Young has described the result as a fusion of the "identity and distribution crises . . . through the phenomenon of fragmented perception of deprivation." He explains:

> The degree to which the maldistribution of benefits of independence affected lower strata differed markedly; the Lower Congo (i.e., the Kongo area) and Southern Katanga remained relatively affluent, whereas the heartland of the central basin, North Katanga, and Northeastern Congo (i.e., Orientale) were particularly affected. The sentiment of deprivation was especially acute among groups which felt themselves excluded from political power . . .[138]

There had been some expectation that the smaller provinces would be stronger than the big ones, because they were more homogeneous. Virtually the reverse proved to be the case. During the period 1963–65, rebellion broke out in the new provinces of Kwilu and Central Kivu, and spread from Central Kivu to cover most of the eastern half of the country. (It is probably significant that Kwilu and Central Kivu were among the provinces which were left behind when other areas seceded, rather than being formed as new provinces on the initiative of local leaders.)

In the following sections, the politics of ethnic sub-nationalism will be discussed as it occurred in five of the political fields of the rebellion: Kwilu, Central Kivu, North Katanga, Maniema, and Sankuru, then in the rebel zone as a whole.

Rebellion in the Political Field of Kwilu

The government of the new Kwilu Province was PSA/Kamitatu in majority, with minority representation of PSA/Gizenga and ABAZI. This government, given some fanfare as a model of effectiveness, launched a program of "planned village development." The villagers resented this interference with their affairs, especially as it came from people they saw as living high on their taxes while their own living conditions worsened. The value of the Congolese franc was falling, the distribution of goods was breaking down, and unemployed men were returning to their villages. Among the latter were PSA supporters who had been recruited into the police in Léopoldville, then sacked when they struck for higher pay.[139]

The Pende and Mbun saw these problems as affecting them more than other ethnic groups. They held only three of twelve ministries in the provincial government, although they made up almost half the population of the province and thus had contributed heavily to the electoral victory of the PSA in 1960. The Pende favorite son, Gizenga, was in prison.

In 1963, Pierre Mulele (a PSA/Gizenga leader who had been a minister in the Lumumba cabinet) organized camps in Mbun country, at which ideological and tactical training was given. A rebellion was launched in October. By that time, Mbun support for the rebellion was nearly unanimous. The Pende were contacted second. Some chiefs hesitated and were assassinated.[140] In due course, most of the Pende of Kwilu supported the rebellion, and it spread from them to Pende living in Kwango, to the west, and to those in Unité

Kasaienne Province, to the east. However, not all ethnic groups joined the rebellion:

(1) The Yaka followed their King, who opted for the central government against Mulele. Moreover, the Yaka had just obtained a Kwango Province, in which they were dominant, and probably saw the rebellion as another attempt by Kwiluites to dominate Kwango.

(2) The Mbala and related peoples, living around Kikwit, identified with the provincial government. Perhaps more importantly, they were identified with the government by the Mbun and Pende and for that reason were the subject of rebel attacks.

(3) The Yans tended to favor creation of a new North Kwilu Province, but Mulele with his background of Lumumbist unitarism could not be expected to favor the proliferation of small provinces.

(4) The Ding, who had split on the question of whether to support PSA or ABAZI in 1960, split again on the issue of support for the rebellion. Due to the opposition of these neighboring groups as well as the efforts of the Congo army, the rebellion was encapsulated.

Eventually the Mbun and Pende, who had a tradition of living together, split. At the moment of the establishment of Belgian overrule, the situation of the Pende had been precarious. Their land had been invaded by the Cokwe and they escaped complete defeat thanks to the Belgians who pushed back the Cokwe and freed the Pende who had been enslaved. Many Pende had taken refuge among the Mbun, where their position was distinctly subordinate. However, the subsequent process of assimilation operated to the advantage of the Pende culture. Today the language barrier has been overcome, in that all Mbun and Pende adults know both languages. Mixed marriages are frequent. There also were some antecedents for conflict: according to one tradition, the Pende could collaborate with the Mbun but not submit to their leadership.[141] Moreover, since independence the Pende had revived their

former custom of circumcision; the fact that the Mbun did
not practice circumcision meant that they were not really
men in Pende eyes.[142]

The basic demand of the rebels is summed up in the slogan
Mulele used: "the second independence." The "second independence" would give the Kwiluites the benefits which
they had been promised in 1959–60 but which had failed to
materialize. There are striking parallels between the Kwilu
rebellion, the idea of the "second independence" in particular,
and the millenarian movement *Mpeve* ("Spirit"). *Mpeve* was
an offshoot of a secret society, *Lupambula*, which had appeared in 1947, coinciding with the return of some Pende
who had been imprisoned in connection with the Pende revolt of 1931. *Mpeve* enjoyed considerable support in 1959–
60, especially among the Ding and Mbun. The sect had identified the 1960 independence with the coming of the millen-
nium, yet it enjoyed a resurgence after 1960 (among the
Ding and Lwer) despite the failure of the promised millen-
nium to materialize.[143]

Rebellion in the Political Field of Central Kivu

The old Kivu Province had two principal towns: Bukavu,
the capital, and Kindu, principal town of Maniema District.
Each town was better connected with Orientale and Katanga
provinces than each was to the other.[144] Of the four peoples
of Eastern Kivu, who were most active in politics there, two
(the Shi or Bashi and the Furiiru or Bafulerso) belong to
Vansina's "Interlacustrine Bantu" cultural region (i.e., they
are culturally closer to the peoples of Rwanda, Burundi, and
adjacent areas of Uganda and Tanzania than they are to the
other Congolese). The other two peoples, the Lega (Warega)
and Bembe (Babembe belong to his "People of Maniema"
cultural region). The Shi and Furiiru had centralized, stratified chiefdoms, each headed by a ruler called the Mwami. By
contrast, Lega and Bembe had segmentary systems. What is
more important for recent political history, however, is that

two of these peoples had rulers widely regarded as illegitimate; among the Bembe, these were "chiefs" who had been imposed by the Belgians on the previously acephalous system, whereas among the Furiiru it was a Mwami considered corrupt.[145]

Bukavu was unusual among Congolese cities in that its immediate hinterland was densely populated by a single ethnic group, the Shi. This had the consequence that intra-Shi conflicts were felt immediately in the city.

According to Verhaegen, "three foci of tensions of tribal origin" conditioned political life in Bukavu from 1959 to 1963, namely rivalries among:

(1) Kusu from Maniema and peoples of Eastern Kivu;

(2) the Shi and immigrant minorities at Bukavu;

(3) the two major Shi chiefdoms, Kabare and Ngweshe.[146]

The first two of these rivalries of course were cross-cutting, in that the Shi are one of the peoples of Eastern Kivu, and the Kusu one of several peoples represented at Bukavu by immigrant minorities.

During the period 1960–63, many changes in the provincial government occurred, gradually leading to a polarization of forces. At Bukavu, the MNC/Lumumba (Kusu-dominated) was opposed by PDC (anti-Kusu, led by Lega). The faction of the Furiiru associated with Musa Marandura, claimant to the Mwamiship, had switched its allegiance to the MNC/L. Among the Bembe, hostility between the youth, members of the Young Wing of the MNC/Lumumba, and the chiefs had increased; in the 1962 debate on dismemberment of Kivu Province, the youth favored inclusion of Fizi District in the new Maniema Province (dominated by a Kusu, MNC/Lumumba majority) whereas the chiefs favored union of Fizi with North Katanga (where there is a Bembe minority). The Lega were divided into three camps: those wanting to remain with Central Kivu (capital, Bukavu), those wanting to join Maniema, and those wanting a separate Lega Province of south Kivu. (It should be noted that those wanting to join

Maniema wanted the boundaries drawn so as to exclude the Kusu.)

Willame observes that these "two poles of agitation"—Bukavu, with its Kusu vs. anti-Kusu conflict, Fizi, with its youth vs. chiefs conflict—"constituted a milieu particularly propitious for the implantation of 'Mulelist' rebels six months after the creation of the province (of Central Kivu)."[147] This may be so, but in Central Kivu as in Kwilu the rebellion lined up opponents as rapidly as it did supporters.

The rebellion in Central Kivu began as an attempt by the Marandura faction to overthrow the current Mwami of the Furiiru. As in Kwilu, there was some ideological preparation: Marandura's son had organized "a series of ideological retreats" in which "a somewhat less refined version of Mulele's doctrine" was taught to young Furiiru and some MNC youth from Bukavu (ethnic affiliation not specified).[148] The provincial President, a Furiiru, was supporting the incumbent Mwami. Therefore, the rebellion may have had an objective as broad as the overthrow of the provincial government, but there is no evidence that the objective was broader. The broadening of the objective of the rebellion to the overthrow of the Congo government came in with the takeover of rebel leadership by a faction led by Gaston-Émile Soumialot and Nicolas Olenga, both Kusu associated with the MNC-L. The Bembe became active participants in the rebellion. The Shi and Lega both came to oppose it, after some hesitation.[149]

A network of enmities, some long-standing and others of recent origin, seems to have contributed to those decisions to support or oppose the rebellion. According to Masson, traditional enmity between the hill-dwelling Shi and the plains-dwelling Furiiru, and between the hill-dwelling Bembe and plains-dwelling Lega, was important as regards the decisions to defend Bukavu and Mwenga against rebel attack.[150]

This process of lining up supporters and opponents should not be thought of as automatic. In particular, the position of the Shi seems to have been decided at the last moment after a visit to Bukavu by then-Premier Tshombe during which he promised the Mwami Kabare that he would reinforce traditional rulers.[151] Some of the Lega seem initially to have favored the rebellion; their opposition crystallized after some Lega were massacred by the rebels at Kindu.[152]

Encapsulation of the rebellion (such as occurred in Kwilu) was avoided when the Soumialot faction supplanted the Furiiru leadership and carried the rebellion into Maniema. About the same time, the Bembe came to constitute the "shock troops" of the rebel forces and as such the main target of the animosity of other groups.[153]

As early as 1964, some tension was evident between Furiiru and Bembe, but this became more acute in 1965 when central government victories began to restrict the area under rebel control. The Bembe would not accept that the Furiiru put their regional interests before those of the revolution, whereas the Furiiru were irritated by the arrogance of the Bembe.[154]

Rebellion in the Political Field of North Katanga

The core of the new province of North Katanga was inhabited by Luba/Katanga. It had voted heavily for the BALUBAKAT in 1960, and then fought a bloody insurrection against the Tshombe regime. The rural Luba population had played an active part in the insurrection, but in 1964 it remained passive.

Albertville, the provincial capital, lay outside the Luba core area. In 1960 Albertville territory had split three ways, one of its seats in the Katanga Provincial Assembly going to the *Union Congolaise* (PNP affiliate), one to the BALUBAKAT-MNC/Lumumba cartel, and one to an individual candidate. Albertville was the largest center of population in North Katanga, and the only one which was really a city.[155] Two further characteristics apparently combined to give political competition in Albertville an elite character:

(1) It was an old town which had had many "strangers" for a long time, and had grown up slowly.

(2) The African *cites* were scattered, and thus had little influence on events in the center of town.

By 1964 the BALUBAKAT government of North Katanga had disintegrated:

a complex factional rivalry, dating back to 1960, existed between Sendwe, first leader of the BALUBAKAT, and Prosper Mwamba-Ilunga, who had led the insurrection against Tshombe in 1960–62. In August 1963, Sendwe had managed to oust Mwamba-Ilunga as provincial President; in March 1964, the Mwamba-Ilunga forces turned the tables, and Sendwe in turn was forced out. At this juncture, Sendwe requested central government intervention to restore him to power, alleging procedural irregularities in the provincial assembly vote of no confidence. Sendwe was restored to office by the army in April, but the situation then deteriorated rapidly.[156]

A coup organized by younger Luba politicians with the help of the BALUBAKAT Youth, ousted Sendwe again; he was again restored to power by the ANC, which exercised indiscriminate repression against the population of Albertville. Thus, when Bembe rebels from Central Kivu entered Albertville seeking revenge for an ANC massacre,[157] the population welcomed them. In addition to Bembe, the rebel column included Vira, Rundi, and Rwanda from Central Kivu, the Boyd, Bangubangu, and Tumbwe villagers from areas along the route south.[158] A small proportion of the BALUBAKAT Youth of Albertville enlisted to defend the city, in response to an appeal from Sendwe, but resistance was slight.

Following the fall of Albertville, large numbers of soldiers and police joined the rebel army, as did some members of the BALUBAKAT Youth, who had fled from Albertville following their abortive coup a few weeks earlier.

During the period of rebel administration of North Katanga (July–August 1964), hostility grew between the population and the rebel army; although the main cause of this hostility was the indiscipline of the rebel army, the fact that the latter was composed mainly of "strangers" probably exacerbated matters.

A number of ethnic conflicts occurred among the rebels themselves. The "provisional government" installed four days after the seizure of Albertville was headed by I. Masengo, a Luba. This government was seen as unrepresentative by leaders of other political and/or ethnic factions at Albertville, and Soumialot intervened to decide that each "nationalist" party represented at Albertville (MNC/L, CEREA/K, PSA/G, BALUBAKAT) should have a share in the government. This new government thus was relatively representative of organized political forces in the city, but to the same extent unrepresentative of the province as a whole. In the meantime, however, Masengo had gone on filling the bureaucracy with BALUBAKAT members, with the result that tensions between government and bureaucracy took on ethnic overtones. Similarly, conflict between military and civilian authorities, due to the greater concern for the welfare of the population on the part of the latter, also took on ethnic overtones because the officers were mainly Tetela/Kusu.[159]

The fact that the rebellion in North Katanga was operating against a background of apathy in the countryside and involved such chaos in the city, goes far to explain Soumialot's decision (August 1964) to withdraw from Albertville in the face of mercenary counterattacks and to operate from the more promising base being opened up farther to the north.[160]

Rebellion in the Political Field of Maniema

Maniema had less ethnic unity than most of the other new provinces. Each of its principal peoples was divided by a border:

(1) The Lega were found both in eastern Maniema and in Central Kivu Province.

(2) The Komo (Bakumu) were found both in northern Maniema as well as in Haut-Congo, south of Kisangani (Stanleyville).

(3) The Songye were found in southern Maniema as well as in Lomami.

(4) The Tetela-Kusu were found in western Maniema and in Sankuru, and were represented by important immigrant minorities in Bukavu and Stanleyville.[161]

This situation meant that ethnic conflict was as likely under rebel rule as in earlier periods. At the same time, it meant that Maniema was an excellent center from which to export rebellion to other areas.

Among the Komo, the millenarian cult Kitawala was widespread. The tendency toward noncooperation with the authorities which Kitawala had inherited from the parent Watch Tower movement (Jehovah's Witnesses) had been reinforced by repression, both before and after independence. Hence it is not surprising that the Komo, and especially the Kitawalists among them, welcomed the 1964 rebellion and took advantage of it to kill local officials who had been unfavorable to them. Nor is it surprising that the Kitawalists came to pose a problem for the rebel authorities.[162]

The Komo and Songye were relatively unimportant in Maniema politics; Songye leaders were attempting to secede, to join the Songye Province of Lomami. The rivalry which dominated Maniema politics was that between Kusu and Lega. The Lega politicians had led the anti-Kusu coalition at Bukavu, and had attempted to have the Kusu excluded from the new Maniema Province.

The rebel conquest of Maniema began with the gradual infiltration of small bands of rebels from Central Kivu. A witness reported that rebels who clashed with Lega "warriors" along the Mwenga–Kasongo road in late June 1964 were mostly Bembe from Fizi.[163]

The Lega marshaled substantial resistance to the rebels, defeating an attempt to capture the town of Mwenga.[164] In contrast, Kindu fell without a fight. The rebels who took Kindu included many Bembe and people from Kasongo, especially so-called "Wazimba." The Wazimba are in fact Southern Binja, and as such they had "cousins" at Kindu, the Northern Binja or "Wasongola." Binja and Lega were traditionally hostile at Kasongo.[165] The seizure of Maniema seems to have constituted, for some of the participants, an anti-Lega crusade.

During the period of rebel administration at Kindu, there was sharp rivalry between the provincial government and the *conseil des sages*. This rivalry reflected the differing ethnic and social composition of the two bodies:

> In terms of its composition the government was neither "popular" nor "revolutionary." It very well could have been elected by the Provincial Assembly under the previous regime. Its principal characteristic was that it was formed of the "counter-elite," that is, of that fraction of the politico-administrative elite which possessed the same characteristics as the group in power but had previously been pushed into the opposition . . .[166]

In contrast, the *conseil des sages* (which combined judicial and legislative functions and owed its title to strong Muslim influence, in Kindu) consisted of twenty territorial presidents of the MNC/L and one of the CEREA/Kashamura. The President was a Bembe, the First Vice President a Lega:

> The choice of two non-Kusu figures could indicate a wish on the part of the rebel leaders of Kindu to gain the confidence of Lega and Bembe sub-nationalists. In 1962, considerations of the same order had led the Kindu nationalists to install Kanga and Kisanga, two Lega, at the head of Maniema Province. It was not so much a question of creating a really balanced sharing of power—all the important functions, civil as well as military, were in the hands of the Kusu and peoples of South Maniema—as of taking into account the sensitivities of the minorities by safeguarding representative forms, and of profiting from the already existing divisions among the Lega.[167]

The Rebellion as Linkage of Political Fields

The rebel army (*Armée Populaire de Libération,* or APL) met with no resistance traveling upriver from Kindu to Stanleyville. Once they controlled Stanleyville, the communications hub of Northwest Congo, the rebels were able to begin linking regional political fields into a Congolese People's Republic. From Stanleyville, APL columns took all of the former Orientale Province in six weeks.

In Sankuru, Ekonda, and Eswe factions had been struggling for dominance since independence. These factions were not wholly ethnic or regional, in that each had an ideological dimension as well. The Eswe faction attracted some Ekonda who favored Lumumbist nationalism, whereas the Ekonda faction was anti-Lumumbist and attracted some Eswe on that basis. The APL took Sankuru without resistance, overthrowing the provincial government and installing a Lumumbist regime in its place. However, the Ekonda-Eswe split worked to the disadvantage of the rebels, as of course the Tetela-Kusu of Maniema appeared to the Ekonda to be more Eswe coming to dominate them. The rebels were driven out of Kole, in the forest zone, without much difficulty. In contrast, Katako Kombe and Lubefu resisted the ANC (Congolese National Army) counterattack for more than a month.[168]

At its peak, the rebel zone extended to within a hundred miles of Luluabourg, and to within seventy-five miles of Coquilhatville in Équateur Province. However, the farther the APL got from the Lumumbist heartland, the thinner its ranks became and the more it was seen by local people as being composed of "strangers." Thus, it was vulnerable to the counterattacks of the ANC (re-equipped and reinforced by white mercenaries and Katangan *gendarmes*). The Belgian-American parachute drop on Stanleyville deprived the rebels not only of the capital of their People's Republic, but more importantly of the hub of their communications system, virtually ending the possibility of their taking over the country:

> Both the heterogeneity of the ranks and the ethnic homogeneity of the officer corps (made the APL) an alien force in the countryside outside of Maniema. As long as the garrisons were posted in towns this did not matter. When it was forced into rural refuge, it was unable in most areas to be as fish in water, following the Maoist metaphor.[169]

The dominant symbol, Lumumba, connoted something equivalent to the "second independence," i.e., supporters of the rebellion were given a second chance to support Lumumba and gain the rewards which had not been forthcoming in 1960.

The Mobutu Government

Since the military *coup* of November 1965, successive governments headed by General Joseph Mobutu have had as a major preoccupation the reduction of ethnic and regional sub-nationalism.[170] In the first government, Colonel Leonard Mulamba served as Prime Minister. After meeting with political figures from each province, Mulamba named a cabinet of twenty-two members, one from each province and one from the city of Léopoldville. This cabinet did not differ markedly from the previous one: six ministers stayed in office. Several former ministers (members of the 1960 political generation) also were included.[171]

The first major change occurred in October 1966: Colonel Mulamba was ousted, and the post of Prime Minister abolished. The motives for the change seem mixed; some of them involve jealousy of Mulamba, and criticisms of the manner in which he was performing his duties. The abolition of the post of Prime Minister eliminated a source of instability which had been particularly acute in 1960 (Kasa-Vubu vs. Lumumba) and in 1965 (Kasa-Vubu vs. Tshombe).[172]

Major cabinet reshuffles in December 1966 and October 1967 represented successive cuts in the number of 1960 politicians in the cabinet, and successive increases in the number of university or *école supérieure* graduates.[173]

Another area of major change is that of the provincial structure. Mobutu halted, then reversed the process of fragmentation which began in 1960–61 with the secession of Katanga and South Kasai and was legitimized in 1962–63 by the laws establishing new provinces and in 1964 by the federalist Constitution. From twenty-one provinces in 1965 at the time of the *coup,* the number was cut first to twelve, then to eight, representing a nearly complete restoration of the provincial boundaries of June 1960.

The weakness of the twenty-one small provinces had become evident, especially in 1965 when rebellion swept through many of them. Even before the *coup d'état* which brought Mobutu to power, tendencies to reunification had appeared in Katanga, Orientale, Kasai, and Équateur, but these had failed due to local forces canceling one another out.[174]

Mobutu's intention to remedy the situation was signaled in February 1966 by an editorial in the publication *Actualités Africaines* (widely regarded as mouthpiece for the President) in which it was noted that Kwango, Lac Léopold II, Unité Kasaienne, Sankuru, and North Kivu provinces all were too small in population and/or too weak economically to stand alone.[175] In March the High Commissioner for the Plan, Alphonse Nguvulu released a proposal (in his personal capacity, not on behalf of the Mobutu government) for amalgamation of the twenty-one existing provinces into nine:

(1) Western Congo (combining Central Kongo, Kwango, Kwilu);

(2) Équateur (Cuvette Centrale, Lac Léopold II, Moyen Congo);

(3) Northern Congo (Ubangi, Uele);

(4) Eastern Congo (Haut-Congo, Kibali-Ituri);

(5) Kivu (North Kivu, Central Kivu);

(6) N'Bonga Baluba (South Kasai, North Katanga);

(7) Central Congo (Maniema, Sankuru, Lomami);

(8) Katanga (Eastern Katanga, Lualaba);

(9) Kasai (Luluabourg, Unité Kasaienne).

Léopoldville would be a Federal District.[176]

Nguvulu is a Kongo who was a member not of the ABAKO but of the *Parti du Peuple,* and served in Lumumba's government. Nonetheless, he resurrected the ABAKO proposal of 1960 for a province of Central Kongo, except for the exclusion of Léopoldville. In general, his proposals show a greater regard for linguistic-cultural boundaries than for the colonial provinces. Under this plan the weakness of the little provinces would be avoided, but their ethnic basis continued. The Nguvulu plan stirred up a great deal of controversy in Léopoldville, but the controversy was cut short by the release four days later of a memorandum from Mobutu proposing the following changes in provincial boundaries:

(1) The "former province of Léopoldville" (i.e., as it stood in 1960) would now include two provinces:

    a. Kwango, Kwilu, and Lac Léopold II, amalgamated under a name to be announced, with Banningville as capital;

    b. Central Kongo, as it stood in 1966;

(2) The former province of Équateur would be reinstated, by amalgamation of Moyen Congo, Cuvette Centrale, and Ubangi;

(3) The former Orientale Province would be left in three pieces because the three pieces (Haut-Congo, Uele, Kibali-Ituri) were "viable";

(4) The former Kivu Province would now include two provinces:

    a. Kivu, amalgamating Central Kivu and North Kivu;

    b. Maniema, as it stood in 1966;

(5) The former Kasai Province would now include three provinces:

    a. Central Kasai, amalgamating Unité Kasaienne and Luluabourg;

    b. North Kasai, amalgamating Sankuru and Lomami;

    c. "The present province of South Kasai keeps its present limits because of the circumstances which created it."

(6) The former Katanga Province would be left in three pieces because the three pieces (East Katanga, North Katanga, Lualaba) were "viable."[177]

The discrepancies between the Nguvulu and Mobutu formulations are marked. Mobutu's formulation starts with the six colonial provinces, thus avoiding the possible emergence of new "supertribal" solidarity groupings which the Nguvulu plan might have fostered. Further, Mobutu's home province of Équateur would be the only one restored to its 1960 boundaries. Katanga and Orientale, the two major foci of counter-governments (the Katanga secession 1960–63); in Stanleyville the Gizenga regime (1960–61), and the rebel regime or People's Republic (1964–65) were left in fragments.

However, by the time the changes became law in April, three further alterations were made:

(1) East Katanga and Lualaba were amalgamated into a new province of South Katanga. According to Willame, "it doubtless was a question of a last-minute concession to pressures in favor of a reunification of Katanga, made in exchange for pledges of loyalty from the leaders of Élisabethville to the central authorities";

(2) Maniema rather than North Kivu was amalgamated with Central Kivu; Willame attributes this shift to the insistence of Governor Palaku of North Kivu Province, who felt that North Kivu would be unable to counterbalance the political leaders of Bukavu;

(3) South Kasai and Lomami were joined; Willame sees three possible explanations, possibly complementary:

a. perhaps the leaders of Lomami preferred to benefit from the advantages of South Kasai: an experienced administration, a rapidly developing urban center, a roughly similar culture (the Songye of Lomami being Luba-speakers);

b. perhaps the Luba/Kasai leaders, numerous in Léopoldville, convinced Mobutu that Lomami constituted a natural hinterland for the overcrowded province of South Kasai;

c. perhaps Mobutu and his immediate entourage decided on their own to reconstitute the pre-independence district of Kabinda.[178]

In a Christmas Message, 1966, the President announced that the 1960 boundaries of Orientale, Kivu, and Katanga were being restored. Willame observes that the regrouping of the provinces

> could in theory lead to substantial economies, especially in the neglected field of public finance, as well as to certain improvements in public administration. As it turned out, the regrouping was the prototype of an "irrational" change —that is to say, a move failing in its primary objective. The reorganization of the provinces was not followed by a decrease in the number of provincial ministers; it engendered squabbles over the appointment of governors, and created seemingly insurmountable difficulties in the posting of civil servants.[179]

These difficulties were met by "depoliticizing" the provinces, which were converted into mere administrative entities, lacking their own legislatures and governments. The governors were career civil servants, appointed by the central government to posts outside their home areas, and rotated rather frequently. The central government retained the right to name and to rotate district commissioners and territorial administrators, regardless of the wishes of the governors in question. The governors were not to communicate with the central government except through the Ministry of the Interior. (Similar restrictions exist for the communes into which Kinshasa, ex-Léopoldville, is divided.) The police, formerly provincial, were made national.[180] To these centralizing reforms might be added the symbolic dimension; the rehabilitation of Patrice Lumumba, the adoption of a more aggressive policy toward UMHK and the Belgian government, and the launching (top-down) of a political party, the *Mouvement Populaire de la Révolution*.[181]

President Mobutu undoubtedly has restricted the scope within which ethnic and regional sub-nationalisms can operate. However, the problem of differential modernization of the various ethnic groups not only continues to exist, but is perhaps more acute than ever before. Table 2 gives the enrollment in general secondary education by province for the period 1962–63, for nineteen of the twenty-one provinces then in existence. It will be observed that the Kongo retain an enormous lead over other peoples. It should be noted that this table is somewhat misleading because the data for Southern Katanga are missing and South Kasai has been disrupted by the massive immigrations of Luba from other parts of Kasai. Table 3 indicates enrollments in two of the three Congolese universities as of 1963; the totals for Léopoldville and Kasai provinces reflect the advantage enjoyed by the Kongo and Luba/Kasai.

Today the Congo seems more integrated than at any time since independence, in the sense that its political life is less fragmented, there is more interaction between the various regions. Broader-based rivalries exist now than ever before. Vansina has suggested that a north-south rivalry is emerging, between a bloc led by the "Bangala" (including Mobutu himself) and a bloc led by Kongo and Luba/Kasai.[182] Such a rivalry, if it exists, would partly coincide with a generational split, given the overrepresentation of southern peoples among young, educated elements.

The regime can manipulate symbols: (1) it can employ symbols which have the same meaning for all Congolese, e.g., leopard skins as a symbol of authority, (2) it can rename cities as a symbol of a new national self-assertion, and (3) it can attempt to prevent rivals to the regime from invoking popular symbols, e.g., the MNC-Lumumba or ABAKO label.

However, many symbols have negative connotations for some. For example, the canonization of Lumumba may help the regime in Orientale, Sankuru, Maniema, and some other areas. However, this symbol has negative connotations in South Kasai, where the Luba remember Lumumba as having ordered the invasion in which many civilians were massacred.

Linguistic integration of the Congo is coming about: Lingala seems to be making progress at the expense both of Kikongo and of Kiswahili. However, to attempt to symbolize national unity and liberation from European rule by adopting Lingala as the national language would certainly be premature and would only antagonize those for whom the other vernac-

ular languages are symbols with positive associations as well
as keys to social mobility.

Conclusion

Most Congolese ethnic labels seem to have been picked up
by the Europeans, sometimes from the people to whom they
applied, but often from neighboring peoples. The Europeans
attempted to pin down the identities of the peoples they were
encountering, but an element of anticipated response was
involved. The Congolese seem to have interpreted questions
such as, "Are you Bangala?" or "Are your neighbors Baluba?"
to mean, "Yes, we (they) are what you Europeans call Bangala (or Baluba)," and to have replied on that basis.

The "Bangala" identity is "artificial" in the sense that it had
no precolonial basis, but most Congolese identities seem "artificial" to some extent because they have undergone substantial
modification since the coming of the Europeans.

Some of the European labels stress unity, others stress
separateness. For example, Europeans promoted the myth of
the Kingdom of Kongo; they might well have promoted the
idea that all the Luba-speakers of Katanga and Kasai derived
from the Luba empires of Northwest Katanga, but instead
they applied labels stressing the distinctness of Lulua, Luba/
Kasai, Songye, Luba/Katanga, etc.[183]

As Monnier and Willame note regarding the Luba-speakers
of Kasai, various actions of the Europeans contributed to the
acceptance of their ethnic labels by the Africans. Administratively, the Luba-speakers of Kasai were divided among various
districts, territories, and sectors. Thus, the various subgroups
lost contact with one another. Politically, the Europeans
sought the support of certain ethnic groups which they favored at the expense of others.[184] Not mentioned by Monnier
and Willame but probably at least as important in leading the
Africans to accept the various ethnic labels were the decisions
of the Europeans (missionaries) as to where to locate their
schools, and which languages to employ as media of instruc-

tion. The content of the schoolbooks and the comments of schoolteachers probably served to promote the stereotypes, myths, and symbols of ethnicity.

At several points in this article, reference has been made to "traditional" enmity, e.g., between Kongo and Yaka, or between Lega and Bembe. However, such enmity seems to be relevant to contemporary politics mainly as it fuses with current grievances, for example, those involving one group's edge in competition for jobs. One must reject the notion, popular in Belgian journalistic circles, that "fifty years of Pax Belgica simply contributed to damping down the racial and tribal antinomies without eliminating them."[185] In fact, as has been shown, most of the ethnic identities, and thus most of the ethnic antagonisms, have arisen or undergone substantial modification during the colonial period.

One must also reject the opposite extreme, the suggestion that ethnicity has no explanatory power in itself. In a country such as the Congo, the symbols of ethnicity remain of greater saliency in most situations than those of African unity in the face of European domination or peasant unity in the face of exploitation by the politicians of the 1960 generation. The Congo rebellions are instructive in this respect; the rebels made very clear their opposition to the "politicians" yet (because the rebels appeared to be "strangers") they were not always able to win the support of peasants who had the same objective grievances against the government.

On the eve of independence, and again in 1964–65, the salience of various identity patterns and symbols changed abruptly, as the boundaries of political fields shifted. The transition from municipal elections in 1957–58 to provincial and Congo-wide elections in 1960 is equivalent to the transition from rebellion within a single province to the establishment of a counter-government in Stanleyville. In this respect, changes in the saliency of certain ethnic identities and symbols meant that some politicians and groups were unable to operate within the larger fields and ceded their places to other politicians and groups.

The breaking up of the six provinces into twenty-one smaller ones produced new configurations of competing ethnic groups. Perhaps the most dramatic example is the split which occurred among the Luba/Kasai; animosity between highland and lowland Luba became so intense that some of the latter demanded formation of a new province of "Central Kasai" in their northern zone of South Kasai Province.[186] This fractioning, like that described in detail in the sections dealing with the Léopoldville and Sankuru political fields, involved (1) initiative on the part of ambitious elite members who felt that they did not have a share in political power and rewards commensurate with the population or wealth of "their" area or ethnic group, and (2) response on the part of the region or ethnic group from which the ambitious elite members came, in terms of a grievance felt by the general population.

All of the governments since independence have reflected "ethnic arithmetic" in the sense that they included members of many ethnic groups, from many parts of the country. Perhaps the only government that was clearly *unrepresentative* in an ethnic and regional sense was the second Ileo government (February–August 1961) in which groups and areas associated with secessionist Katanga or with the Stanleyville-based Lumumbist counter-government of Gizenga were underrepresented. For example, this government included no Lunda, Yeke, Luba/Katanga, or Tetela-Kusu. However, it must be stressed that the apparent representation of a given area or ethnic group in a given government was less important than the *feeling* of people in certain areas that they were represented. For example, the third Adoula government (April 1963–June 1964), under which the rebellions broke out, was nominally representative, including even several MNC-L and PSA members. However, this government clearly was seen as unrepresentative of Lumumbist nationalism.[187]

General Mobutu has been careful to preserve an ethnic and regional balance in his successive governments, and also to involve persons considered genuinely representative of the Lumumbist tendency. However, other pitfalls are less easily avoided. For example, the fact that he is of the "Bangala" group, whereas many senior civil servants are Kongo and

Luba/Kasai, means that a problem between him and the civil servants as a group is likely to acquire ethnic overtones.

The question of what can be done to limit or overcome ethnic sub-nationalism (cultural nationalism) cannot be answered without first establishing what this phenomenon involves. The pattern of ethnic sub-nationalism as it has unfolded in the Congo, seems to confirm both the hypothesis of Young that,

> political behavior can be analyzed in terms of a multiplicity of roles, the relative importance of each at any given time dependent on the situation . . .[188]

and the observation of Mercier that ethnic conflict is "a *form* of expression common to oppositions which can in fact be very different in nature."[189] Each of the multiplicity of roles is defined in terms of oppositions: they include African as opposed to European, Congolese as opposed to non-Congolese, peasant as opposed to city dweller, and a series of ethnic roles, e.g., Kongo as opposed to "Bangala," Yombe (Kongo-subgroup) as opposed to Ntandu (Kongo-subgroup), and so on. The pattern of successive splits within an ethnic group, which occurred in various parts of the Congo, did not seem to involve the creation of new groups, so much as it did the activation of pre-existing cleavages which became much more salient in the new situation. There seems to be no limit to such fragmentation when the political situation encourages it as it did in the Congo between 1960 and 1966.

The shifting from one role to another can involve evolution. As Young suggests, the more frequently and intensively a given solidarity role is activated by perceptions of situation, the more deeply engrained this role becomes. A related but slightly different form of change is the partial fusion of the MNC-Lumumba identity with ethnic identity in Maniema and elsewhere in the Eastern Congo, a type of change Mercier had suggested (without mentioning this example).

If this interpretation of ethnic sub-nationalism is valid, then the task before the Congolese government (and presumably other African governments) had several facets:

(1) to attempt to respond to grievances in various sectors of the population, as these grievances could easily be expressed in the form of ethnic conflict;

(2) to attempt to supplement or supplant the symbols of ethnicity with national symbols;

(3) to structure competition and the expression of grievances in such a way that expression in ethnic form is not encouraged.

The steps Mobutu has taken thus far represent a beginning, e.g., abolishing the small provinces, blocking the formation of ethnic parties, attempting to monopolize the use of the symbols of Lumumbism. However, the more positive aspects are the more difficult to implement; a crucial step will be the development of the MPR into a channel which screens but does not shut off communication of grievances from the masses upward.[190]

NOTES

1. O. Boone, "Carte ethnique du Congo belge et du Ruanda-Urundi," *Zaire* (1954), pp. 451–66.

2. René Lemarchand, *Political Awakening in the Belgian Congo* (Berkeley: University of California Press, 1964), p. 7.

3. Jan Vansina, *Introduction à l'ethnographie du Congo* (Kinshasa: Éditions Universitaires du Congo, 1966), pp. 28–29, 42–44, 214.
I am grateful to Professor Vansina and to Professor Crawford Young, both of the University of Wisconsin, for their many helpful suggestions regarding this article.

4. *Ibid.*, p. 10.

5. *Ibid.*, pp. 10–11.

6. *Ibid.*, p. 18.

7. *Ibid.*, p. 12.

8. Max Gluckman, "Malinowski's 'Functional' Analysis of Social Change," in Immanuel Wallerstein, ed., *Social Change: The Colonial Situation* (New York: John Wiley & Sons, 1966), p. 27.

9. Crawford Young, *Politics in the Congo: Decolonization and Independence* (Princeton: Princeton University Press, 1965), p. 11.

10. *Ibid.*, pp. 12–13.

11. *Ibid.*, p. 14.

12. Benoit Verhaegen, "Révolte au Congo Belge," *Esprit,* March 1959, p. 499.

13. Michel Merlier, *Le Congo de la colonisation belge à l'indépendance* (Paris: François Masperoll, 1962), p. 210.

14. *Ibid.*, pp. 210–11.

15. Thomas Hodgkin, *Nationalism in Colonial Africa* (New York: New York University Press, 1957), p. 118.

16. J. Denis, *Le phénomène urbain en Afrique centrale* (Brussels: Académie Royale des Sciences Coloniales, 1958), p. 140.

17. Young, *op. cit.*, p. 441.

18. *Ibid.*

19. Vansina, personal communication, 1968.

20. Young, *op. cit.*, pp. 187–91.

21. *Ibid.*, p. 195.

22. *Ibid.*, p. 74.

23. W. J. Ganshof van der Merrsch, *Fin de la souveraineté belge au Congo* (Brussels: Institut royal des relations internationales, 1963).

24. Such an approach slights the northern portion of the Congo, especially Équateur Province, but I do cover events in four of the six colonial provinces, and discuss four of the most important ethnic groups in terms of modern politics: the Kongo, "Bangala," Luba-Kasai, and Tetela-Kusu.

25. Vansina, *Kingdoms of the Savanna* (Madison: University of Wisconsin Press, 1966), Chapters 2, 8.

26. Young, *op. cit.*, p. 247, citing Georges Balandier, *Sociologie actuelle del' Afrique noire* (Paris: Presses Universitaires de France, 1955, 1st ed.), p. 39.

27. Young, *op. cit.*, pp. 285–86.

28. Lemarchand, *op. cit.*, p. 129.

29. Joseph van Wing, *Études Bakongo* (Brussels: Desclée, de Brouwer, 1959, 2d ed.).

30. Henry Morton Stanley, *Through the Dark Continent* (New York: Harper and Brothers, 1878), Vol. II, pp. 301–2.

31. Young, *op. cit.*, pp. 242–43, citing Camille Coquilhat, *Sur le Haut-Congo* (Paris: J. Lebegue et Cie., 1888), pp. 202, 244.
The figure of 110,000 was repeated in Cyr. van Overbergh, *Les Bangala* (Brussels: Institut international de bibliographie, 1907),

p. 65, and in G. P. Murdock, *Africa: Its Peoples and Their Culture History* (New York: McGraw-Hill, 1959), p. 280.

32. D. Rinchon, *Les missionnaires belges au Congo* (Brussels: 1931), p. 18.

33. Malcolm Guthrie, "The Lingua Franca of the Middle Congo," *Africa*, XIV (1943), pp. 118–29.

34. John H. Weeks, *Among Congo Cannibals* (London: Seeley, Service & Co., 1913), pp. 48–49.

35. Walter H. Stapleton, *Suggestions for a Grammar of 'Bangala'* (Bolobo: Baptist Missionary Society, 1914).

36. Vansina, personal communication, 1968.

37. Young, *op. cit.*, pp. 244–47.

38. Lemarchand, "The Bases of Nationalism among the Bakongo," *Africa*, XXXI (October 1961), p. 346.

39. Young, *op. cit.*, p. 247.

40. The complete text, translated, appears in Rupert Emerson and Martin Kilson, eds., *The Political Awakening of Africa* (Englewood Cliffs: Prentice-Hall, 1965), pp. 99–103.

41. Verhaegen, ed., *ABAKO 1950–1960: Documents* (Brussels: CRISP, 1962), pp. 37–44.

42. *Ibid.*, p. 56.

43. *Congo*, April 17, 1957, cited in Lemarchand, *Political Awakening in the Belgian Congo*, p. 193. His translation, his omissions.

44. Verhaegen, *op. cit.*, p. 95.

45. *Congo*, April 17, 1957, cited in Lemarchand, *op. cit.*, p. 193.

46. Verhaegen, *op. cit.*, p. 120.

47. Young, *op. cit.*, p. 120.

48. Herbert Weiss, *Political Protest in the Congo: The Parti Solidaire Africain during the Independence Struggle* (Princeton: Princeton University Press, 1967), p. 9.

49. Lemarchand, *op. cit.*, p. 195.

50. Young, *op. cit.*, p. 290.

51. *Ibid.*, pp. 37, 152.

52. Lemarchand, *op. cit.*, p. 195.

53. Vansina, *Introduction à l'ethnographie du Congo*, pp. 129–43, 145–59; Malcolm Guthrie, *The Classification of the Bantu Languages* (London: Dawson's of Pall Mall for the International African Institute, 1967; first published, 1948), pp. 33, 50–51.

54. Henri Nicolai, *Le Bas-Kwilu: ses problèmes géographiques* (Brussels: Centre Scientific et Médical de l'Université Libre de Bruxelles en Afrique Centrale, 1957).

55. Weiss, *op. cit.*, p. 81.

56. *Ibid.*, p. 78.

57. *Ibid.*, passim.

58. Jules Gérard-Libois and Benoit Verhaegen, *Congo 1960* (Brussels: CRISP, 1961?), Vol. I, pp. 161, 163.
This source cites a document in which ABAZI refers to itself as the "Alliance des Badzing." Usually the party was known as the "Alliance des Bayanzi." Apparently there was a disagreement as to whether the Yans were a subgroup of the Ding, or vice versa.

59. John M. Janzen, "A Lower-Congo Example of the Regional Council as Micro-Polity," paper presented to the 10th annual meeting, African Studies Association, New York, November 1967. See also Gérard-Libois and Verhaegen, *op. cit.*, pp. 152–54.

60. Verhaegen, *Rébellions au Congo* (Brussels: CRISP, 1967), Vol. I, pp. 50–51.

61. Hermann von Wissmann, *My Second Journey Through Equatorial Africa, from the Congo to the Zambezi* (London: Chatto & Windus, 1891), p. 306n.

62. Von Wissmann, *op. cit.*, p. 121.

63. B. Moritz, "L'Histoire de la fondation du poste de Luluabourg (Malandji)," *Bulletin du Centre d'Étude des Problèmes Sociaux Indigènes*, 1946–47, no. 4, p. 53.

64. Von Wissmann, *op. cit.*, p. 86.

65. Moritz, *op. cit.*, p. 167.

66. Von Wissmann, *op. cit.*, p. 144.

67. M. W. Hilton-Simpson, *Land and Peoples of the Kasai* (London: Constable & Co., 1911), p. 72.

68. Young sets forth two theories as to the receptivity of the Luba/Kasai to modernization:

(i) "A major, if not *the* major factor in their situation was the state of dislocation in which this society found itself at the moment of European penetration," i.e., due to slave raids;

(ii) "Another theory was that the social mobility possible within traditional Baluba structures, as with the Ibo in Nigeria, had instilled in them a sense of drive for promotion within customary society." Young, *op. cit.*, pp. 258–59.

69. H. Nicolai, "Conflits entre groupes africains et décolonisation au Kasai," *Revue de l'Université de Bruxelles,* XIIe Année (1960), 1–2.

70. H. Nicolai and J. Jacques, *La transformation des paysages congolais par le chemin de fer, l'exemple du B.C.K.* (Brussels: Académie Royale des Sciences Coloniales, 1954).

71. Young, *op. cit.*, p. 264.

72. Nicolai, *op. cit.*, p. 136.

73. Chambre des Représentants, *Rapport sur l'administration du Congo Belge pendant l'année 1954,* p. 78, cited by J. C. Willame, "Les provinces du Congo: structures et fonctionnement," *Cahiers Économiques et Sociaux,* Collection d'Études Politiques, no. 1, p. 74.

74. Willame, *loc. cit.* According to Kalanda, the Belgians became concerned about the Luba/Kasai following the 1944 *Force Publique* revolt (see note 133, below); after 1944, according to Kalanda, the Belgian policy had been to divide the Luba from the Lulua: "flattering the ones for their advancement, thereby feeding their vanity, and evaluating the others negatively for their passivity, which reinforced their feeling of frustration and jealousy." Mabika Kalanda, *Baluba et Lulua: une ethnie a la recherche d'un nouvel équilibre* (Brussels: Éditions de Remarques Congolaises, 1959), p. 97.

75. Young, *op. cit.*, p. 246.

76. Jules Chomé, *Le Drame de Luluabourg* (Brussels: Éditions de Remarques Congolaises, 1960, 3d ed.), p. 21.

77. Young, *op. cit.*, p. 124. Perhaps some non-Lulua voted for *Lulua-Frères.*

78. Chomé, *op cit.*, p. 23.

79. *Ibid.* There is nothing in the citations from the report which

supports conclusively Chomé's allegation that the Belgians were backing the Lulua at all costs, over Nicolai's argument that the Belgians had decided that the only way to resolve the Luba-Lulua conflict was to satisfy at least part of the Lulua demands.

80. Nicolai, *op. cit.*, p. 131; Chomé, *op. cit.*, p. 31.

81. Nicolai (*op. cit.*, p. 142n.) expresses surprise at this attack on the village of the Zappo Zappo, a Songye subgroup. However, there is nothing very surprising about the attack. The Zappo Zappo were Songye who fled from the slave raids of the 1880s, crossed into the Kasai, and were given the right to settle near Luluabourg by Von Wissmann's successor, Le Marinel. In 1891, when Kalamba attacked the State post, the Zappo Zappo helped the Europeans drive him back. In 1895 the Zappo Zappo sheltered the Belgian, Cassart, from the "mutineers." During the continuing attacks by Lulua against the post at Luluabourg in subsequent years, the Zappo Zappo continued to side with the Europeans. Morita, *op. cit.*, pp. 61, 64.

82. Willame, *op. cit.*, no. 2, p. 30.

83. Young, *op. cit.*, p. 395.

84. Young, "The Politics of Separatism: Katanga, 1960–63," in Gwendolen M. Carter, ed., *Politics in Africa: Seven Cases* (New York: Harcourt, Brace & World, Inc., 1966), pp. 171–72. See Vansina, *Kingdoms of the Savanna* (Madison: University of Wisconsin Press, 1966).

85. F. Grevisse, *Le Centre Extra-Coutumier d'Élisabethville* (Brussels: Académie Royale des Sciences Coloniales, 1951); Bruce Fetter, "Élisabethville and Lubumbashi: The Segmentary Growth of a Colonial City, 1910–1945" (Unpublished Ph.D. dissertation, University of Wisconsin, Madison, 1968).

86. Young, *op. cit.*, p. 173.

87. *Ibid.*, p. 175.

88. *Ibid.*, p. 173.

89. See Gérard-Libois, *Katanga Secession* (Madison: University of Wisconsin Press, 1966).

90. Young, *op. cit.*, p. 189.

91. On Sankuru-Maniema, see also:
   1. Thomas Turner, "L'Ethnie tetela et le MNC-Lumumba,"

Études Congolaises, XII, 4 (October–December 1969), pp. 36–57.
    2. Turner, "Mouvements de résistance et de révolte chez les Mongo du Sankuru," *Revue Congolaise des Sciences Humaines*, 2 (January 1971).

92. J. Jacobs, "La situation linguistique d'une région du Congo. Les langues et les dialectes de la région du Sankuru (Kasai) et des régions voisines," in *Premier congrès international de dialectologie générale, Communications et rapports* (Louvain: Centre international de Dialectologie, 1965), p. 100. There are Tetela minorities in Katanga Province and in other parts of Kasai; as these are small we shall ignore them.

93. O. Boone, *Carte ethnique du Congo: quart sud-est* (Tervuren: Musée royal de l'Afrique centrale, 1961), p. 233.

94. Ahmad ibn Muhammad ibn Juma el Mujerbi, *Maisha ya hamed ibn Muhammed el Mujerbi yaani Tippu Tip* (Mémoires of Tippu Tip), Supplement to *East African Swahili Committee Journal*, 28 (1958), 2, and 29 (1959), 1, par. 97.

95. Stanley, *op. cit.*, Vol. II, p. 101.

96. Wissmann, *op. cit.*, pp. 53, 222.

97. *Ibid.*, p. 222; S. Hinde, *The Fall of the Congo Arabs* (New York: Thomas Whittaker, 1897), p. 89.

98. There were two important qualifications to the homogeneity of a hundred years ago:
    (1) The fact that some lived in the forest and some in the savanna had important consequences as regards diet, land tenure, importance attached to hunting, etc.
    (2) The southern Tetela influenced and were influenced by their Luba-Songye neighbors, whereas the northern Tetela influenced and were influenced by *their* neighbors, other Mongo.

99. Vansina, *op. cit.*, p. 239.

100. Hinde, *op. cit.*, pp. 208–10.

101. A central issue (sometimes implicit) in writings on the "Batetela mutinies" is whether the mutineers were avenging the death of Ngongo, reacting to bad treatment, or revolting against colonialism. In addition to Hinde, *op. cit.*, see for example:
H. Lassaux, "Les évènements de Luluabourg de 1895. La révolte des Batetela," *Congo*, I (1926), pp. 567–83.
Auguste Verbeken, *La révolte des Batetela en 1895* (Brussels: Académie Royale des Sciences Coloniales, 1958).

A. van Zandijke, "La révolte de Luluabourg de 4 juillet 1895," *Zaire,* IV (1950), pp. 931–65, 1063–82.
A. Zousmanovitch, "L'insurrection des Batetela au Congo Belge au XIXe siècle," *Présence Africaine,* no. 51 (1964), p. 164.

102. J. Barden, *A Suggested Program of Teacher Training for Mission Schools Among the Batetela* (New York: Columbia University Teachers College, 1941), pp. 26–27.

103. Our interviews, Sankuru, 1970.

104. Georges Brausch, "Origines de la politique indigène belge en Afrique, 1879–1908," *Revue de l'Institut de Sociologie* (1955), 3, p. 455.

105. Willame, *op. cit.,* no. 5, p. 91.

106. A. Corman, *Annuaire des missions catholiques au Congo Belge* (Brussels: L'Édition Universelle, 1924, 1st ed., and 1935, 2d ed.).

107. A. De Rop, *Les langues du Congo* (Coquilhatville: Éditions Aequatoris, 1960), p. 12.

108. Corman, *op. cit.*

109. Thomas Ellis Reeve, *In Wembo-Nyama's Land* (Nashville: Publishing House of the M. E. Church, South, 1925), p. 118; J. Alexander Reid, *Congo Drumbeat* (New York: World Outlook Press, 1964).

110. E. Bradkman, *Histoire du Protestantisme au Congo* (Brussels: Éditions de la Librairie des Éclaireurs Unionistes, 1961), pp. 189–90, citing *Congo Mission News,* No. 154 (April 1951), p. 7, and No. 167 (July 1954), p. 8.

111. Congo Belge, Gouvernement général, Affaires économiques, Direction de la Statistique, "Résultats des enquêtes démographiques: population indigène de la Province du Kasai, *"Bulletin mensuel des Statistiques générales du Congo Belge et du Ruanda-Urundi,"* série spéciale, no. 3, fasc. f (October 1959). Congo Belge, 2e Direction générale, Ie direction AIMO, *Enquêtes démographiques:* District du Maniema, fasc. 7 (March 1959).
In Sankuru, Sambala were concentrated around the towns and missions and apparently received a disproportionate share of the schooling dispensed. There does not seem to be a separate Sambala category in Maniema.

112. Reid, *op. cit.*, *passim*. Corman, *op. cit.* (2d ed.), pp. 150–51.

113. P. Raucq, "Les relations entre tribus au Kasai: leurs incidences géopolitiques et économiques," *Africa-Tervuren*, VII (1961), 2, p. 51.

114. A. Lux, *Le marché du travail en Afrique noire* (Louvain: 1962), pp. 680–81.

115. Lusambo, which might have served to draw more Sankuru Tetela into the urban sector, was stunted in its development. The transfer of the Kasai capital from Lusambo to Luluabourg sealed the fate of Lusambo, which actually lost population during the 1950s. (Willame, *op. cit.*, no. 5, p. 85)

116. Lux, "Migrations, accroissement et urbanisation de la population congolaise de Luluabourg," *Zaire*, XII (1958), no. 8, p. 837.

117. Lemarchand, *op. cit.*, p. 194; Willame, *op. cit.*, no. 5, p. 96.

118. Grévisse, *op. cit.*, p. 312; Fetter, *op. cit.*, pp. 143–44. However, a prominent Kusu reports that he served as President of the Association des Batetela around 1950; hence at Lubumbashi at that moment the two were united (our interview, Kisangani, 1970).

119. Fetter, *op. cit.*, p. 120.

120. *Ibid.*, citing Union Minière du Haut Katanga, Service de Main-d'Oeuvre indigène, *Rapport Annuel*, 1935–41.

121. J. Denis, "Élisabethville, matériaux pour une étude de la population africaine," *Bulletin du CEPSI*, no. 34 (1956), pp. 137–95; Fetter, *op. cit.*, pp. 212–13.

122. V. Pons, et al., "Social Effects of Urbanization in Stanleyville, Belgian Congo," in *Social Implications of Industrialization and Urbanization in Africa South of the Sahara* (Paris: UNESCO, 1956), p. 29; V. Pons, *Stanleyville: An African Urban Community under Belgian Administration* (London: Oxford University Press, 1969), p. 76.

123. Pons, et al., *op. cit.*, pp. 655–56.

124. *Ibid.*, pp. 477–78.

125. Corman, *op. cit.* (2d ed.), p. 286.

126. Denis, *Le phénomène urbain en Afrique centrale*, p. 136.

127. Gérard-Libois and Verhaegen, *op. cit.*, p. 1072.

128. "From the viewpoint of privileged and ruling groups the utility of presenting one's own society in terms of a non-egalitarian classless society is apparent. In the world of today, both in the bourgeois democracies and the people's democracies, such a presentation affords no bases for group solidarity amongst the underprivileged . . ." (S. Ossowski, *Class Structure in the Social Consciousness*, London, 1963, cited with reference to Africa by P. C. Lloyd in his *The New Elites of Tropical Africa*, London: Oxford University Press, 1966, p. 335)

129. Lumumba was uniquely qualified to draw upon the Tetela ethnic group as a political resource. He was born and educated in Wembo-Nyama (Katako-Kombe *territoire*). He worked in Maniema as a clerk for the mining company Symétain, then went to Léopoldville where he attended the post office training school. Sent to work in the Stanleyville post office, he became active in trade union and *évolué* activities, and became President of the aforementioned *Mutuelle des Batetela*. Following a brief term in prison for embezzling funds from the post office, he returned to Léopoldville and became sales director of a brewery. (See Lemarchand, *op. cit.*, pp. 199–200.) Thus when Lumumba went into politics he was able to draw upon a network of pre-existing contacts, partly but by no means exclusively Tetela-Kusu, in Sankuru, Maniema, Stanleyville, and Léopoldville.

130. Willame, *op. cit.*, no. 5, p. 92.

131. Gérard-Libois and Verhaegen, *op. cit.*, Vol. III, "Annexes," pp. 8–10.

132. Willame, *op. cit.*, no. 5, p. 96.

133. African millenarian movements diffused from field to field, but in the case of Kitawala no organizational links resulted; Kimbanguism was limited mainly to Kongo until 1960. (See Young, *Politics in the Congo*, pp. 252–53.) The 1944 Luluabourg mutiny had its origin in a conspiracy which represented the first African attempt at interprovincial organization. The conspiracy began in Élisabethville among Luba-Kasai and was supposed to involve uprisings in various cities, coordinated by Luba telegraphers along the B.C.K. railroad. However, already in 1944 relations between Luba "strangers" and Katangans were sufficiently bad as to constitute the fatal flaw in the conspiracy. Fetter, "La révolte de Luluabourg à Élisabethville," *Études Congolaises*, XI, 4 (October–December 1968).

134.

Ethnic Parties	Groups Represented	Seats Won
ABAKO	Kongo	12
MNC-KALONJI	Luba-Kasai	8
BALUBAKAT	Luba-Katanga	6
RECO	Shi-Ngweshe	4
LUKA	Yaka	3
MOUVEMENT UNITAIRE BASONGE	Songye	3
UNC	Lulua	3
ASSOCIATION NGWAKA	Ngwaka	2
MEDERCO	Other "Sudanic" peoples of Équateur	2
UNIMO	Mongo	1
UNEBAFI	Bembe	1
ATCAR	Cokwe	1
		46

Regional Parties
With Ethnic Overtones

CONAKAT	Lunda, Yeke, Tabwa	7
PUNA	Ngombe and other "Bangala"	7
COAKA	Small tribes of Kasai	3
		17

(Based on Weiss, *op. cit.*, pp. 70–72, and Lemarchand, *op. cit.*, p. 224)

135. Gérard-Libois and Verhaegen, *op. cit.*, Vol. II, p. 522.

136. Young, *op. cit.*, pp. 217, 315.

137. *Ibid.*, pp. 525–52.

138. Young, "Congo and Uganda: A comparative assessment," *Cahiers Économiques et Sociaux*, V (1967), no. 3, p. 398.

139. This section on rebellion in Kwilu is based primarily on two sources:
        (i) Renée Fox, et al., "La Deuxième Indépendance—étude d'un cas: la rébellion au Kwilu," *Études Congolaises*, VIII (January–February 1965);
        (ii) Verhaegen, *Rébellions au Congo*, Vol. I, pp. 35–186.

140. Verhaegen, *op. cit.*, Vol. I.

141. *Ibid.*, p. 44.

142. *Ibid.*, p. 43.

143. *Ibid.*

144. *Ibid.*, Vol. II (Brussels: CRISP, 1970?), p. 4.

145. Vansina, *Introduction à l'Ethnographie du Congo*, pp. 201–10, 105–14. In the interest of clarity I am omitting consideration of the Rundi and Rwanda populations around Bukavu, and of the northern portion of Kivu, which became the province of North Kivu.

146. Verhaegen, *op. cit.*, Vol. I, p. 265.

147. Willame, *op. cit.*, no. 4, p. 133.

148. Young, "The Congo Rebellion," *Africa Report* (April 1965), p. 9.

149. Verhaegen, *op. cit.*, Vol. I, p. 335.

150. Paul Masson, *La bataille pour Bukavu* (Brussels: Charles Dessart, 1965, 2d ed.).

151. Verhaegen, *op. cit.*, Vol. I, p. 342.

152. *Ibid.*, Vol. II, pp. 615–28.

153. Young, *op. cit.*, p. 9.

154. Gérard-Libois, *Congo 1965* (Brussels: CRISP, 1966?), p. 157.

155. Denis gives the following criteria for city status in Central Africa: (1) minimum population of 20,000; (2) coherent structure; (3) multiple functions (Denis, *op. cit.*, pp. 25–29). Of the towns and centers in North Katanga, Kongolo had a population of only 13,000 in 1958. Kamina and Manono had more than 20,000 each but Kamina consisted of a military base and a *centre extra-coutumier*, some 15 km apart, and Manono was not a coherent city but a scattering of villages around a center, the single modern function of which was mining. (Willame, *op. cit.*, no. 1, p. 112; Denis, *op. cit.*, p. 39)

156. Young, *op. cit.*, p. 9.

157. *Ibid.*

158. Verhaegen, *op. cit.*, vol. I, p. 435.

159. *Ibid.*, pp. 443–82.

160. Young, *op. cit.*, p. 9.

161. Verhaegen, *op. cit.*, vol. II, pp. 17–66.

162. *Ibid.*, pp. 19–22. Daniel Biebuyck quotes an informant who said he became a Kitawalist *because* he was a Komo ("La société kumu face au Kitawala," *Zaire*, XI, 1, January 1957, pp. 7–40).

163. Verhaegen, *op. cit.*, vol. II, p. 291.

164. *Ibid.*, vol. II, pp. 291–96.

165. *Ibid.*, vol. II, pp. 627–28. As mentioned above, Bembe and Lega also seem traditionally hostile.

166. *Ibid.*, p. 399.

167. *Ibid.*, p. 408.

168. Willame, *op. cit.*, no. 5, pp. 117–20.

169. Charles W. Anderson, et al., *Issues of Political Development* (Englewood Cliffs: Prentice-Hall, 1967), p. 138.

170. An immediate danger was opposition from the Kongo, whose favorite son Kasa-Vubu had been deposed. Mobutu was of course a "Bangala" in Kongo eyes. However, this danger did not materialize. The ABAKO political bureau appealed for calm, the Governor of Central Kongo Province pledged his support for Mobutu, and Kasa-Vubu denied any intention of organizing rebellion in the Kongo area. Gérard-Libois, *op. cit.*, pp. 415–16.

171. *Ibid.*, p. 420. One of the former ministers was forced out only five months later: this was the long-time "Bangala" leader Jean Bolikango, dismissed as Minister of Public Works. Bolikango (who had run against Kasa-Vubu in 1960) reportedly still cherished the ambition to become President. Apparently, he also disagreed with Mobutu as to the manner in which the provinces of the Congo were to be reunited.

172. Gérard-Libois, *Congo 1966* (Brussels: CRISP, 1967?), pp. 18–20.

173. *Ibid.*, pp. 24–25; *Africa Report*, January 1968, p. 28.

174. Willame, "La réunification des provinces du Congo," *Études Congolaises*, IX, no. 4 (July–August 1966), pp. 74–80.

175. Gérard-Libois, *op. cit.*, p. 221.

176. *Ibid.*, p. 222.

177. *Ibid.*, pp. 222–23. Both Banningville and the new province subsequently were named Bandundu.

178. Willame, *op. cit.*, pp. 81–82.

179. Willame, "Military Intervention in the Congo," *Africa Report*, November 1966, p. 45.

180. Gérard-Libois, *op. cit.*, p. 117.

181. Mobutu had banned political party activity after he seized power. In January 1967, Antoine Kiwewa, President of a faction of the MNC-Lumumba, called for a two-party system in the Congo with his group as the "majority party." He claimed that the MNC-L alone "is capable of channeling nationalist forces." Another grouping should be organized as an opposition party. Kiwewa was speaking at a reception organized in Lumumba's memory, in the presence of Mobutu.

The new Constitution (announced by Mobutu in April 1967, and approved by national referendum in June) limited the number of political parties to two. On April 18 Mobutu refused to allow a revival of the MNC-L. On April 19 a spokesman for ABAKO asked official recognition of a *Union des Nationalistes de l'Afrique Révolutionnaire*, grouping ten previously dissolved parties. These initiatives were forestalled when Mobutu installed himself as founder-President of the MPR, and government spokesmen made it clear no opposition party would be recognized. *Africa Report*, March 1967, p. 26; *ibid.*, June 1967, p. 37.

In October–November 1970 the first elections were held since 1965. Mobutu was elected unopposed, as were the four hundred national deputies.

182. Vansina, speaking before Wisconsin Africanists Association, Madison, 1968.

183. There is a sound reason for the Belgians not to have promoted Luba unity in the way some of them promoted Kongo unity. At the time of the establishment of the Congo Independent State, a Luba-Katanga kingdom was still functioning, and in fact posed a threat to European domination for a number of years, as did the Lulua of Kalamba. In contrast, the Kongo state was only a memory, and no officials higher than clan chiefs retained authority.

184. L. Monnier and J. C. Willame, *Les provinces du Congo: structure et fonctionnement*, no. 2, pp. 34–35.

185. *Le Pari Congolais* (Brussels: Charles Cessart, 1960?), p. 38.

186. Monnier and Willame, *op. cit.*, pp. 69–70.

187. Young, *Politics in the Congo,* pp. 346–48.

188. *Ibid.,* p. 239.

189. Paul Mercier, "Remarques sur la signification du 'triba-lisme' actuel en Afrique noire," *Cahiers internationaux de sociologie,* XXI (1961), p. 63. The stress is his.

190. An example of an attempt to cope with all three facets is Tanzania's electoral law which permits meaningful choice between two candidates for each seat, but requires that each candidate use Swahili rather than a local language, and forbids discussion of race, tribe, or religion. (Ruth Schachter Morgenthau, "African Elections: Tanzania's Contribution," *Africa Report,* December 1965, pp. 12–16) The Congolese elections of 1970 did not permit such choice.

TABLE 1

Total Draft Quotas for Force Publique by Province, 1892–1914

Province	1960 Province of which it became part	Total of annual quotas
Lower Congo	Léopoldville	7,428
Lac Léopold II	Léopoldville	2,393
Équateur	Équateur	6,445
Maringa (Lopori-Lulonga)	Équateur	692
Bangala and Mongala	Équateur	7,256
Ubangi	Équateur	5,512
Uele	Orientale	11,970
Orientale (including Maniema)	Orientale/Kivu	10,172
Ruzizi-Kivu	Kivu	428
Katanga	Katanga	405
Lualaba-Kasai	Kasai	8,407
Lado Enclave	(Became part of Southern Sudan)	147
		66,340

(SOURCE: F. Flament, *La Force Publique de sa naissance à 1914*, Brussels: Académie royale des sciences coloniales, 1952)

TABLE 2

**Enrollment in General Secondary Education
1962–63, by Province**

Province	Enrollment
Léopoldville city	9,499
Central Kongo	5,015
Kwango	500
Kwilu	2,770
Lac Léopold II	1,162
Moyen Congo	552
Cuvette Centrale	1,482
Ubangi	447
Haut-Congo	1,956
Uele	1,333
Kibali-Ituri	838
Central Kivu	1,063
North Kivu	3,827
Maniema	491
North Katanga	956
Central Kasai	2,268
Unité Kasaienne	759
North Sankuru	929
Lomami	732
South Kasai	1,331
Undetermined	46
TOTAL	37,926

(SOURCE: *Études Congolaises*, December 1963. South Katanga is not included, except for two schools in Jadotville.)

TABLE 3

A. Students at Lovanium University, 1963, by Province of Origin

	Number	Per Cent
Léopoldville	260	38.4
Équateur	37	5.5
Orientale	63	9.3
Kivu	70	10.3
Katanga	61	9.0
Kasai	178	26.3
Undetermined Congolese	8	1.2
	677	

B. Students at Free University of Congo, 1963, by Previous Origin

	Regularly Enrolled	Pre-University	Total
Léopoldville	17	7	24
Équateur	2	11	13
Orientale	5	9	14
Kivu	7	2	9
Katanga	2	–	2
Kasai	11	2	13
	44	31	75

(SOURCE: *Études Congolaises*, December 1963.)

V
KENYA

❖ ❖ ❖

EDITOR'S INTRODUCTORY NOTE

Decision-makers in Kenya are faced with the dilemma of reconciling equity in elite recruitment with economic development. In pre-independent Kenya, non-Africans, who commanded key skills and capital, controlled the political and economic institutions. This hegemony was ensured by a manipulation of social services. For example, Europeans, Asians, and Africans were taught in different schools with distinct curriculum. As a consequence, Europeans were prepared for decision-making positions, Asians for skilled labor, and Africans for unspecialized tasks. It is no surprise that upon independence Africans demanded a fundamental revision in the priorities of colonial times. The African community was united in their demand for an opportunity to hold high level positions. In response, the government emphasized Africanization as a way to rectify the imbalances of the colonial era. At the same time, the government desired to maintain a high level of economic growth. Elite recruitment policies, therefore, placed high priority on individual achievement and experience. As a result, Africanization corrected racial imbalance while creating intertribal inequities. For example, Kikuyus who enjoyed greater educational opportunity than other Africans under the colonial administration were recruited for decision-making positions. Smaller less-advantaged tribes were quick to recognize that without increased resource allocation for social services and economic development in their provinces, they might never possess the necessary skill to share in the administrative and economic opportunities accompanying Africanization.

In response to the complaints of tribal minorities, the government insists that all imbalances were inherited from the colonial administration, that recruitment is based on merit, and that resources are allocated according to need. The government also attempted to recruit candidates for leading civil service positions from among the less-advantaged groups and promised to allocate expenditures to overcome tribal imbalance. However, it made no frontal attack on ethnic inequities through a quota system which, according to government planners, might jeopardize economic development. Since 1968 the government has yielded to increased minority tribal pressure and has placed increased emphasis on the advancement of less-developed people and areas. The government's success in blending Africanization with the private enterprise system may indeed determine the survival of Kenya's national integration.

ETHNIC INEQUALITIES IN KENYA*

By Donald Rothchild

UNIVERSITY OF ZAMBIA

"The time has come," writes James S. Coleman, "to recognize the professional respectability as well as the practical essentiality of the ancient and honorable hybrid discipline of political economy."[1] Such an approach to the study of developing countries is as timely as it is prudent. This article attempts to apply the approach of political economy to the question of elite recruitment, the process by which individuals are selected and assigned to strategic, political, and administrative roles.[2] It seeks to examine recruitment as a conflict of interests facing decision-makers in Kenya. Such a task seems most meaningfully handled by enlarging the boundaries under examination to include recruitment of the elite who are to manage Kenya's economy as well as its political structure. This method of analysis leads almost inevitably, under Kenyan circumstances, to a discussion of the crucial issue of resource allocation, for the priorities established in expenditure patterns are of direct relevance to the opportunity for members of various ethnic groups to compete in the market place for political and economic positions.

I shall also discuss ethnic conflicts, ranging both the less favored against the more favored traditional groupings and the non-Africans (Europeans and Asians) against the Africans. I shall attempt to gauge for these two situations the priorities that the Kenya government places upon the somewhat conflicting claims of equity and economic development.

* The Journal of Modern African Studies, 7, 4 (1969), pp. 689–711. Reprinted by permission of Cambridge University Press.

Clearly the government faces a number of dilemmas as it plans its policies on recruitment and resource allocation. It must attempt to reconcile the pressures for equity with the pressures for development in an essentially poor country experiencing steady but limited economic growth. I shall describe these pressures below. A failure in either direction could cause political instability.

On the one hand, the government must satisfy the legitimate demand for African opportunity. In pre-independent Kenya, non-Africans, though few in number, held nearly all the key positions in the government and the private sector. Many of these Europeans and Asians have remained in Kenya as citizens and expatriates. For a forward-moving economy, their skills are still badly needed in many, but by no means all, of the positions they held before. The majority community, ill-trained but expectant, now looks upon independence as not simply a transfer of sovereignty into African hands but as implying a new emphasis upon African participation in high-level posts in the bureaucracy, the army, agriculture, and industry. Equity means, for Africans, a fundamental revision in the priorities of colonial times. The extent to which the government fails to measure up to these mass expectations will have a direct bearing upon the general public's sense of frustration and, in turn, upon the regime's stability. The government's emphasis upon Africanization—a policy of recruiting Africans for existing high-level positions in the public and private sectors, rather than creating new opportunities—is a conscious attempt to relieve pressures upon the regime.

African pressures as such are only one aspect of the larger drive for equity. Within the ranks of the African community, the members of the less-favored tribes often express a keener dissatisfaction with their lot than do their more skilled and educated neighbors. Ethnic imbalances of opportunity exist among Kenya's indigenous peoples which have resulted from such factors as differing regional patterns of colonial settlement and investment, social outlooks, soil and rainfall conditions, educational circumstances, and so forth. And, even though Africans may bear little responsibility for these conditions, the less-favored indigenous peoples naturally chafe at the resulting differences in both elite recruitment programs and public welfare expenditures. The consequent demands for representativeness and reallocation of expenditure acts as a constraint upon the government, deflecting it from the policy it might otherwise take of recruiting Africans and allocating resources among regions solely on the basis of such criteria as merit and development needs.

On the other hand, the government's recruitment and expenditure policies must assure the continued growth of the economy, creating the basis for a conflict between the claims of economic development and those of equity discussed above. With more and more African school-leavers coming on to the market in search of jobs, additional employment opportunity is essential to meet rising popular demands and expectations. Unemployment problems in Kenya could be exacerbated by simply conceived programs of Africanization, which have the effect of driving away scarce capital or much-needed high-level personnel. Moreover, the adoption of a rash policy of industrial location, seeking to compel industrialists to set up new plants in the less-developed areas of the nation, would run the risk of reducing new investment in the country as a whole, should businessmen refuse to cooperate on these terms.

Kenya's leaders recognize that the country's modernization cannot be moved ahead by politically inspired policies which have the result of encouraging either a capital or a brain drain. President Kenyatta has given frequent assurances to the business community that his government's Kenyanization policy will not jeopardize the nation's rate of growth. In his 1968 presidential address to Parliament, he declared that "it is not the intention of my government to endanger the buoyant state of the economy, by forcing the pace of localization beyond the point which the private commercial sector can absorb or accommodate."[3] Kenyanization will, according to the Vice-President, "move forward without disruption of the business and the economy of the country,"[4] a pledge which may well secure economic stability at the price of political conflict.

It is now time to examine more closely the various pressures on the government and the consistency of its responses to these different demands. The reasons for a conflict between the claims of equity and economic development will be looked at in greater depth, and an analysis will be made of how the Kenya government is attempting to meet this problem.

The Facts of Inequality

Before examining the kinds of racial imbalances inherited from the past and the urgency of the demands for rectification, it is important to note an essential difference between racial and tribal imbalances. Whereas tribal minorities demanded a proportionate share of administrative and economic opportunities, racial minorities strove to retain their privileges against African calls for equity. Tribal minorities backed Africanization enthusiastically and sought equity within this policy; racial minorities were apprehensive over the effects of Africanization and stressed their rights under the Constitution. Thus the former group stressed corrective equity while the latter sought legal equity.

Imbalances of opportunity between tribal groupings remain a stubborn fact of life in Kenya today. Although they may be attributable to a variety of inherited circumstances, these inequalities inevitably cause political tensions to rise to the surface. The success of Central Province (chiefly Kikuyu in composition) in securing support for social welfare activities and, in consequence, in building up a pool of trained manpower and an array of commercial enterprises has not been lost upon the less-advantaged peoples of the country.[5] Regional discrepancies in education—illustrated by Tables 1 and 2—seem particularly significant in this regard, for they emphasize not only the priorities of the past but the resultant supply of manpower for the future.[6]

TABLE 1

Primary School Enrollment and Child Population by Province in 1964[a]

Province	Population aged 7–13 (*thousands*)	Enrollment (*thousands*)	Enrollment (%)
Central	265.9	250.0	94.0
Coast	120.3	55.1	45.8
Eastern	337.4	166.9	49.5
Nairobi	29.0	39.8	137.3
Nyanza	354.1	193.7	54.7
Northeastern	44.8	0.9	2.1
Rift Valley	373.7	144.2	38.6
Western	232.5	164.2	70.6
Kenya	1,757.7	1,014.8	57.7

TABLE 2

Secondary School Enrollment, 1966[b]

Province	Boys	Girls	Total
Central	11,277	3,630	14,907
Coast	4,938	1,815	6,753
Eastern	4,722	1,186	5,908
Nairobi	9,740	5,490	15,230
Nyanza	5,128	1,423	6,551
Northeastern	56	–	56
Rift Valley	4,946	1,468	6,414
Western	5,995	1,379	7,374

[a] SOURCE: Republic of Kenya, *Kenya Education Commission Report, Part II* (Nairobi, 1965), p. 9.

[b] SOURCE: Republic of Kenya, *Ministry of Education Triennial Survey, 1964–1966,* and *Annual Report for 1966* (Nairobi, 1967), p. 77.

The effects of this social welfare investment over the years can be seen in part in the tribal distribution of loans made by the Industrial and Commercial Development Corporation. The statistics on I.C.D.C. loans up to April 1966 show that Kikuyus, who formed 20 per cent of the male population, received 64 per cent of the industrial and 44 per cent of the commercial loans.[7] The consequences are also apparent in the figures on income distribution among provinces. Even though the available data seem incomplete and, for our purposes, somewhat distorted by the inclusion of the more affluent non-African residents of Nairobi, Mombasa, and the Rift Valley, "substantial inequality" of income between regions does become apparent.

TABLE 3

Monetary Gross Domestic Product *per capita*
by (Old) Province, 1962[a]

Provinces	Monetary product (£,000)	Population (thousands)	Monetary product per capita (£)
Nairobi E.P.D.	79,494	315	252
Coast	28,224	728	39
Rift Valley	23,691	1,049	23
Central	23,404	1,925	12
Nyanza	17,885	3,013	6
Southern	5,481	1,014	5
Northern	1,834	590	3
TOTAL	180,013	8,634	21
Total excluding Nairobi and Mombasa	76,618	8,139	9

[a] SOURCE: Republic of Kenya, *Development Plan, 1966–1970* (Nairobi, 1966), p. 29.

The non-African's privileged position stems largely from such interrelated factors as a command of key skills and capital, discriminatory investment and employment practices, and the manipulation of the social services of the colonial state to assure continued non-African hegemony. A manpower survey conducted in 1964 illustrates the extensive role played by non-Africans at the time of independence. A racial breakdown of jobs requiring university or higher education showed that, out of 6488 positions surveyed, 23 per cent were held by Africans, 27 per cent by Asians, and 50 per cent by Europeans. Africans held only 2 per cent of the highest-level positions in the leading banks and motor firms; and less than 6 per cent of the town planners, lawyers, doctors, engineers, surveyors, and similar professional men were Africans. In the semiprofessional and technical categories, Africans held an average of 76 per cent of the posts; however, their share of careers as aircraft pilots and navigators (1 per cent), senior and supervisory nurses (4 per cent), and noncertified accountants (17 per cent) was low in proportion to their numbers in the total population.[8] Despite immigration controls and trade licensing, this non-African predominance at the upper levels is changing only gradually, for many of the newly trained Africans are absorbed by the new posts created in an expanding economy.

A situation of non-African command over key skills inevitably gives rise to significant income inequalities—and dissatisfactions. It is important to note just how wide are these disparities. In Kenya's public service in 1966, 88 per cent of African males earned up to £359 per annum; among European men, 51 per cent earned between £1200 and £2399 and 33 per cent earned more than £2400; and among Asian men, 51 per cent earned between £360 and £719 and 37 per cent earned more than £720.[9] The disparities in annual incomes were only slightly less extreme in private industry and commerce.

Non-African leadership in the private sector of the economy is also buttressed by its access to the capital available at home and abroad and, in colonial times, by discriminatory legislation aimed at supporting its enterprises. The Kenya economy, like that of many of its ex-colonial counterparts, is heavily dependent upon private domestic or external capital. Some 55 per cent of the £325 m. required for developmental purposes over the plan period from 1966–70 is to be raised from private investment sources.[10] What this means in practice is substantial, but lessening, dependence upon those who have managed over the years to effect savings, primarily non-African peoples. Although the number of African-owned and managed corporations is increasing rapidly (see Table 4), the continuing need for non-African capital is apparent so long as a continuance of the capitalist pattern of development is planned.

In addition to the non-African predominance implicit in the statistics of Table 4, it is also notable that the increases of capital in previously registered companies followed a similar pattern. In 1964, for example, Europeans increased the capital in their businesses by £6,803,770; comparable figures for the other communities show £657,750 for the Asians, £25,000 for the Africans, and £2,430,500 for racially mixed

TABLE 4

Companies Incorporated, Classified by the Communities of the Shareholders[a]

Year	European		Asian		African		Partly European/ Asian/African	
	No.	Nominal capital (£)	No.	Nominal capital (£)	No.	Nominal capital (£)	No.	Nominal capital (£)
1955	246	8,875,892	99	3,559,400	1	250	6	789,100
1957	229	8,306,017	101	2,539,325	2	6,450	9	610,500
1959	136	1,100,664	116	1,126,300	5	14,000	13	48,350
1961	105	813,718	134	1,073,175	18	113,250	14	61,470
1963	161	3,085,130	153	1,198,850	17	52,350	29	2,465,800
1964	151	4,205,050	147	1,512,500	81	503,875	48	891,050
1965	122	918,350	144	1,205,550	108	803,550	53	425,050
1966	138	941,910	165	1,412,725	87	428,550	68	834,350

a SOURCE: Compiled from the Kenya Registrar-General's *Annual Reports*.

companies.[11] This overall non-African control over private investment capital, combined with the former colonial discrimination, both official (by prohibitions on such cash crops as coffee) and unofficial (in access to loans and jobs), gave the European and, to a lesser extent, the Asian communities a great advantage in securing the entrenched positions of privilege they hold today. The schemes for Africanizing employment and business opportunities have not only eliminated the most obvious areas of discrimination but have made steady inroads upon the reserves of privilege itself. Even so, it will be a long time before wealth loses its present racial implications.[12]

Finally, it is necessary to point to the manipulation of the social services of the colonial state as a means of ensuring non-African hegemony in Kenya. Housing, medical facilities, pensions, and schools were all separate and very unequal. It will suffice for our purposes to concentrate upon the crucial area of education during colonial times. Except in a few unusual cases—such as the Royal Technical College of East Africa, the Kenya Technical Institute, Nairobi, the Mombasa Institute of Muslim Education, and an experiment in multiracial education at the Hospital Hill Primary School, Nairobi —Africans, Asians, and Europeans were educated in separate racial schools.[13] The country's integration was held back by this separatism, for the different racial schools emphasized distinct curricula. Moreover, African opportunity was thwarted by colonial budgets which spent more money on European and Asian than on African education, although the latter community represented 97 per cent of the population. As the Kenya Education Commission which reported these facts concluded:

> Unfortunately these differences were largely self-perpetuating. A European child, brought up in that station in life to which it had pleased a colonial destiny to call him, was effectively trained for a corresponding social role. Like the independent school boy in pre-war England, it never entered his head that he would not occupy a position of authority; still less did the idea of an African "boss"

appear either possible or appropriate. These assumptions were to a large extent reflected on the African side. Except among nationalists and other idealists, the horizon, for practical educational purposes, was for long limited by the occupations of a rural, semi-tribal society and the lowest levels of the public administration.[14]

Although the Kenya government has abolished the racial system of schools and required a substantial intake of African students in the lower levels of formerly non-African schools, it would appear that the effects of differing educational opportunities among races will continue to spill over into the economic sphere for a long period to come.[15]

African Attitudes Toward Tribal Inequality

The less-favored indigenous peoples of Kenya are quick to express indignation over the disparities outlined above. Several indications of this resentment emerge from an analysis of their attitudes on the distribution of amenities and on recruitment into the civil service.

In 1966 this author conducted a survey of African attitudes which included a number of questions on intertribal relations in Kenya.[16] As the responses to the statements posed in Table 5 suggest, there is broad feeling that the smaller, less-advantaged peoples should receive considerable government encouragement.

A greater, and more revealing, spread of attitudes emerged when the respondents were asked two open-ended questions on the neglect of the less-advantaged tribes as well as the obligations of the government toward them. As Table 6 shows, there is a substantial group of Kenyans (and the survey covered all main tribal groups) who feel that the less-favored peoples are neglected in regard to education, transport facilities, and medical services. Although 7 per cent of the responses to the question fell in the "don't know" category and 9 per cent did not accept that any neglect existed, the breakdown of positive responses emphasizes the ways in which Africans reacted to the issues at hand.

TABLE 5

Reactions of 653 Africans to the following statements:

(a) "The government should spend more on building secondary schools for the smaller tribes, even if this means less money spent on more advanced tribes."

(b) "The government should spend more money on industries, water, and electricity in areas where the smaller tribes live, even if this means less money spent on more advanced tribes."

(percentages)

State-ment	"Strongly agree"	"Agree"	"Dis-agree"	"Strongly disagree"	"Don't know"	Refused to answer	Total[a]
(a)	41	30	15	12	1	1	100
(b)	29	31	23	16	1	1	101

[a] Several percentages, in this and the tables which follow, do not add up to 100 because of rounding.

TABLE 6

Responses to the question "In the past, have these smaller tribes been neglected in any ways?"

	Responses[b]	
	No.	%
1. Neglected in the following ways:		
(a) Poor medical services/facilities	174	15
(b) No communications or transport	159	14
(c) Poor educational facilities	383	33
(d) No agricultural/land management training	67	6
(e) No development of the area/not given good land by the Government	74	6
(f) Treated like wild game/part of the tourist attraction	18	2
(g) No instruction in food nutritional values	7	1
(h) No instruction in personal hygiene/dress/left like savages	23	2
(i) Unrepresented in government jobs and in political representation	62	5
(j) Neglected but gave no example	17	2
2. Don't know	81	7
3. Not neglected	107	9
TOTALS	1,172	102

[b] The 653 individuals were permitted more than one response.

These figures become even more meaningful when related to statistics on tribal affiliation. As might be anticipated, there was a close correlation between large size and favorable position on the one hand and small size and less favorable status on the other.[17] The percentage of each tribal group that believed the smaller and less-favored tribes were not neglected was much higher among the Kikuyu and Luo—22 and 19 per cent respectively—compared to 16 per cent of the Kamba respondents, 13 per cent of Luhya, 7 per cent of Kisii, and 4 per cent of Embu/Meru. Whereas 61 per cent of the Kikuyus and 55 per cent of the Luos mentioned neglect in the key field of education, corresponding percentages rose to 68 among the Luhya, 72 among the Embu/Meru peoples, and 84 among the Kisii. It is also interesting to note that younger males with greater education tended to place the greatest stress upon educational neglect among the less-favored peoples; the most outstanding exception to this pattern were the tribal elders, 77 per cent of whom spoke of neglect among the less-advanced tribes in the area of education.

In what ways would these respondents want the government to do more to help the smaller and less-advantaged peoples improve their conditions? A follow-up question in the survey asked for suggestions, revealing new areas for public initiative (see Table 7). In particular, it is significant that the Kikuyu respondents placed at least as much emphasis upon agricultural and land improvement schemes as they did upon adult literacy, while the less-advantaged tribes placed greater stress upon educational improvement than any other single factor.

It is now time to look at the demands for increased tribal minority recruitment into the civil service. It would appear that these claims have emanated from a somewhat different source than have the appeals for amenities.[18] Whereas an evident concern with education, transport, communications, and irrigation and land improvement schemes existed at the grass-roots level, the general public placed less emphasis in this survey upon increased tribal minority representation in the civil service than did their parliamentary representatives. This conclusion is borne out by Table 7, which draws atten-

TABLE 7

Ways the Government Could Do More to Help the Smaller and Less-Advantaged Peoples Improve Their Conditions

	Responses[a]	
	No.	%
1. Suggested improvements		
(a) Improve health facilities/build clinics	133	13
(b) Build adult literacy centers/send teachers to their areas	175	17
(c) Initiate self-help schemes, i.e., cooperatives and trade centers	68	7
(d) Start an exchange scheme sending experts to these areas and local people to more advanced areas to learn and have more contact	93	9
(e) Start irrigation/land improvement schemes	82	8
(f) Train people in land development and agriculture generally	115	11
(g) Improve roads/communications/transport	126	13
(h) Encourage people (strongly) to give up certain traditions and customs	22	2
(i) Give people more political representation and train them for posts in the government and the private sector	32	3
2. Don't know	48	5
3. Not neglected	118	12
TOTALS	1,012	100

[a] See note to Table 6.

tion to the fact that only 3 per cent of the responses stressed elite recruitment as a means available to further the opportunities of the less-advantaged African peoples. This survey would seem to suggest that, although the spokesmen of tribal interests are aroused over this particular issue, their followers are less so.

The call for increased tribal minority representation in

high-level positions, in both the public and private sectors, had been made with great frequency. Around the time of independence in 1963 the critics assailed "Kikuyu–Luo domination" of the country;[19] however, by 1966, the focus of attack became more and more limited to the Kikuyu alone. Wariness of Kikuyu hegemony became so pronounced that a new term, "Kikuyuization," came into use.[20]

M.P.s especially backbenchers of the Kenya African National Union (K.A.N.U.) and members of the Kenya People's Union (K.P.U.), have led the assault upon the imbalance in elite opportunities in the public and private sectors. A typical charge was put forth by a K.P.U. member in Parliament:

> Today, when we look at the top jobs in the government, we find that in most of the ministries, including certain co-operatives, practically all these have been taken over by people from the Central Province . . . If one tribe [the Kikuyu] alone can take over about 72 per cent of the Kenya jobs, and they are less [than] two million people, how can you expect 25 per cent of the jobs to go to more than eight million people who belong to other tribes?[21]

Time and again these spokesmen for the less-advantaged African peoples have alleged that tribalism is a significant factor in determining appointments and promotions in the civil service.[22] To substantiate their contentions, they have pointed to the staffing of various government ministries, describing them as predominantly Kikuyu or Luo in composition.[23] In support of his argument that the Ministry of Agriculture was Kikuyuized "from top to bottom," Martin Shikuku, a leading spokesman for tribal minority interests and the government chief whip, listed the permanent secretary, the deputy permanent secretary, the under secretary, the director of agriculture, and a number of other Kikuyus in this ministry.[24] Another member alleged that Kikuyu people from Kiambu controlled security in the country, citing the attorney-general, the commissioner of police, the director of intelligence, and the controller of State House in support of his contention.[25] Yet another gave data on personnel in the Ministry of Commerce and Industry to back up his charge that it was indeed a "Kikuyu Ministry."[26] Others have declared that district officers, provincial officers, and land surveyors have been recruited primarily from among the Kikuyu.[27]

Dissatisfaction with the tribal imbalances in opportunity led finally, in March 1968, to a demand that Parliament should elect a select committee to investigate allegations of tribalism and to "report the findings to this House for immediate government rectification of the situation."[28] Introducing the motion, a member urged that the select committee should examine "the senior positions held by Kikuyus," particularly in the railways, the statutory boards, the police force, and the Ministry of Agriculture.[29] The proponents of the committee argued at length for the principle of group equity: namely, that positions should be distributed so far as possible according to the group's numerical proportion in the total population. In the end, Parliament rejected the motion, but not before there were grim allusions to the role of ethnicity in the turbulence and disunity currently facing Nigeria.[30]

African Attitudes Toward Racial Inequality

The dilemma of equity and development, albeit in different form, is also present in Kenya's race relations. In the colonial situation, Europeans, Asians, and Africans were socially compartmentalized and politically and economically stratified. The colonial state placed Europeans in top decision-making positions in the public and private sectors, allowed Asian predominance in middle-level positions, and left the unspecialized tasks for the Africans. The state itself was an instrument of a ruling, alien order. In time, nationalism successfully wrested political power from British authority, but only slowly were inroads made upon the non-African dominance of the economic order. Such a situation confronted African nationalism with a difficult choice in setting priorities for Africanization and development: whether to be carried along by the momentum of nationalism despite economic consequences, or whether to ensure economic growth despite political consequences. The government chose to blend African opportunity with the continued operation of the private enterprise system—the Africanization of capitalism. Whether such a solution will be able to satisfy the objectives of equity *and* development remains the essential test of the regime's capacity to survive in the face of extensive and overlapping pressures.

The continuance of the non-African's privileged position inevitably leads to majority impressions of neglect as well as to majority demands for Africanization and the reallocation of resources. Repeated speeches at public gatherings and in Parliament have underlined African resentment over their lack of opportunity and called for Africanization as the logical fulfillment of political independence. A note of urgency was evident in these appeals. "Mr. Speaker, I wish to submit," one member of Parliament stated in the debate on the Trade Licensing Bill, "that just now the public of Kenya is quite impatient with the rate of Africanization of business in this country . . . what we want . . . is that the business in Kenya should be Africanized today, so that all the black citizens of Kenya get first priority."[31] In speaking for the less-advantaged African, he, and many of his colleagues in both parties, echoed the thoughts of a large number in the majority community.

A number of the responses, throughout the survey of African attitudes toward Kenya's minority groups, indicated a deep sense of neglect and a broad sentiment that African opportunity must be enhanced. A majority of respondents felt that Asian citizens should not be allowed to buy farming land, that non-African control over business and commerce should be ended, that private schools owned and managed by European citizens should be taken over by the government, and so forth. Table 8 demonstrates that the parliamentarians' priority for hiring Africans first is endorsed by the general public.[32]

Related to the generalized sense of neglect is the African suspicion that Europeans and Asians seek to perpetuate their privileged status by refusing to share their skills with fellow African workers. Africans recognize the connection between

TABLE 8

Reactions of 653 Africans to the statement "Big businesses in Kenya should employ Africans rather than Europeans"

(percentages)

"Strongly agree"	"Agree"	"Dis-agree"	"Strongly disagree"	"Don't know"	Refused to answer	Total
44	26	20	7	2	1	100

skill and income, in their demands for education and training. Any unwillingness on the part of expatriates to share their knowledge gives rise to deep African resentment. As Table 9 indicates, a considerable body of African opinion felt that Europeans and Asians were not cooperative in helping Africans acquire job skills.

TABLE 9

Reactions of 653 Africans to the following statements:

(a) Europeans and (b) Asians "don't like Africans to learn anything that will help them to get good jobs"

(percentages)

Statement	True	False	No opinion	Total
(a)	32	65	4	101
(b)	78	18	4	100

It is evident that Africans were more suspicious of Asians' lack of cooperation in passing on skills than that of Europeans. This may perhaps be attributed to more direct relations with less professionally trained Asians, who feel immediately threatened by African entry into the skilled labor market and who therefore are unwilling to teach Africans their trade. Moreover, a breakdown of these figures in terms of age, education, and tribe shows some interesting results. There was a clear correlation between age and apprehension about non-African cooperativeness; the younger the group, the less likely was it to be uneasy about either Asian or European intentions in this regard. However, divergences of opinion emerged when cross-tabulated by tribe and education. Whereas there was little difference between tribes in their attitudes toward Asians, Kikuyus were notably less uneasy about European assistance than were Luos, Luhyas, and Kambas.[33] The divergence in education-group attitudes is shown in Table 10. Distrust of Europeans decreases with education, while distrust of Asians rises.

TABLE 10

Percentages of Each Educational Group Who Thought the Above Statements "True"

Statement	Completed primary	Some secondary	Completed secondary	Elders
(a)	40	24	29	34
(b)	73	77	82	92

Thus the less-privileged core community insisted upon a redress in the inequality of racial opportunities inherited from the past. In contrast to the tribal situation discussed above, the African community was united behind its leaders in demanding a rectification of racial imbalances. This unity of purpose created a great pressure for change; there was no doubt in government circles of the need to recruit Africans as rapidly as possible into leading positions in the public and private sectors. The main countervailing factor was the need to maintain a high level of economic development in the country. As a consequence, governmental freedom to Africanize the economy was limited by the lack of skilled manpower and capital. These constraints compelled a search for a formula which would reconcile the legitimate call for group equity with the requirements of civil service efficiency and economic development.

In civil service recruitment, a policy of rapid Africanization was pursued. Considerable success was shown here, as indicated by President Kenyatta's assertation of December 1967 that 92 per cent of the civil service had been Africanized.[34] Concerning recruitment into high-level positions in the economy, the government displayed determination tempered with caution. In response to somewhat divergent influences, private firms were pressed simultaneously to expand both their investment and African participation. Government controls over immigration and trade licensing were to be used to encourage African opportunity; but, in the last analysis, as President Kenyatta informed Parliament, "it is up to employers to undertake this Kenyanization on a voluntary basis."[35] But, to the extent that the administration's gradualist and capitalist-oriented approach conflicted with popular desires for radical change, a potentially unsettling situation came into being.

Government Responses to Claims for Equity

The government has responded to tribal minority complaints and dissatisfactions in three basic ways: by insisting that existing imbalances were inherited from past administrations, by setting a high priority in recruitment policies upon individual merit and industriousness, and by assuring the less-advantaged peoples that resources would be allocated according to need. The government sought to reconcile development and equity; but, where a choice between the two was inescapable, it seemed ultimately to place greatest emphasis upon the nation's economic growth.

Government spokesmen have all along taken pains to reject any implications that it has made "a deliberate effort to assist Kikuyus to the detriment of others."[36] Although they admit that imbalances in opportunity do in fact exist, these are seen as the consequence of colonial indifference and not current intentions. The fault is attributed to different rates of regional educational opportunity. As the minister of housing, Paul Ngei, a Kamba, declared:

> It is clear therefore, that if there are more members of one tribe, or the other, in our public service, it is a situation which must have a reason, not because of impartiality [sic]

nor favoritism, but purely because of the merits of the members, and of the educated people in one particular group. Mr. Speaker, I am saying so because it must be admitted by this House, without fear, that certain areas have enjoyed better educational facilities . . . If I may be allowed, Mr. Speaker, to see the position of educational institutions according to provinces, I am sure the hon. Members will agree that the people have been taken because of their educational attainment rather than the color of their face, rather than because they belong to one tribe, or rather than because they live near Lake Victoria.[37]

For another minister, opportunity came with education. The inequalities of the moment were "not our fault. It is a challenge to us but not our fault."[38]

As part of the emphasis upon economic growth and nation-building, government recruitment policies have set a higher priority on personal achievement than on intergroup equity. Government spokesmen stress individual education and experience as essential qualities for appointment to the public service, ruling out any frontal assault upon tribal imbalances by such artificial remedies as the creation of tribal preferences or quotas.[39] A neat tribal balancing in each ministry would, they argue, "create chaos in the Civil Service," causing not only inefficiency but new dissatisfactions with the classification of peoples according to tribe, clan, and, ultimately, family.[40]

This emphasis upon individual merit inevitably means continuing to favor the Kikuyus in civil service recruitment—at least until such time as the rest of the population secures the same educational opportunities and accepts the same values as do this people.[41] Constitutionally, the most effective safeguard against favoritism is the Public Service Commission, an independent body, created under the Constitution, which exercises considerable control over the disposition of civil service positions. Politically, the government is careful to take special pains to recruit candidates for leading civil service posts from among the less-favored peoples in order to blunt charges of preferential treatment.[42] Nevertheless, because individual merit and achievement remain of paramount importance in the recruitment process, the tribal imbalance continues as a live political issue on the Kenya scene.[43]

Finally, the government has promised to allocate expenditure in such a way as to overcome existing tribal imbalances of opportunity. How are development objectives to be reconciled with this goal? Government planners have consistently argued that investment in the less-favored provinces should not take place at the expense of overall national development. This will mean continued economic disparities between regions. However, the commitment to the less-favored is upheld by distinguishing between developing an area and developing a people. Thus the Kenya paper on African socialism refuses to retard the development of the nation as a whole through heavy investment in areas "deficient in resources" but calls for investment in human beings, such as education, training, health, the movement of peoples to areas richer in resources, and the development of "those limited resources that are economic."[44] The policy throughout seeks to ensure the *effective* use of scarce resources, to make it possible for the peoples of the less-favored areas to compete on more even terms with their more fortunate neighbors.[45]

With the passage of time and increased pressure from the representatives of less-favored areas, a perceptible change in the government approach to the problem of tribal imbalance in opportunity became evident. A more direct, area-oriented approach emerged. President Kenyatta, at the opening of the sixth session of Parliament in 1968, announced that the new development plan would place "particular emphasis" on the advancement of the less-developed areas.[46] In line with this policy, the Ministry of Commerce and Industry has encouraged traders and industries in some "so-called neglected areas";[47] the Ministry of Cooperatives and Social Services has reserved a special fund for "comparatively slow" areas;[48] and the Ministry of Agriculture has decided to spend a larger share of development capital in Kenya's pastoral areas in an effort to redress present imbalances.[49] The most striking evidence of the government's determination to help the less-advanced areas through the reallocation of resources was the sponsoring of an Act which transfers 50 per cent of the proceeds of the graduated personal tax collected in Nairobi and Mombasa, less 50 per cent of the cost of collection, to county councils in the rural parts of the country.[50] In a practical sense, then, the government has placed increased emphasis upon group equity—even at the expense of national development goals where necessary. As Aristotle pointed out long ago, political stability requires that the multitude be saved from extreme poverty:

> Measures must therefore be contrived that may bring about lasting prosperity. And since this is advantageous also for the well-to-do, the proper course is to collect all the proceeds of the revenues into a fund and distribute this in lump sums to the needy, best of all, if one can, in sums large enough for acquiring a small estate, or, failing this, to serve as capital for trade or husbandry, and if this is not possible for all, at all events to distribute the money by tribes or some other division of the population in turn.[51]

It is useful now to compare the Kenya government's response to the pressures for racial equity with corresponding ones for tribal equity. What emerges from the comparison is an impression of striking similarities. Where a divergence of approach does occur, it is primarily a matter of degree and not of kind.

The racial situation parallels the tribal in that existing imbalances of opportunity are seen as inherited from the colonial past. Government leaders, mindful of the background data on the bases of racial privilege discussed above, have been quick to note that existing disparities are a hangover from imperial days.[52] The colonial state was a racial state which discriminated against African opportunity and enterprise. The African-led state of post-independence times would apply reallocative justice so as to right the imbalances of former times. For Senator J. P. Mathenge, the leader of government business in the Senate, the K.A.N.U. government was not "a racialist government" and would treat citizens of all races equally; yet it would also redress the existing imbalances between races, a policy which means that "the proportion of officers in the Civil Service, and we hope in all other walks of life, will more accurately reflect the racial composition of the population as a whole."[53]

Do these references to group numericalism amount to a form of discrimination in reverse? African leaders themselves seem to disagree on this issue. Most spokesmen deny that ethnic quotas are discriminatory in a negative sense; they are interpreted instead as a color-conscious reaction to the three-tier structure erected by the colonial state.[54] For Tom Mboya, it was not "being racial" to insist in 1960 that the African be given special opportunity and special treatment.[55] Dr. J. G. Kiano has more recently contended that "if we appear to be attempting to correct the economic imbalance by giving some priorities to Africans, it is not that we are discriminating against our friends."[56] And J. K. Gatuguta defended the action taken by the Nairobi City Council in replacing Asians with Africans in the municipal market stalls as follows:

> Again here, Mr. Speaker, Sir, I must make it quite clear that it is very wrong for anybody to think that this is discrimination. It is not. All the government is trying to do now is to remove the imbalance in commerce and industry. If the government thinks that some section of the community has advanced so far in commerce and industry and that something should be done to remove the imbalance, that is not discrimination.[57]

On the other hand, some speakers have justified discriminatory measures as a means of evening up an unequal situation. One of the frankest statements putting forth this point of view occurred in the debate on the Trade Licensing Bill. Martin Shikuku, ridiculing the meaning of fair competition between unequals, maintained:

> So it is useless, although we are all citizens, to talk in terms of fair competition against the people who have been established for a time and who have the money and the know-how, just because they happen to be citizens. I reject this. We must discriminate, Mr. Speaker.[58]

The difficulty obviously arises over the values attached to discrimination itself. If discrimination is seen as corrective justice, it may be given high priority as being in the interest of the greatest number. The dilemma arises in its most painful form when parliamentarians seek to reconcile the equity required by the Constitution with the principle of "corrective redistribution."[59] On such occasions, many parliamentarians are tempted to follow the advice of the former Vice-President, Oginga Odinga, and "not emphasize this word 'discrimination'."[60]

Tribal imbalances inherited from the past also lead to government efforts for a reallocation of resources which would benefit those currently disadvantaged. In both cases the principle of corrective justice is applied in order to lay the basis for equal opportunity. Thus education and training of Africans are emphasized, and loans and licenses are channeled into African hands. Although preference is given to the majority African community in one instance, and to the smaller and less-advantaged African peoples in the other, the principle is basically similar.

Historically, a trend toward greater and greater stress upon a corrective redistribution of resources has been discernible. In the period immediately after independence a high priority was put upon development. This meant that government leaders placed great emphasis upon gross economic profitability in the use of resources, a policy which involved the most gradual kind of attack upon existing disparities in society. In time, however, a change in priorities became discernible and increasingly the achievement of group equity was stressed. In 1967 the government signaled the change of emphasis with the passage of the Immigration Act, the Trade Licensing Law, and a host of measures aimed at speeding up the Africanization of the economy. Political pressures were building up, and a policy which led to the acceleration of African participation in the life of the society was as prudent as it was genuinely nationalist. "The new, tough line which the Kenya government is taking in order to speed up Africanization in commerce and industry," concluded an editorial in the *East*

Africa Journal, "is long overdue and most welcome." The Africanization of high-level positions in the private sector was, in editorial eyes, "so small as to be almost meaningless."[61] Similar political pressures for intertribal and interracial equity brought about a progressive revision of priorities in the direction of corrective justice.

Interesting differences in African attitudes toward intertribal and interracial relations did in fact emerge, but these differences were essentially a product of a part-real, part-mythical sense of African solidarity. The shared experiences of colonialism and racism, as well as the common struggle against these forces, created a sense of identity which enhanced coherence within the African community. As a consequence, tension management within a community of Africans united by common experience, citizenship, and friendship was smoother and easier to effect than between racial communities, which were disconnected in many instances because they had different values, experiences, and allegiances.[62]

These variations in the closeness of intercommunity connections were reflected in diverse government responses to the tribal, and the racial, minority claims regarding elite recruitment. Dissimilarities are evident, for example, in the readjustments in priority between personal achievement and intergroup equity. In the immediate post-independence period, the recruitment of Africans was based essentially upon education and experience. Since African efficiency was essential to supplant non-African hegemony, these qualities represented a prized asset—even if not distributed evenly within the population. With respect to the minority racial communities, however, African solidarity strengthened the majority group's attack upon European and Asian dominance and privilege, despite the latter's considerable skill and experience.

Independence was viewed by the African community as the signal for a new era of African opportunity, and inevitably this opportunity would have to be offered at the expense of the predominantly noncitizen jobholders. Thus the needs which gave rise to solidarity, and which placed a high priority upon a combination of rapid Africanization and merit, opened

the way to inequalities among Africans. Inter-African inequities became the price for securing the more pressing objective of interracial equity—at least temporarily. The greater
urgency of Africanization led the government to move more
swiftly on the racial than the tribal front; it sought, through
such means of tension management, to achieve political stabilization, without which no development is possible.

The Balance Between Equity and Development

The government, then, adjusts its priorities as between
equity and development partly in terms of group demands.
Because racial divergences involve wide cleavages, demands
on the part of the majority African community for equity
receive careful and sympathetic attention from political leaders.
But, where common experiences and aspirations create a
sense of solidarity on the part of the African community, the
intertribal boundaries are reduced and the demands for equity
become intermeshed with the common goal of development.

As a result, there emerge two overlapping clusters of groups.
In one cluster are minority tribes and the African community
as a whole in its relationship with the non-Africans. In the
other cluster are Europeans, Asians, and some Africans.
Whereas the former emphasizes group equity, the latter
stresses individual equity under the Constitution. Each holds
different objectives and values, and thus makes different demands on the government. The corrective reallocation sought
by the less-privileged groups is employed to the end of numerical justice but possibly at the expense of rapid economic
development. The more privileged groups claim that individual equity will foster rapid economic growth. However, the
government of Kenya recognizes that ultimately equity and
economic development are mutually interdependent and
must be pushed simultaneously.

The government has limited flexibility of movement as it
goes about the task of according priorities. Too much emphasis upon group equity may slow down growth and con-

tribute to instability; and too complete an acceptance of individual equity may lead to such wide divergences of opportunity as to cause a breakdown in the system. The government's ability, within this rather circumscribed situation, to achieve successful recruitment and resource allocation policies is one of the acid tests of leadership for Kenya and all third-world countries.

NOTES

1. "The Resurrection of Political Economy," in *Mawazo* (Kampala), I, 1, June 1967, p. 31.

2. For an analysis of the concept of elite recruitment, see Lester G. Seligman, "Elite Recruitment and Political Development," in Jason L. Finkle and Richard W. Gable, eds., *Political Development and Social Change* (New York, 1968), pp. 328–38, and Lewis J. Edinger and Donald D. Searing, "Social Background in Elite Analysis: A Methodological Inquiry," in *American Political Science Review* (Menasha, Wisconsin), LXI, 2, June 1967, p. 428.

3. *National Assembly Debates* (Nairobi), XIV, sixth session, 26 February 1968, col. 3.

4. Republic of Kenya, *Statement on Application of the New Immigration Act in Relation to "Work Permits" and Kenyanization,* by the Hon. D. T. Arap Moi (Nairobi, 1968), p. 3.

5. Kenyans have been quick to relate educational opportunity to elite recruitment. Thus the writer of one letter observes, "we should appreciate the fact that all tribes are not alike in educational fields. You may probably agree with me that some tribes are lagging behind. Hence, it will not be surprising to perceive that some advanced tribes will not be debarred from playing a bigger role in the public service." *East African Standard* (Nairobi), April 3, 1968.

6. The value of the statistics in Table 2 as an index of regional distribution of opportunities is reduced by virtue of the fact that many of the schools recruit from all over Kenya.

7. This information appears in Peter Marris, "Entrepreneurship and Development: A Study of African Businesses in Kenya" (draft copy), and is used with his permission.

8. Republic of Kenya, *High-Level Manpower Requirements and Resources in Kenya, 1964–1970,* prepared under the direction of Calvin F. Davis (Nairobi, 1967), pp. 28–30.

9. Republic of Kenya, *Statistical Abstract, 1967* (Nairobi, 1967), p. 153.

10. *Development Plan, 1966–1970*, p. 44.

11. Registrar-General, *Annual Report, 1964* (Nairobi, 1965), p. 13.

12. Because wheat is normally grown on large, mechanized farms of a thousand acres or more, it has long been regarded as a European undertaking. By 1968, however, African farmers, many of them planting as little as fifteen or twenty acres of wheat, provided 22 per cent of the total production of this commodity. John Dalling, "Wheat Grows into a Surplus Crop," in *Sunday Nation* (Nairobi), June 9, 1968.

13. For a description of colonial policies and practices in the field of education, see Colony and Protectorate of Kenya, *Report on Asian and European Education in Kenya, 1958* (Nairobi, 1958).

14. Government of Kenya, *Kenya Education Commission Report, Part I* (Nairobi, 1964), pp. 21–24.

15. Dissatisfaction with noncitizen predominance in the higher levels is noticeable. In a public speech, C. G. Maina asserted that the Kenya government was concerned about the rather high proportion of sixth-form places being taken by noncitizens. *East African Standard*, October 27, 1967.

16. Results are based upon 653 completed questionnaires out of a total sample of 730. Refusals were recorded for 50 interviews, and 27 interviews were rejected as incomplete or dishonest. Those interviewed had completed primary school or more; the place of interview was divided roughly evenly among urban (Nairobi), peri-urban, and rural areas. For a companion piece based on the same survey, see Donald Rothchild, "Kenya's Minorities and the African Crisis over Citizenship," in *Race* (London), IX, 4, April 1968, pp. 421–37.

17. The 1962 population census of Africans by tribe shows the following results:

Kikuyu	1,642,065	Mijikenda	414,887
Luo	1,148,335	Kipsigis	341,771
Luhya	1,086,409	Turkana	181,387
Kamba	933,210	Nandi	170,085
Kisii	538,343	Masai	154,079
Meru	439,021	Others	1,315,441
	Total	8,365,942	

18. Parliamentary spokesmen for tribal minorities have made many appeals for amenities and agricultural and industrial improvement schemes. See, for example, *National Assembly Debates*, XI, fifth session, February 21, 1967, cols. 219–20; X, fourth session, October 6, 1966, col. 472; and XIV, sixth session, March 29, 1968, cols. 1329–52.

19. "The Civil Service as it stands at present is divided up into two groups; you will find that most of the jobs in the Civil Service are going to two tribes, the Kikuyu and the Luo." A. R. Tsalwa, *Senate Debates* (Nairobi), I, first session, July 25, 1963, col. 495.

20. "I abhor the present policy of 'Africanisation' which is just a synonym for 'kikuyuisation' in its application." Letter to *The Reporter* (Nairobi), May 19, 1967.

21. G. F. O. Oduya, *National Assembly Debates*, XIV, sixth session, February 27, 1968, col. 66.

22. *Daily Nation*, December 10, 1966.

23. *Senate Debates*, IV, first session, July 21, 1965, col. 464.

24. *House of Representatives Debates*, X, fourth session, October 14, 1966, cols. 879–80. For a similar charge by Senator O. M. Chilo, see *East African Standard*, October 14, 1966.

25. *House of Representatives Debates*, X, fourth session, October 14, 1966, cols. 883–84. See also cols. 1385–86.

26. *Ibid.*, October 11, 1966, col. 636.

27. For example, *ibid.*, September 30, 1966, cols. 259 and 270–71. Similar charges have even been made of the recruitment policies of the East African Common Services Organisation. See *Proceedings of the Central Legislative Assembly Debates* (Nairobi), III, 2, August 18, 1964, cols. 529–30.

28. *National Assembly Debates*, XIV, sixth session, March 29, 1968, col. 1303.

29. Motion presented by Luke Obok, *ibid*.

30. *Ibid.*, cols. 1305 and 1310. In an earlier debate, the Assistant Minister for Labour, L. W. Oselu-Nyalick, declared that if the present trend were not changed, Kenya might be headed toward "another Biafra." *Ibid.*, February 28, 1968, col. 110.

31. J. W. Khaoya, *National Assembly Debates*, XIII, fifth session, November 7, 1967, col. 1803.

32. The less educated members of the sample tended to be more positive in their response to this question than did those who had achieved a higher level of formal education. The positive answers, grouped by intensity of agreement, were as follows:

Intensity of Agreement	Completed primary	Some secondary	Completed secondary	Elders
Strongly agree	53	47	33	41
Agree	23	22	32	34

33. Percentages agreeing with the question were Kikuyu, 23; Luo, 37; Luhya, 38; and Kamba, 47. A separate study conducted by Peter Marris shows, too, that African businessmen think Europeans generally helpful toward African advancement, Asians not so. They are bitter about the unwillingness of Asians to help Africans, either by training or in business.

34. *Kenya Newsletter* (Nairobi), December 15, 1967. The President further declared, "All major decisions of the Government are now made by our sons and daughters. Despite this rapid Africanisation, there has been no fall in the standards of efficiency."

35. *National Assembly Debates*, XIV, sixth session, February 27, 1968, col. 3.

36. Mwai Kibaki, *House of Representatives Debates*, X, fourth session, October 11, 1966, col. 655.

37. *National Assembly Debates*, XIV, sixth session, March 1968, col. 561.

38. Mbiyu Koinange, Minister of State, President's Office, *ibid.*, March 20, 1968, col. 1316. The former head of the civil service, Duncan N. Ndegwa, was equally explicit on this point: "The tribal imbalances in the Public Service and elsewhere will be adjusted only by the development of equal educational opportunities." See "Loyalty and Dedication in the Public Service" (Kabete: Kenya Institute of Administration, January 5, 1967, mimeo), p. 20.

39. Ndegwa, *op. cit.*, p. 20.

40. Mwai Kibaki, *House of Representatives Debates*, X, fourth session, October 11, 1966, col. 662.

41. Kikuyu initiative and industriousness have frequently been noted by non-Kikuyu leaders. E.g., *ibid.*, October 20, 1966, col. 1394; *National Assembly Debates*, XIV, sixth session, March 7, 1968, cols. 561–62; and *East African Standard*, February 22, 1967.

42. John S. Roberts, *A Land Full of People: Life in Kenya Today* (New York: Frederick A. Praeger, 1968), pp. 72–73.

43. "It is not the Government's intention or policy to promote or appoint people in the Public Service on the grounds of their tribes or tribal connections." J. Nyamweya, Minister of State, President's Office, *House of Representatives Debates*, X, fourth session, October 14, 1966, col. 891.

44. Republic of Kenya, *African Socialism and Its Application to Planning in Kenya* (Nairobi, 1965), p. 47.

45. *Development Plan, 1964–1970*, p. 35.

46. *National Assembly Debates*, XIV, sixth session, February 26, 1968, col. 3. For a follow-up statement, see the remarks of the senior planning officer with the Ministry of Economic Planning and Development, B. H. Ogola, to the Western Provincial Planning Committee, *East African Standard*, April 12, 1968.

47. *House of Representatives Debates*, X, fourth session, October 11, 1966, cols. 653–54. See also *National Assembly Debates*, XIII, fifth session, October 17, 1967, cols. 803–6.

48. *East African Standard*, February 10, 1967.

49. *Ibid.*, February 27, 1967; *Kenya Newsletter*, March 1, 1967.

50. *National Assembly Debates*, XIII, fifth session, December 18, 1967, col. 3461. The following year the Nairobi City Council raised its rates by more than one third to cover an estimated deficit of £570,000. Councillors passed a resolution urging the government to rescind its decision on reallocating part of the city's GPT revenues to subsidize other councils. *East African Standard*, December 3, 1968.

51. Aristotle, *Politics*, tr. by H. Rackham (Cambridge, Mass., 1959), p. 511.

52. Charles Njonjo, quoted in *Daily Nation*, September 20, 1967; Tom Mboya, letter to the editor, *Daily Nation*, February 6, 1967; and *African Socialism*, pp. 28 and 51. For a radio commentary along these lines on "Voice of Kenya," see *Daily Nation*, January 11, 1969.

53. Mathenge went on: "This means that 99 per cent of the civil servants and other people will be black people," *Senate Debates*, I, first session, July 25, 1963, col. 518.

54. No doubt, as Daniel P. Moynihan has observed, ethnic quotas

can cause hardship for certain groups: "If ethnic quotas are to be imposed on American universities and similarly quasi-public institutions, the Jews will be almost driven out. They are not 3 per cent of the population." (*The New York Times,* June 5, 1968)

55. *Legislative Council Debates,* LXXXVI, fourth session, October 27, 1960, col. 439.

56. *National Assembly Debates,* XII, fifth session, July 20, 1967, col. 2503.

57. *House of Representatives Debates,* X, fourth session, December 14, 1966, cols. 2784–85.

58. *National Assembly Debates,* XIII, fifth session, November 6, 1967, col. 1765.

59. Reinhard Bendix, *Nation-Building and Citizenship* (New York: John Wiley & Sons, 1964), p. 130.

60. *National Assembly Debates,* XII, fifth session, July 7, 1967, col. 1977.

61. *East Africa Journal* (Nairobi), IV, 1, April 1967, p. 42.

62. Cf. Manfred Halpern, "Conflict, Violence, and the Dialectics of Modernization," a paper presented to the American Political Science Association, Washington, D.C., September 1968.

INDEX